Preying Indians

By

Thomas Adams

Copyright: September 2011

Introduction

It is of necessity for the author of this work, myself, Thomas Michael, to explain the premise of the following piece the reader may intend to read. It is impossible for the author to understand how to label this work. The narrator, Thomas Adams, and his seventeenth century life experiences within "Preying Indians" are all fictional. The facts throughout the story on the downfall of the Southern New England Indian civilization and the genesis of the expansionist conquest through the powers of the United Colonies, however, are all from non-fictional sources. It was easiest to use a fictional character to connect the factual events throughout several different Southern New England regions into one theme.

I have spent the last several years researching Southern New England Indians and this is what has spawned from my interest. I have lived in Southern New England my entire life and have such a love and curiosity of how it has come to be. I must thank all of the previous writers through hundreds of centuries who sacrificed vast amounts of time to put forth information to supply future generations with a description of the past. True firsthand accounts and the avoidance of other authors' opinions were very important for this work. I have tried to use information to provide evidence to support the narrators opinion, as well as, for the reader to form his or her own.

I must say that throughout this work material from other books is indented to credit the writer. The last thing I want to do is take credit for anyone else's efforts and intellect. I hope when the reader comes upon an indent they are not thrown off as it is just as an important part of the story as the narrator's voice. I came across certain works that were descriptively written far better than I could ever come close to writing and thought it was necessary for "Preying Indians" to share the message. Still, through the narrator I have tried to make it as entertaining a story as possible with the intention to share information to the reader.

I hope to share a portion of history that is not told. We are taught so much on the Revolutionary War, but what happened before freedom was ever possible. The truth is discovered from knowledge of all events and participants. However, what if only one perspective is disclosed?

What is to be of a people who do not live within reality?

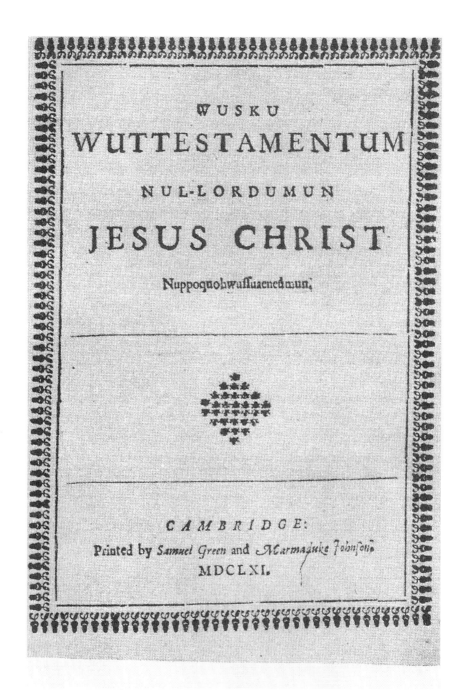

John Eliot, New Testament Translated into the
Massachusett Indian Language, Cambridge, Massachusetts, Samuel Green and
Marmaduke Johnson, 1661

Part I: Thomas Adams

"Ask of me, and I shall give thee, the heathen for thine inheritance, and the uttermost parts of the earth for thy possession."[1]

In Southern New England I have come to distinguish that three types of Indians reside within these bounds, those that pray, those that prey, and those that are preyed upon. During my entire life living in new settlements and townships throughout this region I have become fascinated with the one type of Indian who chooses to pray upon the gospel. It is my greatest hope to express to the reader the extraordinary, selfless, sacrificing, men these Indians were, even as they will always be viewed as colonial subjects.

There may be a great hesitation for the reader to believe that an Indian could actually become a Christian. For "idleness and improvidence are the Indians' great sins", as claimed by the colonists. These certain habits simply satisfy the Indian lifestyle, even though the belief among some of the colonial magistrates is that through proper example and fit laws, these sins will be "rooted out."[2] Many successful cases of Christian Indians do exist.

What led to Indian conversion was the concern held by the English government of Massachusetts upon the Indians' affairs within that jurisdiction. Before the Indians began to pray to Jesus, they had submitted their lands unto the jurisdiction and government of the colony of Massachusetts. Massachusetts would afterward approve and settle several townships and plantacions for these Indians to pray and live within.

It is true that the Indian holds a far different level of human dignity than that of a white man as he has no Christian heritage. Therefore, how is there any possibility for this simple creature to evolve in an ever-changing society, which is claimed to be moving toward a completely Christian state?

The purpose of the Christian religion may simply be to use scripture to evolve the soul within into a perfectly moral spirit comparable to that of Jesus Christ. Not, on the contrary, to use religion externally as a means to expand and conquer land from those of a different awareness. Some white men have held a great desire on transforming this Christian spirit upon the Indian. I am in favor to this and to all the efforts made by English missionaries to share the life and sacrifice of Jesus Christ with the Indians, but if there were ulterior motives that developed through the dangerous control religion could enforce upon a man who contemplated his conscience in a different manner, I would not consider those acts as those of a Christian.

It was difficult enough for the Christian Indians to be consolidated into praying villages rather than to just learn a new religion. These praying villages consequently opened up vast amounts of land for the Massachusetts Colony. In order for the Indians to obtain residency within the sanctioned praying villages they must have submitted their land and rights to the Massachusetts commonwealth. The praying villages neighbored townships which served to increase a sense of security with the local Indians for the white man. The close proximity followed the assumption that if the Indian dwelt a long distance away they would not care to pray or subject themselves.

Land is a powerful acquisition in this New World and reckless measures at times may have been made for its acquirement. The English took land through different means, such as written contracts not in accordance with the verbal agreement, using sinuous and lesser sachems to make deals with, and also getting Indians drunk and manipulating them out of their territory. Yet too eager for land, the white men were distanced from the true divinity of religion, which resulted in the denial for the spirit to evolve and improve the world universally. The excessive amount of land man pursued could not equivalently be controlled and maintained, which forced men to dedicate all their efforts upon improving their land for their own benefit.

More and more the white race has invaded New England and destroyed long standing Indian traditions. It can be argued that all the white men brought in exchange for beautiful wilderness were cloth goods, weapons, and vices. With the rapid population growth and development of civilization throughout the settlements, by the 1670s, there was little choice for the Indians, they could submit to the English and depend on the white man, or they could deny submission to the colony and expect sanctions and possible war. Even if the tribe remained neutral by submitting to the King of England and not the colony, the Indians were still viewed as servants of the colonies. Many Indians that submitted land in order for colonial protection did not receive the expected security and lost much more than land, but on the contrary, there were Indians who were too proud to submit anything to colonial authority and had wars' forced upon them.

The issues accumulating between the two different people led to many misunderstandings and suspicions. The English would ultimately be unbearably harsh upon the Indians with their ever-growing authority. The Indians would always be considered their subjects, not friends or equals. The English felt the necessity to remove all of the Indians guns from Indian subjects, as well as, demand that certain tribes must send hostages in order for English alliance. Christian

Indians, neutral Indians, and those that rebelled from the white men all had every right to be upset with the Massachusetts authorities. Every example of an Indian subject defecting away from Massachusetts authority occurred because of colonial conduct. There were also rumors that would spread amongst all Indians that the English held a "design to cut off all the Indians." Interestingly enough, the younger Indians wanted to take a violent course against the white men rather than their sachems and senior relatives. The younger Indian bands were eager and audacious for war, while the elders were interested in maintaining peace.

The Christian Indians were in the heart of this struggle in 1675, and it is only a small group of Indians that have come to be known as true Praying Indians, all because of the labor of missionaries from England. This group of Indians has practiced peaceful conduct and adjusted their lifestyle accordingly with every demand made by colonial order. Yet, these Indians still have had to withstand unprovoked suffering from both the white men and other rival Indians. The praying Indians continuously developed into true followers of Christ; however other Indians, who were stubborn to change into the civilized nature required by the colonies, disrupted the development of the Christian Indians. The Indians who rejected Christianity were blamed as the troublesome Indians who formed the enemy force in the great Indian war of 1675 known as King Philip's War.

The great tragedy King Philip's War expressed was the failure of the tremendous missionary efforts made by the Christian Englishmen who held such righteous intentions. All the money and time invested in Christianizing the Indians grew distant following the war just as the Southern New England Indian had. The missionary effort greatly depended on strong and continual support from England in turn to convert the Indian. However, there were men within the authority who held such disregard for Indian honor and friendship that they pushed many Indians to rebel against colonial rule.

The missionaries in New England, small in number, held true Christian motives. Of these motives there were three of most importance:

> First, the glory of God, in the conversion of some of these poor desolate souls.

> Secondly, his compassion and ardent affection to them, as of mankind in their great blindness and ignorance.

> Thirdly, and not the least, to endeavour, so far as in him lay, the accomplishment and fulfilling the covenant and promise, that New England people had made unto their king, when he granted them their patent or charter, viz. That one principal end of their going to plant these countries, was, to communicate the gospel unto the native Indians.[3] [Daniel Gookin]

The sponsored funding for the missionary program in New England opened many possibilities for the growth of praying Indian communities and greatly influenced Indians who were searching for guidance and order. In 1649 Parliament passed an act for the formation of a charter that held a purpose to raise the funds for the support of the missionary program in New England, which English missionaries had previously funded privately. The Propagation of the Gospel in New England was organized under the provision of an act of Parliament and whose original members were wealthy Puritan merchants of London. The propagation of the Gospel in New England was also designated as the New England Company.

The corporation's intention was to supply funding for the peaceable conversion of the Indian into Christianity through working with English missionaries. The New England missionaries depended upon this funding greatly, especially John Eliot, who traveled throughout Massachusetts, Connecticut, and Rhode Island in hopes of leading the Indians toward the Gospel, as well as Thomas Mayhew Jr., who successfully converted the Indians of Martha's Vineyard. Both men invested large amounts of time and money with no compensation from the English or the natives of New England before the Propagation of the Gospel in New England was founded in 1649. I have chosen to share a quote from the great Indian missionary John Eliot, who developed many colonial-sanctioned Praying Villages. John Eliot reflects the intention of the missionaries:

> "And this Vow I did solemnly make unto the Lord concerning them; that they being a people without any forme of Government and now to chuse; I would endeavor with all my might, to bring them to embrace such Government, both civil and Ecclesiastical, as the Lord hath commanded in the holy Scriptures; and to deduce all their Lawes from the holy Scriptures, that so they may be the Lord's people, ruled by him alone in all things."[4] (John Eliot)

This missionary's explanation of the intended conversion for the Southern New England Indian describes exactly where my passion has manifested itself throughout my life. Will forming someone else's civil and ecclesiastical laws and government become successful? Even if it is God's law to be practiced, it is still a man that is to establish order and administer the gospel. It could be argued that the only successful example of the ideal life for a Christian Indian was found on Martha's Vineyard under the missionary Thomas Mayhew, Jr., which I had witnessed, not on the mainland under John Eliot, where many Christian Indians rebelled.

The great failure of John Eliot was his ignorance in the distrust that his fellow Englishmen held toward the Indian. Eliot spent so much time on the advancement of the Indian that he lost sight of educating the English on what the Indian became through the success of conversion. There is no doubt, though, that Eliot felt great sympathy for the Indians, as when King Phillip's War began he was very troubled. He felt the war would not have occurred if Plymouth had honest land dealings with Philip. Eliot wrote to John Winthrop, Jr., "I humbly request that one effect of this trouble may be to humble the English to do the Indians justice and no wrong about their lands."[5]

The Praying Indians endured much grief and separation from their traditional ways in order to convert to this Christian religion. There have been some words spoken that the true reason of the mission was to increase the colony's bounds and strength at the natives expense. Yet, it was considered of greatest necessity by the English missionaries to join the converts into praying villages in order to remove the chance of the uncivilized influence from the non-converted

Indians. The great factor for the unsuccessful conversion of the Indian is that these praying Indians became considered scandalous by members of neighboring townships because of the conduct of hostile non-converting Indians. Anger towards bands of troubling Indians expanded into an overall hatred for all Indians. Colonists and farmers who held land near a praying village doubted that conversion was more important to the Indian than the Indian's own tribes and it was also assumed that the praying Indian would join an Indian uprising at the moment of an outbreak. Again, however, the counter argument could have been that the main reason for the colonies objection toward praying villages was the desire for praying town land.

It must be said that the colonial legal system did make some fair decisions on false accusations made against the praying Indians, however, it came to the point that the court could not deny public outcry against all Indians living in praying villages, mostly because these villages bordered townships and there were cases of peaceful Indians rebelling. The court chose to punish many innocent praying Indian tribes through interning them on a frigid isolated island called Deer Island.

Negatively affected by so much injustice, this peaceful group of Praying Indians did not react violently throughout any of the unfair hardships and false accusations they would face. For most Christian Indians in praying villages, English accusations would point to these neighboring Indians whenever barns and houses were burnt, even though they had no part in it. Still, however, the Praying Indians would ultimately sacrifice their lives for the colonies very own survival in New England's first civil war (King Philip's War) fought between the colonists and the hostile Indian. There existed some supernatural strength within these Indians which allowed them to be ready to fight at any moment upon the colonies request, even as they were interned on an island in Boston Harbor.

These men known as the praying Indians were also variously called friendly Indians, Christian Indians, Converts, or peaceful Indians. They were on the side of the English, though some rebelled at the time of King Philip's War. The other group of Indian I will categorize in this work were unfavorable to the English. I define this group as preying Indians, non-converts, rebellious Indians, neutral Indians or hostile Indians. These are the Indians who did not align with the English culture, rebelled from Christian conversion, or simply manifested hatred toward the colonization of their homeland and did not understand the legal system of the English. The Christianizing of Indians stirred anger in some Indians because in the past it was customary for individuals or broken tribes to be accepted into larger tribes, yet, once conversion grew in numbers and villages, it became viewed by nonconverts as simply the adoption of Indians into white settlements increasing its strength[6].

To confuse matters, there were tribes, such as the Massachusetts, Wampanoags, and Nipmucs, whose members separated, either remaining peaceful or rebelling. The Mohegans of Eastern Connecticut held a strong alliance with Connecticut throughout many years and greatly influenced the outcome of the two Southern New England Indian wars. The Mohegans preyed upon tribes unfavorable to the English or themselves.

Even more confusing is that tribes most resistant to Christianity were those with the strongest leadership. Yet, the two most influential chiefs in promoting the colonies growth denied the conversion of their tribes: Massasoit of the Wampanoag Confederacy, responsible for the original peaceful settlement of Plymouth in 1620-21, and Uncas, chief of the Connecticut Mohegans.

The attempt to conform the natives toward the civilization religion would foster brought about many different reactions within the Indian tribes throughout Southern New England. There are many interpretations as to what or who was responsible for the creation of Indians preying upon the colonies, but the one certainty of the Indian is the change to their lifestyle that disease and the arrival of the English spawned.

I am now finally writing what wanders in my mind in this year 1676. I question the justice in altering a man dependent upon his natural environment, cherishing every small aspect which forms the universe. The Indian I hope to reveal holds no means for destruction upon an environment to increase a material wealth.

As the abovementioned Eliot quote reveals, it is a Christian Missionary who finds it of necessity for an aboriginal species to peacefully convert in order to succumb to a government. With the encroachment of colonization the Indian becomes labeled uncivilized and must change and become persuaded by material wealth and private property. It was the Indian family that took as much firewood as it needed within its tribes bounds and then moved on for others to only use what they needed.

My name is Thomas Adams and I am the son of a Puritan who followed the original Pilgrims of Plymouth. I was born in Plymouth in the year 1625. I have lived in five New England towns and experienced different communities, but I was too young to have a recollection of a couple of the early ones. I was born in Plymouth and don't remember anything of it; then to Watertown and don't remember much; third to Wethersfield, where my interest in Indians began, but I was not allowed by my father to have contact with them; fourth to Great Harbor, Martha's Vineyard, where I was amazed how faith transformed the Indian into a convert. My present residence has been Springfield, Massachusetts for around twenty years. Here on the mainland, faith, on the other hand, became a weapon for the Indian and colonists to fight in a war.

Since I was a small boy, I wondered if Indians lived the proper way of life and if we were the ones imposing on nature and the life dependent upon it. I had been sheltered from the Indian culture through my adolescence and was somewhat led to believe the Indian was a savage heathen. I had no definitive comprehension until I moved to Martha's Vineyard in 1645 with my parents during my early twenties.

I have decided it is important to write in print a collection of information on the colonial past I have accumulated. I feel a genesis of something big has happened. I know there is much I will have left out and the most accurate information can only be provided by an on hand account, but please accept my effort.

Now, in the year 1676 I feel a divine force leading me towards the paper to write down what I have lived through and learned. It has become very difficult to separate heresy from reality, which is why I have decided to share my account. I do not, however, feel comfortable sharing all this with my neighbor, as I am not sure the character of every New Englander would understand the information I am sharing. Every locality seems to have an unfavorable theory on the Indian.

I don't remember much of Plymouth or Watertown because of my age, but the other three towns I reflect back to often. The thing I remember most is the interaction and perception of the Indian. When respect was given, respect was received. However, when valuable land was sought after by any means, retaliatory action followed. It seems to me, also, that communities are a reflection of the men that plant them, and in Southern New England, aside from Rhode Island, Puritan theology held precedence. Indians, on the other hand, were once a reflection of their sachem, but became broken communities for a number of reasons.

Now I am sitting in Springfield, Massachusetts at the age of seventy-one reflecting through these words my journey throughout Southern New England where I have experienced a much different perspective of the colonization process of Indian land as held by other settlers. In 1629, Governor John Winthrop and the Massachusetts Bay Company held the hope of creating a Christian state within the New World, only to become possible through the conversion of the heathen toward the Gospel.

For me, the great insult applied to the Indian is that an entire population of newly established neighbors, including Christian missionaries, displayed superiority toward the inferior Indian. At first, the Indian lived perfectly fine in the wilderness with no dependence upon any foreign entity. The colonists upon their arrival, on the other hand, depended upon the Indian for their very survival in a desolate wilderness. Yet, with the continual influx of English into New England the tide would turn and the Indian way of life would cease. As the colonial force strengthened, the Indian behavior changed, and it would become the Indian who became dependent upon the English.

When we look back on the age of the Southern New England Indians, their existence may be described as one of no importance. Their lives, on the contrary, are of the greatest significance. The development of self-government and what has become of New England is all the result of a Puritan design for civilization first enforced upon the New England aborigine. What happened to the Indians of Southern New England is simply the genesis for the expansionist conquest at the hands of the United Colonies.

The United Colonies was formed in 1643 by three of the New England Puritan colonies: Massachusetts Bay, Plymouth, and Connecticut. The three formed the organization known as the New England Confederation or Commissioners of the United Colonies, as a way to solve common problems together. This Confederation held the power to grant permission for war, which in the Indian community was held by the Sachem, thus the United Colonies approved themselves to be the highest authority, or Sachems, of the region. The conditions across the Atlantic in England also led to the formation of the United Colonies as the English Civil War began around 1642. Expanding differences over the authority of king and parliament, at the time when settlement in New England was forming, led to much opposition against the king and the uprising of Oliver Cromwell, who led England into a parliamentary commonwealth away from a monarchy. New England colonists supported Cromwell's rule and many of Cromwell's refugee's were given refuge here. Charles Burpee wrote regarding the United Colonies formation:

> It seems the formation for the United Colonies was a matter of great importance. The great civil war of England was on and with early results in favor of Charles. In Virginia there were indications that royalists might assume an attitude unfriendly to the New England Puritans. News came to remote New England only at intervals but it could be interpreted readily and sadly. On the face of it, it meant that in case of apparently immediate need of aid for the colonies, there could be none. More recent news from the homeland would be more favorable. Cromwell had reorganized a mob-like army with his more sober-minded, farmer "Ironsides"- a matter of cropped-hair Puritan Roundheads against Cavaliers. It is obvious foreign issues influenced colonial policy. With conditions in England preventing protection it came to be September 7th, 1643 when [New Englanders] came to advance the kingdom of Christ and enjoy religious freedom; the settlements were more dispersed than was first intended and they were surrounded by people of several nations and strange languages which might prove injurious now or for future generations; the natives had proved troublesome and dangerous and have of late combined themselves. [Charles Burpee][7]

This great land of Southern New England now seems to have been fashioned by removing the heathens from their home and replacing them with a civilized state of English Puritans (aside from Rhode Island); the changeover was not so simple, though. It is true that Puritanism had dedicated itself to warfare against sin[8], and within New England the destruction of war against sin devastated the strongest Indian tribes holding the most valuable land.

Still, a vast loss to the Indian culture and property was undoubtedly the result of illness. Death because of foreign diseases became a common occurrence to the native families of the Massachusetts, Wampanoag, and other Southern New England tribes throughout the period of settlement until the end of their existence. Around 1612 in Norumbega, what New England was once called, a lethal strain of infectious fever, as defined by William Bradford, was first spawned through fisherman and explorers infecting the Atlantic coast. The illness decimated the coastal Wampanoag and Massachusetts tribes for the next three years and the mighty sachems could offer no protection for their tribes. The arrival of European diseases left the Plymouth settlers able to encamp upon the uninhibited fields of the Wampanoags' land in Patuxet in 1620.

The destruction brought on by war and disease were the major factors in changing the Indians' way of life and affiliation throughout the building of colonial settlement. Thus the ever-changing tribes increasingly entered into a state of confusion. Tradition held by families and tribes were slipping away with the passing of entire families through both disease and war. It came to the point that there stood no man to pass down the tradition inherited from the previous generations as they continuously succumbed to some form of illness or violence. What formed tribes after pandemic outbreaks or violence was the joining together of fragmented tribes.

An infusion of Indian customs into English colonial society thus occurred as the tribal traditions became lost. The weakened tribes were open to find some type of structure for living in the same, but now changed environment. Some Indians, searching for guidance, chose the path of conversion to Christianity after witnessing many misfortunes of their brethren.

A great factor in this change of belief for the Indian was that the sachem—or Sagamore, or Shaman, or powwow—who served as the tribe's leader, or the tribe's priest and doctor, now failed to protect the community from the outbreak of pestilence or war. The tribe would make a payment of tribute (bushels of corn, deer, breaking up acres of land, and so on) to the sachem in return for his ability to protect. But as unprecedented calamities befell nearly every tribe, the leading Indians were viewed as not fulfilling their obligations toward their subjects. The great tragedy is that protection would be sought from Puritan officials who thought they were themselves God's chosen people. The flood of pestilence surged in cycles in 1612, 1613, 1618, 1633, 1643, 1646, and 1652, and disease would continually afflict tribes and never lay dormant for long. The other loss of security for many of the stronger tribes came during the two great New England Indian Wars in 1637 and 1675.

The devastating effect of disease reduced the Indian population, but war also served as a potent factor in the breakdown of the Southern New England tribes, especially the tribes that increased their strength because they had not been eliminated by pandemic as their Indian rivals had.

The means, by which the removal of the Indian took place, as the following work intends to reveal, was not through civilized and Christian behavior, which the New England Puritan claimed to practice after a rebirth into the kingdom of God. The colonial action upon the Indian, on the contrary, was one of discrimination and prejudice. Puritan settlers who were practicing in a divine nature- as it was a requirement for the Puritan to obtain rebirth and enter the Kingdom of God only through living a holy life- were committing acts on account of a selfish ego not a humble spirit

The Indians, however, were welcoming and kind. They did not expect to change any form of the new arrivals behavior. The Indians shared their land with the colonists under the presumption that the colonists would use the land and share it as the natives had. The successful development of the colonies reversed the roles of the Indian and the white man. At first, wilderness survival for the English settlers was dependent on the Indian; however, following a generation's perseverance of constructing a settlement both structurally and spiritually, many Indian tribes became dependent upon the colonists. The colonists, there is no question, were intent to conquer and, in turn, did not wish to equally share the land that would persistently become theirs.

This conquest of the New England Indian lands, moreover, didn't occur rapidly. There was actually peace and civility between the first generation of settlers and Indians. The law of nature practiced by the Indians and the law of man practiced by the Puritans did coexist more or less effectively for a generation.

There were significant hypocrisies, though, within Puritan belief that would permanently separate the two. Such inconsistencies led to a slow decay in the relationship between Indian and settler in New England. The peaceful intercourse maintained by the first generation of Massachusetts settlers with the Indians did not continue with the following generations. The increase of petty insults, disrespect, and ignorance on the part of the Puritans—all of which incited the Indians—shaped an ever-changing atmosphere within New England as material wealth began to take precedence over natural wealth.

There are many men who believe that the expansionist conquest is the natural right of European colonists and that there is no need to appreciate the former inhabitants of the land. As long as it is only necessary to praise the conquerors, there is no need to learn of the struggles and sacrifices of the Indian. This expansionist movement has become successful through the use of legal instruments. That is, colonial law justified almost every act they performed. The colonization of the Indian lands, which were used by the original natives publicly in every democratic sense, from firewood to hunting grounds, had now become private property largely due to submission for protection. Land became only affordable to those with the means to afford such property. Eventually, the Indians' source of commerce, wampam-peag, was eliminated and they had no way to afford the civilized customs the English had adapted them toward. Debts were made the Indian could not repay. Anger and fear developed among both peoples, and offensive preventative violence became necessary in order for colonial protection. War declared upon the uncivilized Indians was always presented by the New England settlers as the will of God. In his famous eulogy to King Philip William Apess expressed his opinion of the misinterpretation of civilized acts.

> Now, if we have common sense and ability to allow the difference between the civilized and the uncivilized, we cannot but see that one mode of warfare is as just as the other; for, while one is sanctioned by authority of the enlightened and cultivated men, the other is an agreement according to the pure laws of nature, growing out of natural consequences; for nature always has her defense for every beast of the field; even the reptiles of the earth and the fishes of the sea have their weapons of war. But though frail man was made for a nobler purpose, to live, to love, and adore his God, and do good to his brother. However, most men are governed by animal passions, which are not true principles of God.
>
> The, pretended, hypocritical Christian says it was the design of God that they shall murder and slay others, because they have the power. Power was not given us to abuse each other, but a mere power delegated to us by the King of heaven, a weapon of defense against error and evil; and when abused, it will turn into destruction. Mark the history of nations throughout the world. [William Apess][9]

These uncivilized acts unjustly done to others, however, will always come back around. If the colonists continue this insane process of removing a race of man from his original habitat—a man different from those familiar with civilization—there will be an overall devastating result. It may not happen overnight, but as it is taken from the Indian it will be taken from the colonists.

The settlers were unwilling to treat the Indians as equals because of their manner, means of torture, and beastly way of life; and the white man used all of these examples of heathenism to easily justify any act committed by the colony upon the uncivilized heathen. Would you call them "civilized," these men who use murder, lies, and war to obtain unnecessary land? We do not call those corrupt men gluttonous; we call them our forefathers. If corrupt measures, presented to be those of a Christian, do indeed work and grow to be celebrated, what will become of our future generations?

A house is only as strong as the way it is built and the foundation which it is supported upon. Yet, if built with compromising measures, will not the house develop cracks in its struts and beams and begin to founder?

The settling of Govenor John Winthrop in 1630 and the great migration of Englishmen into Massachusetts Bay are among the most important events that formed the Southern New England civilized colonies, and set in motion the removal of the uncivilized New England Indians. The continual influx of settlers throughout the 1630s caused the overcrowding of the eastern coastline of Massachusetts by the Massachusetts Bay Company, and this rapid population increase to the once empty, plague-stricken land of the Massachusetts Tribe led Englishmen into Connecticut. However, you will learn further ahead that the Plymouth colony also sent men to Connecticut.

Of importance, in my eyes, is that before Winthrop left England on board the Arbella, he had promised in the governor's oath of office in 1628-29 to bring the natives of this new country to the knowledge of the true Christian God. However, it took sixteen years after Winthrop's arrival to just begin efforts by England to fulfill this expectation and begin converting the Indians toward Christianity. For the reader, this may soon appear to have done more harm than good. With the increasing English population within New England and the expectations held by few of the Puritans serving as missionaries to the Indians, the Indians became separated into two groups: those subject to the colonies and those not. Sadly, many of those for the colonies were treated just as poorly as those against.

It must be said that the term Christian, or praying, Indians is a great hypocrisy in the literal sense. The colonists used Christian Indians more as tools for warfare rather than to spread the word of the almighty Lord. Hence in Southern New England, many years after the arrival of John Winthrop with his proclaimed missionary intentions, there developed preying Indians and praying Indians. For many praying Indians the term preying would apply just as appropriately. It is incredible how much the two intertwine. To determine any difference, if one exists, we must first understand the difference between the two conflicting roles, why Indians chose one path or the other, and how they were driven toward that particular direction.

I hope to share examples upon whether an earnest collective effort for the successful transformation of the heathen toward Christianity existed. And, if so, was it a sincere effort by the English missionaries? The conversion of the true native New Englander was one of the first justifications for the Massachusetts Bay Company to embark toward New England in 1630 following the settlement of

Plymouth and Salem. Why, though, would a group of wealthy merchants even consider having the ability to transform a savage?

Well, to start, they were Puritans and came to New England not for commercial gain, but because of deep religious convictions along with the expectation to build a Christian nation comparable to no other. As we will see, however, the intentions of the Puritan in New England stemmed from much more than just religious acts. The confusion for me falls upon all the military preparedness mandated by the Puritans. I am aware the Puritan in the vast wilderness was to be prepared for an instant Indian invasion, which forced all colonies to mandate all their residents to have guns and powder readily available. Yet, violence is not what the Christian stood for, as the Puritan relinquished wrong to obtain rebirth into the Kingdom of God. The Puritans, in their religious terms, should have been adverse to the intentions of a military power.

Puritanism grew through a religious reformation movement in opposition of the domineering Catholic Church in Rome. John Calvin expanded a dissent toward the Catholic religion during a period of religious reform in the sixteenth century. The Puritans, acquiring a belief in the importance of religious freedoms inherited from the Reformation, sought to keep English liberty away from the Catholic Hierarchy. New England became the ultimate result of this religious and political movement. Most of the leading men in New England were all Calvinists: John Endicott, the presiding magistrate of the Salem Colony during the beginnings of the Massachusetts Bay Company; John Winthrop, governor of the Massachusetts Bay Colony; Thomas Hooker, the founder of Hartford, Connecticut; and Roger Williams, the founder of the Rhode Island Colony.[10]

It must be asked, what is a Calvinist? What is a Puritan, or, otherwise, a Protestant? A protestant is just as the word sounds: one who stands in protest. Also, we need to discover why Calvinism still has such a lasting effect on the Puritan movement.

So why was Calvin so passionate for a reformation? His knowledge and passion led him to believe he held the ability to reform the Catholic Church from within. Most intended reformers were born, baptized, confirmed, and educated in the Catholic Church, they were, however, ultimately banned. Calvin felt it necessary to share the understanding of predestination and election into the Kingdom of God:

> The power for the presence of all things to be created is the most important characteristic to justify the existence of predestination in heaven or on earth. This all-embracing predestination, the Calvinist places, not in the hands of man, and still less in the hand of blind natural force, but in the hand of Almighty God, supreme Creator and Possessor of heaven and earth. It is in the figure of the potter and the clay that Scripture has formed, from the time of the prophets and still continuously developing, an election by God determining those who are to live in the kingdom of God. It is one of His perfections that He has the best possible plan, and that He conducts the course of history to its appointed end. And to admit that He has a plan which He carries out is to admit Predestination. Election in creation, election in providence, and election also to eternal life; election in the realm of grace as

20

well as in the realm of nature; continues His eternal plan. (Loraine Boettner)[11]

It is claimed that election is granted to those who are predestined prior to their birth to join the Kingdom of God. This individual election of certain men to acquire eternal life occurs even before the creation of the physical state of an infant. Those elected, however, will not join the kingdom immediately after birth. All infants will grow to become sinners and join the fall into sin as Adam had. We all are sinners, and it is sin which brings upon death and darkness, eliminating eternal life. Man, ignorant to do good and dead in sin, is not able, by his own strength, to convert himself. The inevitability to sin left man unable to obtain redemption. It is true we are all caught up in sin, as even our forefathers have been trapped because of sin, but it is claimed there is a rebirth predestined to those elected by God to obtain the mercy of the Lord.

Calvinism expresses that as a result of the fall into sin all men are guilty, corrupted, hopelessly lost; their souls dead. Man has to become dependent on divine faith in order for the development of a true spiritual life, but first he must be thrown into humiliation and despair to become lifted by faith toward supernatural strength. From this mass of sinners, God has elected some to find salvation through Christ. Thus the life which Jesus sacrificed has been predestined to certain individuals who obtain his virtues, while passing others by. For me, it seems the concepts of election and predestination claim that the highest creative power has favored some men over others, while the only evidence of who the elected are is found inside the individual, and that sole individual, if he truly is elected, will not disclose to anyone his superior nature because ego does not exist within him.

The theology of Calvin would evolve (or devolve) within the New England Puritan as it had all over Europe. It seems as this reformation gained strength and created its own form of religious dominance in New England, any ulterior beliefs to Puritanism were considered inferior. Ironically, the Puritans fled from the enforcement of religion to force it upon Indians within their own bounds. Through this religious development, we must ask: was it predetermined by the supreme creator that there were God's elect among the heathen Indians within Southern New England? I think most Puritans did not consider any of the Indians to be elected, as the settlers were content to simply justify their actions and beliefs in order to satisfy their material wants.

It is true; one of the major objectives for prominent Puritans immigrating to the new world was to convert the Indians to believe in the Gospel. Yet, if the acceptance toward the belief in Jesus Christ was a major factor in fulfilling the election of God to enter into the Kingdom of God, the Indians had quite a long way to both civilize and educate themselves just to understand the concept of the Christian Religion.

The hypocrisy in the aspirations of the Puritans, for me, falls within their actions which were in contrast to the divinity within the elected, which they proclaimed to follow. The events that transpired against the Indians to colonize the wilderness were far from those of the righteous. The Indians inevitably began to question the validity of the Puritans beliefs, and "whether English men were ever at any time so ignorant of God and Jesus Christ as themselves?"

In response to the Indians question, the Indians were told:

> There are two sorts of Englishmen: some are bad and naught, and live wickedly and basely, and these kind of Englishmen were in a manner as ignorant of Jesus Christ as the Indians now are; but there are a second sort of Englishmen, who though for a time they lived wickedly also, like other profane and ignorant English, yet, repenting of their sins, and seeking after God and Jesus Christ, they are good men now, and now know Christ, and love Christ, and pray to Christ, and are thankful for all they have to Christ, and shall at last, when they die, go up to heaven to Christ: and we told them that all these also were once as ignorant of God and Jesus Christ as the Indians are, but by seeking to know him, by reading his book, and hearing his word, and praying to him, they now know Jesus Christ; and just so shall the Indians know him, if they so seek him also, although at the present they be extremely ignorant of him. [Church Missionary Society][12]

Therefore, could it be possible to save the heathens when they have never even heard of Christ who is the only means of salvation?[13] The answer, if one exists, is where my fascination lies. If the men in New England, who first claimed missionary work, were sincere and sacrificed success to share the knowledge of the Elect with the Heathen, would there have developed such a catastrophic war with the Indians in 1675? The self-interest of the farmers and speculators positioned the missionary work with the Indians at the bottom of colonial affairs, ultimately casting the Indians as an obstacle. At first, though, the worthy men involved with the Massachusetts Bay Company seriously believed that the aborigines of New England were the degenerate descendants of the ten lost tribes of Israel, and it was hoped that they might now be reclaimed from this strange backsliding.[14]

It is true the few missionaries who faithfully believed in converting the Indians into Christians were deprived of funds at first, because the funds were from the missionaries own or other private sources. New England missionaries sent word to England for want of money in order to convert the poor heathen, but why could not God himself convert them where they were if it was of necessity? Instead the missionaries, aside from Thomas Mayhew Jr. in Martha's Vineyard, were to first drive them out of their homeland.

In the beginning of settlement in Plymouth 1620-21 it was an Indian named Samoset, who on entering the English settlement at Patuxet, otherwise Plymouth, repeated those words, "Welcome, Englishmen! Welcome, Englishmen!" Hence the genesis of transforming Patuxet into Plymouth would now come into fruition because of Samoset's great sachem Massasoit, who chose for his Wampanoags to deal peacefully with the invaders.

Massasoit was the first great sachem who peaceably welcomed the planters of Plymouth in 1621 to a new world filled with heathens. The Wampanoag sachem held many smaller tribes together as the Wampanoags were more of a confederacy. Massasoit's home tribe was called the Pokanokets. That Massasoit should be able to hold so many tribes together with constant changes, and hold his subjects to not apply violence on invaders of their territory, required a character belonging to few. The extent of the Wampanoag Confederacy territory over which Massasoit held power has been determined as all of Cape Cod, and that portion of Massachusetts and Rhode Island lying between Narragansett and Massachusetts Bays, and perhaps extending westerly into Connecticut, together with all the neighboring islands.[15]

The idea of converting the heathen would later become somewhat established throughout Massasoit's country as the settlers became planted and settled, even though religious conversion was not favored by Massasoit. Massasoit was largely responsible for the English to settle in Plymouth. How incredible fate has worked so that Massasoit's second son Phillip (otherwise known as King Phillip, Metacomet, Pometacom or Metacom) will forever be known as the leader of the Indians in their do or die fight against the colonists. He would also be the last great sachem of the Wampanoags. King Philip fell to his death during the last Indian War of New England ending in 1676, also ending any remnant of Indian tradition.

Ironically, the beginning of colonial New England was all possible because of Massasoit's peaceful nature toward the English pilgrims. Massasoit's need of protection from the neighboring Narragansett tribe may have been the largest factor toward his welcoming conduct. Thus, at first contact it may have been the Wampanoag Indian who was guided by self-interest rather than the Pilgrim, as the threatening rival of the Wampanoags, the neighboring Narragansett Indians, didn't feel any effect of the 1612-19 plague keeping their strength and numbers.

Fifty years after the birth of Plymouth, though, Massasoit's son Metacomet became to be known as King Philip, the great iconic enemy of the English. The demise of the Southern New England Indian civilization accompanied King Phillip's death along with the demise of the Narragansetts at the hands of the colonists, which all was possible because the settlers were securely established to conquer only because of Philip's father. The consequences of the last great Indian War in 1675-1676, known as the war of King Phillip, the Narragansett War, or the second Puritan conquest, forced Puritan society to neglect their obligation to Christian Indians, who should have been protected by the same laws that governed English settlers.

The relationship between the Christian and non-Christian Indians was one of deceit just as most Indian relations had become with the addition of the English element. The relationship between the sachem and his community had also gone awry. Converts in "colonial-sanctioned praying towns" denied tribute payment toward their former Indian leaders, which threatened the sachems' power.[16]

As the reader will see, the Southern New England Puritan and Indian societies were so greatly intertwined that events occurring twenty years prior had an impact on the conduct of the present-day Puritan or Indian. The relationship between heathen Indian and praying Indian, however, came to its conclusion with the Indian War of 1675, which brought about the permanent separation of the two within the same society. The Indian land, aside from reservations, was all but gone after the war and there was no longer any use for the heathen in day-to-day life.

Indians became looked upon as an obstruction to the Puritan evolution. If there was no benefit to the colony, the Indians were pushed aside at will. It was assumed that God meant this new world for the Puritans, and gave away the lands of the heathen for their inheritance. [17]

By 1674, the Christian Indians in New England had their villages (reservations) in various locations within the English Colonies, and at a considerable distance from each other:

1st: Within the Islands of Martha's Vineyard, resided many hundreds of the Wampanoag Indians that profess the Gospel, who began their practice under the guidance of Thomas Mayhew Jr., around 1643. These Indians had little involvement of the 1675 Indian war. The English that dwell upon those Islands have held a good relationship with those Indians all the time before, during, and after the war.

2nd: A large number of Christian Indians live within the jurisdiction of New Plymouth, called the Cape Indians, once considered of the Wampanoag confederacy: Nauset, Suconesset, Manamet, Mashpee, Shaumes. These Indians have shared great peace with their English neighbors, and several of them have served the English in the war, "especially in the heat of the war". They were courageous and trustworthy during the time of war.

At the beginning of the war, the English of that colony were untrustworthy of them, and delayed in bringing them into the front lines. However, those Christian Indians were continuously ready and willing to join with the English against their brethren. It is so significant to colonial success that those Indians proved so diligent to the English interest, considering the war first began in the Colony of Plymouth and that hostile Indians were also Wampanoags.

3rd: There were a few praying Indians in Connecticut. There were about 40 persons considered to be of the Mohegan tribe that began to embrace the Christian religion. They lived near to New Norwich. However, the chief Sachem, Uncas, and his eldest son, Oneko, were not followers of the Christian religion, even though they and their people still have continuously joined the English in war, going all the way back to the first Indian war in Connecticut in 1637 against the Pequot tribe.[18]

With the unusual foresight Uncas had, he was able to join in an alliance with the whites. With the defeat of the Pequot tribe in 1637 he would thus build up the power of the Mohegans on the ruins of the Pequot confederacy, which had earlier held dominance throughout Connecticut, to the east of and along the river. He held the character of a statesmen as well as a warrior, while continuously inciting the other tribes. He would obtain a strength obtained through alliance comparable to no other Indian throughout New England. Uncas also continually claimed himself and tribe as an injured group by other tribes to generate concern and action out of his Connecticut allies. "Valuable in its results for the Connecticut settlers, this alliance was to be one of the strongest in terms of destroying the confidence of the unfavorable tribes."[19]

The Mohegans were very effective in combating and removing any unfavorable Indians by their skulking practice of warfare, and they grew into a force that didn't receive any colonial consequence for their actions toward opposing tribes, even if the acts were unjust. Uncas also made many accusations against numerous tribes and other sachems. The Mohegans, furthermore, proved extremely faithful toward the English in warfare, especially against their ancient enemies the Narragansetts in 1675.

4th: The final Indian confederations that chose Christianity and deserve recognition are those that inhabit the jurisdiction or Colony of Massachusetts. Many of these tribes belong to either the Massachusetts Tribe or Nipmuc Confederacy. As those of the Massachusetts tribe were: Weechagaskas, Neponset, Punkapoage, Nonantan, Nashaway.

These tribes were taught and instructed in the Christian faith by John Eliot. The great John Eliot labored with the Massachusetts Indians on the Atlantic coast for thirty years and then later introduced Christianity to the Nipmucs further west.[20]

Daniel Gookin also performed laboriously as a Massachusetts Magistrate in the conversion efforts upon the Nipmucks of western Massachusetts.

Major General Daniel Gookin, of Cambridge, who was born in Kent Co., England, and first settled in Virginia, in 1639, and in Cambridge, in 1644 was the superintendent of all the Indians that had subjected themselves to the colonial government. He was accustomed to accompany the apostle John Eliot in his missionary tours. While Eliot preached the gospel to the Indians, Gookin administered civil affairs among them.

In 1636, Plymouth Colony enacted laws to provide for the preaching of the gospel among the Indians, and ten years later the Massachusetts Colony passed a similar act, under which, or in accord with which, the good work of Gookin and Eliot was done, though their efforts went beyond the letter of the law, in the direction of humanity, for the uplifting and Christianization of the Indians.

The aid of the general court was promised to all the praying Indians, through Gookin, in grants of land for their benefits on condition of their subjection to the yoke of Christ, and this promise would have been carried out on those conditions to all of them had not King Philip's war broken out and put a check to many of General Gookin's contemplated projects for the benefit of the uncivilized races. [Nipmuck Indians][21]

With the first generation of planters taking up most of the land by farming and grazing around Boston, their children had to undertake a small amount of land or move farther west. And the farther out they moved, the more they would outstrip ancestral land held by the Indians, and the Nipmucs were witnessing this population influx in the 1670's. The Massachusetts and Nipmuck Praying Indians also felt more of the destructive impact of the 1675 Indian war than all the rest of the Christian Indians. The Nipmuck and Massachusetts praying village populations were:

Natick: 145
Punkapoag: 60
Hassanamessit: 60
Okommakamesit: 50

Wamesit: 75
Nashobah: 50
Magunkaquog: 55
Manchage: 60
Chabananongkomun: 45
Maanexit: 100
Quantisset: 100
Wabquissit: 150
Pachackoog: 100
Waeuntung: 50

White Settlements formed in Concord in 1635, Sudbury in 1638, Lancaster in 1643, and Marlboro in 1654. The Indian would destroy the first attempts at settlement in all four of these towns. Previous to the advent of the white man, there were three tribes of Indians there, having their headquarters on three well-known hills. One of them, the largest tribe, comprising about 100 souls, under Sagamore John, had their seat on Pakachoag Hill. Another tribe under Sagamore Solomon dwelt on Asnebumskit and another smaller tribe was on Wigwam Hill, on the northwestern border of Lake Quinsigamond, under Sagamore Pannasanet.

The rights of these tribes of Indians to all this land, comprising sixty-four square miles, 43,000 acres, were purchased by the Committee of the General Court having in charge the settlement of the place, the consideration given being "twelve pounds of lawful money of New England, or the full value thereof in other specie, two coats and four yards of trading-cloth, valued at twenty-six shillings, and full satisfaction in trucking cloth and corn. [The Nipmuc Indians][22]

One important point I must mention before I start to explain the beginning of the colonization of New England is that if the fidelity and integrity of the praying Indians had been trusted and practiced in the beginning of the 1675 war, great mischief might have been prevented. Superintendent of Indian Affairs Daniel Gookin wrote on the matter of how great a tool the praying Indian could have been:

Most of the praying towns, in the beginning of the war, had put themselves into a defensive position, and had made forts for their security against the hostile Indian. It was suggested and proposed to the authority of New England, that some Englishmen, about one third part, might have joined with those Christian Indians in each fort, an act which the praying Indians greatly desired. The Christian Indian fidelity might have been better demonstrated by bringing in Englishmen, and that with the assistance and company of some of those English soldiers, the Indians would have been freed to scout daily or range the woods from town to town, in their several assigned praying locations. The Indians would have proved themselves very capable to guard the English frontiers, which held such vast bounds. Thus this might have prevented the disaster that afterward ensued. This was not only the thought of some English, but the desire of some of the most wise of the Christian Indians, who in all their actions wanted to show the English of their fidelity and friendship to them and the interest of the Christian religion. The Indians wanted to eliminate the animosity and displeasure that they thought was felt by some English against them.

The Christian Indians were ready to comply with all commands of the English authority. However, the direction of peace and independence became rejected, and on the contrary, many local colonists spawned a spirit of hostility and hatred against those poor Christian Indians. Thus many distressing calamities befell both sides, with many Christian Indians joining the side of King Phillip and the rebellion as the war unfolded.[23] (Daniel Gookin 1612?-1687)

Even before the war of King Phillip in 1675, there wasn't a feeling of firm peace for tribes after the Pequot war in 1637. Furthermore, the Massachusetts tribe was broken and weakened, mostly due to disease, and the remnants of that tribe converted to Christianity, and occupied the villages around the Massachusetts Bay towns, seeking guidance and protection. Upon the east coast of Narragansett Bay lived the Wampanoags, also reduced by the plague. Upon the west shore of the Bay, extending to the Pawcatuck River, lived the Narragansetts who held an army of about a thousand warriors. Between the Connecticut River and the Thames were the remains of the old Pequot confederacy, on whose ruins after defeat in 1637, Uncas, the son-in-law of the Pequot sachem, Sassacus, had now ruled over and used the former Pequots to increase his supremacy as Sachem of the Mohegans. Extending into northeastern Connecticut, central Massachusetts and Providence Plantations were the Nipmucks, or Nipnets [fresh water Indians], this tribe formed about a thousand warriors, smaller bands formed this confederacy.[24]

Massachusetts and Connecticut held very different relationships with their native Indians. In the colony of Connecticut, the Indians performed for the colony's benefit. Connecticut chose the same course during the war in 1675 that they had taken in 1637: they kept a fair stance with their neighboring Indians, the Mohegans. This tribe was not only very helpful to the English in their expeditions, but served as a guard to the Connecticut frontiers. The Mohegan Sachem Uncas had no interest with the principles of Christianity as many Massachusetts tribes had, yet the Connecticut tribe proved to be very faithful and serviceable to the English. The Mohegans were instrumental to the preservation of the Connecticut colony which had but one small deserted village burnt in the 1675 war, and very little of their other substance destroyed by the enemy.[25] On the other hand, throughout the war of 1675 the Massachusetts colonists, on the strength of false accusations, rounded up large bodies of praying Indians who were entirely faithful to the English and interned them on the frigid Deer Island. Superintendent of Indian Affairs Gookin accurately described the discrimination toward the Indians:

It is the hatred of Satan against Christ's work among those Indians that hindered their progress in the Christian religion. The work of the devil is not only to be blamed upon the Indian conduct, but also on men within the

27

colony who are just as guilty of evil doings. Both Indians and Englishmen became enraged in finding other Englishmen and Indians professing the Christian religion toward the non-converted Indian. This conversion, however, would become so injurious to the converts without an earnest reason. To direct them away from the Christian religion; and if the devil with this trick has prevailed, then the whole work of Christ among the Indians is completely wasted. The success of eliminating Christian Indians has satisfied Satan and his instruments [which may now set an unfortunate precedence]. [Daniel Gookin][26]

In all fairness we must take into account the aspect of what the colonists had to face in terms of terror. The Pilgrims were welcomed to stay because of Massasoit's self-interest and they decided to stay and expand. They felt if they were to survive in the wilderness it was necessary to combat any unfavorable Indian Tribe. The Pequot's, for instance, had their fortification destroyed by Captain Mason and his Connecticut force in 1637 after the tribe had murdered and committed many horrific acts against Englishmen. Captain Mason described his intentions upon evil Indians:

The reader may hope, as myself, that the face of God is set against those that do evil and to cut off the remembrance of them from the earth. For the colonists, however, the lord was pleased to strike the evil Indians, and to give the colonist's the Indian land for an inheritance. The Puritans felt the lord remembered them in their low estate, and redeemed them out of the enemies' hands. [John Mason][27]

It may be true that some successful men have benefitted from the works of God, as it has worked out so well for one particular race of men in Southern New England. Only time will tell if combating evil conduct with evil conduct will breed success. My grave concern is if the design for colonization remains to be for private profit, the public good will forever be overlooked, just as the Indian has discovered.

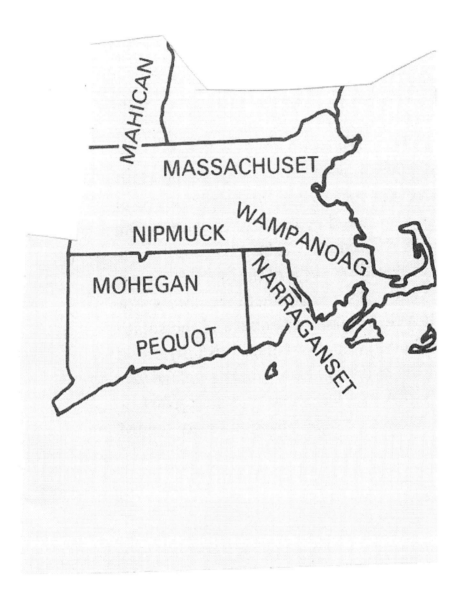

Southern New England Tribes

Adopted from The Indian and the White Man, Chandler Whipple
The Berkshire Traveller Press, 1974

Part II: The Wethersfield Massacre

Well, I am now writing in the year 1676 trying to comprehend what factors influenced Southern New England Indians toward becoming a praying or a preying Indian. I will share what I have uncovered on the origin of the Indian conversion process, as well as the process of colonizing a few New England towns.

The necessary molding of the Christian Indian seems very insincere to me. Only a handful of men seem to have been fully dedicated to the project whereas the majority of men within the towns were for eliminating the Indians. I have become very confused through this process how colonial men who chose deceitful practices are connected and dependent upon the loving God, Jesus Christ. They have become so successful with expansion through violence, which seems the opposite of what a Christian stands for. I must remind the reader, however, that at the initial genesis of Southern New England there was a respect formed between the Indian and Pilgrim. Unfortunately, the following generations did not share that same respect for each other, and that may be in large part because the settlers were not in need of the Indians for protection or food any longer; they now desired land.

Land became easily obtainable as Puritans in New England gained great dominance over Indians for the last forty years, and the conversion of Indians is one of the great factors upon land submission. By submission to the colony the Indian

31

tribe would relinquish its land rights and then be sanctioned to a reservation which was defined as a praying Indian village.

It must be said, though, that the settlers, in most cases, acquired enormous plots of land from different tribes by honest measures. Many poor settlers paid in goods, difficult to acquire, for land held by the Indians, who valued the items as of an equivalent value. The Indians would come to discover that the white man held an entirely different definition on the ownership of land, which classified private property as land where no one else would be allowed to hunt and fish upon it. The realization of losing ancient territory was a slow process because other land was unoccupied where the Indians could find fish and game, but by the time their vast areas became populated with foreigners, it was too late.[28]

In the pages that follow, I will also include three major events of violence by the Puritans toward the Indian that were of great importance in furthering Indian submission: the Pequot War (1637), the murder of Miantonomo (1643), and King Philip's War (1675). In each case, it is not only the actual event that is extraordinary but also the events that had led up to and followed the moment of violence. Above all, we must always keep in mind that none of these events would have come to fruition if Massasoit did not interact peacefully with the plantation of Plymouth settlers. The three events I will describe serve as the root for the great growth of selfishness, arrogance, and ignorance toward Indian, increasing with every successive generation. The passion of the English for territory, their confidence that God had opened up New England for the exclusive occupancy of Puritans, their contempt for the Indians, and utter disregard of the Indians' right; made war with the Indians inevitable, sooner or later.[29]

The Pequot War of 1637, the first New England War, is the first incident I will describe. This war, though more of an invasion in nature, is the first major incident which increased the separation and fear between colony and Indian. The Pequots were a branch of the great Muhhekanew (or Mohican) nation. Their main seat had been on the east bank of the Hudson River, in the area of Albany. The Pequots were driven from their country by the Mohawks and they then chose to invade eastern Connecticut. As a result, the powerful Pequots overwhelmed the Connecticut Tribes whom they encountered, and exacted tribute from the tribes who were inferior. It is true this method used by the Pequots in Connecticut may be comparable to that of the English, in which strength enabled conquest.

The Pequots settled near the seacoast, on territory formerly occupied by the Niantics, which was on both sides of the Mystic River. Not content with the conquest of the seashore tribes, the Pequots made war on the Sequins of the central Connecticut valley around the area of Hartford and Wethersfield. According to the Dutch account, the Sequins were beaten in three encounters, and so became tributary to the Pequots. This was some years after the first visit of the Dutch in 1614 by Adriaen Block, but probably not earlier than 1630.[30]

No event in the early history of New England had a greater influence on its development than the Pequot War had. This war eliminated the possibility of colonial destruction by Pequot violence, which threatened to crush the infant province of Connecticut. The war established a country that would be without a major outbreak of war for nearly forty years and it also brought about a large expansion of settlers throughout Connecticut's wilderness.

The Pequot War's origin could be considered to have begun in the "year 1633, and 1634, as several Englishmen arriving from England, in Massachusetts, went to the Western Country to discover the Connecticut River. The next year the English began to remove there and by the beginning of 1637, Hartford, Windsor, and Wethersfield were settled, along with a fortification built at Saybrook on the mouth of the River."[31]

It was in 1636 when the emigrants from Watertown, Dorchester, and Newton, Massachusetts, had really pushed their way through the dense forests leaving the crowded Massachusetts Bay and occupied the Connecticut Valley. Thus a struggle for existence became inevitable between the settlers and the Pequot Indians who claimed those bounds. The settlers found the country along the Connecticut River down to its mouth dominated by the Pequots, the most dreaded of all the tribes in New England. The Pequots had driven away the weaker tribes or held them under subjection. Their total strength at that time is estimated to have been about three thousand. Their chief sachem was Sassacus, and their principal stronghold was at the mouth of the Thames (Pequot) River.[32]

It may be difficult to feel sympathy for the Pequots who ultimately felt the same wrath by the English that they had committed upon Connecticut River Tribes. The Pequots would also commit heinous acts against the newly settled English whether in revenge for colonial acts or not. Maybe in the universe of true justice the Pequots received what they were due, but it was the generations of Southern New England Indians after the Pequot War who became aware of the consequence of colonial dissent and thus chose not to practice in it. Yet, even with transforming towards a civilized lifestyle, mistreatment ensued upon Christian Indians.

The account of what I have witnessed and heard of on the Pequot War in this ever-changing world of rumor must begin being told at a great distant time and location from my current home in Springfield, Massachusetts. In unraveling the most momentous affair for the entirety of the colonies existence, as well as the first war of Connecticut, where I was a resident at the time, I will open during the time of my father's decision to come to the New World and what events led to it. I feel it is of necessity for the reader to be shared the information my father has shared with me, which is all connected with how we ended up in Wethersfield in search of a new independence, which was also the site of the worst assault on the colonists by the Pequots.

My father, also named, Thomas Adams, taught me the most of what I know on the crossing of the Atlantic by the English Separatists. The Pequot war may have happened because the Pequots would not change their behavior, which the Separatists wanted the English Church to do. The English Separatists wanted to practice the spirit of nationalism and not for the King to be supreme in the matter of religion. There is one bold act performed by Martin Luther, in particular, that strongly represents the beginning momentum of a movement which ultimately brought the Puritan and Separatists courage to foster dissent and reform against the Catholic and English Church. My father described it as the beginning of a new era.

The Puritan exodus was first taught to me when I was about twelve when we lived in Wethersfield, Connecticut around 1637, just after the Pequot War.

Religion, my father explained, was the reason for many problems and it was the reason he ended up in the New World. The important development for the independent religious movement in England arose in 1517. Tetzel, who was a Dominican Friar and the guardian of the Franciscan Friars, had been appointed by the Cardinal Archbishop of Mainz joint commissaries for Saxony and North Germany, to preach to all who would contribute to the rebuilding of St. Peter's Church at Rome. While Tetzel was preaching in the Schlosskirche at Juterbogk, Martin Luther had nailed to the door his ninety-five theses, in which he challenged Tetzel to a defense of his position and took a stand defiant to the established order, from which he refused to withdraw. Martin Luther is considered the first leader in the Reformation. He was the one who first held the strength to protest the feelings that had long been felt of many thoughtful and conscientious people in Europe. No one else up to that point found the courage, energy, or conviction; yet, once Luther was heard, the idea of reforming the Catholic Church began to spread.

Following Luther's motivation, John Calvin, a Frenchman, born in the year that Henry rose to the throne of England, would also expand the reformation and separate himself from the Catholic Church.

John Calvin was born on July 10, 1509 seventy miles northeast of Paris. Around the age of twenty-four he had prepared a speech for his friend, recently elected Rector of the University. On November 1, 1533 this speech to the University was a plea for a reformation on the basis of the New Testament and a bold attack on the scholastic theologians of the day, who were represented as a set of scholars, ignorant of the gospel. It seemed the papacy came to exert great power, political as well as religious, throughout Catholic Europe. The state of morals came to be nearly intolerable and even the priesthood became corrupt, which was expressed by Calvin through the elected Rector.

This speech, nevertheless, made the elected rector and Calvin have to flee Paris for their life. The Parliament regarded this speech as a manifesto of war upon the Catholic Church. Thus Calvin's rooms were searched and the authorities seized his books and papers. Twenty-four innocent Protestants were burned alive in public places of the city from November 10, 1534, till May 5, 1535. For nearly three years Calvin wandered as a fugitive under assumed names from place to place in southern France, Switzerland, and Italy, until he reached Geneva as his final destination. [33]

Luther and Calvin and all the other reformers of that period were predestinarians. It may surprise the reader to discover that the doctrine of Predestination was not made a matter of special study until near the end of the fourth century. This deep truth within Christianity was first presented by St. Augustine, the great Spirit-filled theologian. In his doctrines of sin and grace, he went far beyond the earlier theologians, and taught an unconditional election of grace, and restricted the purposes of redemption only for the definite circle of the elect.[34]

Thus the Reformation Calvin demanded was a revival of Augustinianism and through it Protestantism came into its own. Martin Luther, prior to Calvin, must be remembered for his role in the reformation as well. He was an Augustinian monk and from this rigorous theology he formulated his great principle of justification by faith alone. [Lorraine Boettner][35]

Henry VIII of England (1491-1547) also performed an act contrary toward the Catholic Church, which in consequence resulted because of a quarrel he held with the Pope and Cardinals concerning the ending of his marriage to Catherine of Aragon. Thus he would establish the Church of England as an independent religious body.

It is true Henry VIII. of England was born and died a Catholic, however, his decision in 1534, set his supremacy beyond that of the Pope of Rome. His decision had no religious importance, but simply showed that he wanted to divorce one woman to marry another. Nevertheless it became decided by the Pope to exclude him. This not only influenced Henry VIII, but it stirred the English into a dissenting attitude toward the traditional faith. As it came so shortly after Luther's outbreak, a movement by Englishmen to protest Catholic principles was beginning to arise.

If Luther the priest could oppose the philosophy that he had been taught for a long period of time because of his profession; if the King of England, who had been a supporter of the establishment, and had backed the views of the church of Rome, could set up an independent national church, what was to become of future revolts against religion? What was to prevent the men who followed Luther, the Church of England and Calvin in developing a different theory on their own?

Developing from these independent ideas, the Puritan fight against the hierarchy became a social tool, and the only solution lay in a real and thorough reformation of the religious practices that dramatically influenced society. With the increase of opposition held by the people for reformation, dissent against the government also grew amongst the people. Every ruler in England held his or her own individual persecution practices, while the people continually morphed their own theologies into one of independence. There were, though, various sects of dissenters carrying far different demands for change. Puritanism held many influential voices within the press, parliament, and among the country gentry.

In her opposition to this democratic movement, Queen Elizabeth troubled and tormented the Puritans as far as she thought it practical. In the conservative temper of the people, she found enough support to prevent a Puritan transformation of the church. It was early in Elizabeth's reign that the zeal of this extreme movement, inflamed by persecution, gave rise to the sect of Separatists. They in turn denied the royal supremacy over religious affairs and claimed the right to set up churches of their own, with pastors and elders and rules of discipline, independent of queen or bishop.

By 1576 the Separatists had come to be recognized as a group, under the lead of Robert Browne, a man of high social position:

> The separatists had openly broken with the Church of England, and proceeded to set up a completely separate body. No government in Europe at

that time would have tolerated the existence of such a society, outside and independent of the established institution, and it is no wonder that the bishops and the sheriffs of England got after this congregation with vehemence. Holland alone of all Europe would offer an asylum to these people, though not so much because the Dutch believed in toleration as because the Separatists were good Calvinists, as were the Dutch. [Perry Miller and Thomas H. Johnson,][36]

The Puritans wanted a simpler form of faith, especially with the reign of Elizabeth and the spread of corruption. "They believed in the established church and believed that reformers should come from within." There is no doubt the "Separatists believed that reformers should come out of the church and that church and state should be separate and distinct. It was 1602 when a group of Separatists chose the cultured John Robinson to be minister and, for ruling elder, William Brewster, at whose home in Scrooby the dissenters met and whence, with increasing numbers, they finally succeeded in fleeing to freer Holland in 1608."[37]

It wasn't, however, in the mainstream of Calvinism, but in one of its smaller streams that this world-famous movement originated. During the reign of Elizabeth it wasn't the purpose of the Puritans to separate themselves from the established church of which the sovereign was the head, but to remain within it and reform it according to their own wishes. For a time they were partially successful in this work, especially in simplifying the ritual and in giving a Calvinistic touch to the doctrines. In doing this they showed no conscious tendency towards freedom of thought, but rather a bigotry quite as intense as that which animated the system against which they were fighting. [The Beginnings of New England, John Fiskes] [38]

The year of 1603 was the closing for Elizabeth at the helm, and James Stuart came from Scotland to take her place. The conservative feelings with which the late queen had pursued Puritanism were soft in comparison with the opinions held by her successor. The Puritans, however, continued developing theocratic independence and concealed the true spirit against despotic privilege. People felt both lowly servants and kings must obey the eternal law of God.

The Puritans felt progress would come through resistance, but on the contrary, James Stuart's motives toward the Puritans are best described through the spiteful threat with which the king broke up a conference: "I will make them conform," he said, "or I will hurry them out of the land."

It was in 1606—two years after King James' fierce threat—that an independent church was organized. Another year hadn't even passed before its members had suffered so much at the hands of officers of the law that they began to think of following the example of former heretics and escaping to Holland.

In England, during this time, such a train of abuse and persecution followed the Puritans that they were forced to abandon their homes and quit their means of living. Ridicule exercised its wit and prisons exerted their power, but the power of spirit still triumphed. My father's "own country, which should have been the kind and equal parent of all citizens, became a cruel monster, devouring her own children"[39]; and he eventually would leave during King James' reign forever.

Holland began to grow more liberal by welcoming foreigners, which extensive commerce tends to attract. However, nothing came easy for the Separatists after they left England. Life in Holland, although free from persecution, was hard. The language was alien and after great trials and dangers, the Rev. Mr. Robinson, in 1610, with his congregation, removed to Amsterdam, and the next year to Leyden, where they remained ten years.[40]

According to my father, he experienced the unfamiliar lifestyle in Leyden, but it was not home. He wanted a new beginning for himself and my mother and he opted to come to the New World at their first opportunity. He arrived in Plymouth at the time of a demanding second winter in 1621-22 for the settlers, when they were busy fortifying a settlement and surviving the cold. On the 9th of November, 1621, a ship was viewed off the coast. She was the Fortune, which my father was on. The Fortune sailed into Plymouth Harbor, bringing from England and Holland thirty-five more colonists, most of them lusty young men. It was a welcome reinforcement, but it was lacking the rations of food that could be served during the winter, for the Fortune wasn't well supplied.

> The Fortune, which stayed not above 14 days, disposed late comers into several families, and took an exact account of all their provisions in store. It was proportioned the same to the number of persons, and found that it would not hold out above six months at half allowance, and hardly that. And they could not well give less this winter time till fish came in again. So they were presently put to half allowance, one as well as another, which began to be hard, but they bore it patiently under hope of supply. [Perry Miller and Thomas H. Johnson][41]

When she set sail for England after dropping off the company and rations, she carried a little cargo of beaver skins and choice wood for wainscoting, as a first installment of the sum due to the merchant adventurers. But, my father later discovered, this cargo never reached England, for the Fortune was overhauled by a French cruiser and robbed of everything worth carrying away.[42]

My father had joined the new world of which Massasoit and his band opened the door and supported the creation of this permanent settlement for the English in New England. Massasoit, in the end, promoted the population influx that soon would develop through the Massachusetts Bay Company and eventually support the termination of the New England Indian culture.

The progress of the colony was slow. Their harvests were insufficient to feed themselves and the newcomers. During the famine of 1623, the best dish my father could set before his wife was a bit of fish and a cup of water. After four years they numbered only 184.[43]

I was born in the Plymouth colony on May 1st, 1625 to Thomas and Mary Adams. I was named Thomas as well.

At that time, land was being assigned to each settler and abundance ensued. In 1631, my father chose that the three of us move to Watertown, which was within the Massachusetts Bay Company's jurisdiction. He had high hopes of becoming associated with the great merchants of England who presided around Watertown, which he discovered after he had made a previous expedition there. No simple tradesmen they, as I was told, but persons who dealt in a large way in a wide assortment of goods, such as linen cloths, buckrams, fustions, satins, fine woolen, and other commodities. My father felt strongly that he would yield success in Watertown, and we actually ended up in neighboring Medford as my father found work on the private estate of Mathew Craddock.

It was in Watertown where my father first met the successful merchant, Thomas Mayhew, who immediately offered work for my father in Medford. My father told me Thomas Mayhew and his son Thomas Jr., were two of his favorite people he'd ever met. My father and Thomas Mayhew Sr. struck up a friendship immediately when the two first met.

In business at Southampton in England, Thomas Mayhew, Free Commoner and Merchant, followed the colonizing ventures of the great mercantile companies. My father was told Southampton was filled with merchant adventures concerned in the first settlement and maintenance of plantations in the West Indies and on the mainland of America.

A gentleman named Mathew Cradock at some point discovered the abilities of Thomas Mayhew. Cradock was a successful London merchant and the first governor for the company of the Massachusetts Bay. Mayhew's stature grew through success and this information was shared through the reports and intelligence of others, but the most important information told to Cradock about Mayhew was from the mouth of John Winthrop, with whom Mayhew had been acquainted.

Cradock was a potent merchant within the United Kingdom who traded in all the oceans. He invested in trade with Persia and the East Indies, and also sent ships to the Levantine, the Mediterranean, and the Baltic provinces. As Governor he was financially invested in the Massachusetts Company, in which he supported John Endicott as the chief authority of the small colony at Salem. Cradock wrote a letter to Endicott stating, "omit no good opportunity that may tend to bring [the heathens] out of that woeful state and condition they now are in."

As early as 1629 Cradock sent over shipwrights, gardeners, coopers, cleavers, and a wheelwright to the new plantation. In that year he would settle his personal estate at Medford on the banks of the Mystic. The estate would need management. Thus an appointed agent or a factor would be appointed to have oversight and supervision of his shipping, fishing, trading, and plantation interests.[44]

Mayhew would become one of these factors and my father would obtain employment under him. I don't remember meeting Thomas Mayhew, but he and my father built a formidable business relationship. Anything Mayhew was involved in my father assisted. Anything from farming to carpentry kept my father's finances stable.

According to my father, Thomas Mayhew's first residency was at Medford in the vicinity of Boston. Medford, the private plantation of Mathew Cradock at this time, was not considered a township. The plantation was situated upon a grant of thirty-five hundred acres. As Cradock's factor, Mayhew became the foreman for a large number of employees, who were occupied to develop Cradock's business interests in numerous fields. In 1634, Mayhew and my father built a brilliant water mill in Watertown. Mayhew would eventually buy it for himself, and then sell it and receive great profit.

My father told me the story of how he and a team took two days to help carry the timber for building the mill at Watertown. "The mill, which was the first in Watertown, was built at the head of tide-water on the Charles River at Mill Creek, which was a canal partly or wholly artificial, leaving the river at the head of the falls, where a stone dam was built."[45]

Mayhew also requested that my father receive the delivery of special hemp for calking the pinnace, because of another interest of Cradock's in shipbuilding. When our family moved to Medford, the town was strongly becoming noted for shipbuilding. Cradock sent over expert artisans to grow the industry in Medford. In 1632 they had a ship of one hundred tons on the stocks. In the year following, a vessel of three hundred tons and another of sixty tons were erected.

Stated through Mayhew, my father discovered that Cradock, in London, had become frustrated with Mayhew's results as the Medford factor. Cradock believed his investments in New England should produce great revenue. But New England wealth did not grow over night, "nor did it contain the wealth of the Caribbean". New England timber and the fish that were caught in abundance did not bring about profitable markets in the home country.

Cradock blamed Mayhew's bad dealing for his financial misfortunes within New England. The termination of Mayhew's employment also meant my father's termination from work. It meant removal from Medford for our family. However, we still followed Mayhew and took up residency in the nearby village of Watertown, where they already had business interests.[46]

Mayhew became one of the great landowners of the colony. He held a large farm of two hundred and fifty acres. However, we didn't stay long. My father said the Watertown colonists weren't confident. For example, a man innocently fired his musket into the air to scare wolves away from his cattle and the whole colony went on alert. People who lived within earshot spread the alarm and before morning drums were beating in Boston and settlers were grabbing their weapons.[47] My father, obviously, hadn't much fear, especially after peacefully dealing with the Indian in Plymouth. What happened in Connecticut, however, would change him.

Our migration to Connecticut began in Watertown when my father met up with an old friend of his from their time in Plymouth named John Oldham, who had a reputation as "a colorful and controversial trader" to the Indians. Oldham came to Plymouth in 1623, on the ship Ann. His active involvement, in 1624, with Rev. John Lyford, in plotting both here, and by correspondence with a faction in England, against the interests of the Plymouth Company; his defiance of and drawing a knife on Captain Standish when called upon duty of watch, and ward; his outrageous conduct towards the Governor himself and his cursing—all amazed the dignified gentlemen of Plymouth and finally caused his arrest and expulsion from the Colony.

In the spring of 1625, although Oldham had been forbidden so to do, he came back to Plymouth and again misbehaved, whereupon he was jailed until he had cooled down, and in March of that year was again expelled. He went to Virginia, and had there a great sickness, but recovered and came back up again to his family in the Bay, and lived there until the population greatly increased.

As a resident now of the Massachusetts Bay, in 1629, he was making himself obnoxious to the Governor and Council of that Company, by his persistent pressing upon their notice of plans and claims which they considered to be more for his benefit than for their own. These propositions were apparently based upon a patent, which Oldham had obtained, or in which he was somehow interested. He claimed a title based upon a patent and right by grant which the council felt was void by law. Oldham professed to have been issued a patent "under William Gorges, son of Ferdinando, covering part of the region around Boston."[48]

Oldham admitted no terms of agreement, unless he had liberty to trade for beaver with the natives, which the Bay denied to the best of their own planters. Neither was he satisfied to trade for himself, with his own stock and means, which was probably so small that it would not much hinder the Bay. However, Oldham's trade did interest other men, who were never likely to reap any benefit from the planting of the country, but their chief aim and intent was their own profits from Oldham's intercourse.

Returning to New England in the late summer of 1629 foiled of his great plans for a land patent in Massachusetts, Oldham would be admitted a freeman of the Massachusetts Colony, May 18th, 1631. He was an early settler at Watertown, a church member there and apparently trusted and respected. In May 1632, he was one of the two Watertown deputies chosen to advise with the Governor and Council about raising a public stock. In the summer of that year he had a small house near in Watertown, made all of clapboards, but it burnt down by making a fire in it when it had no chimney.

In May, 1634, he was one of that town's three representatives to the first General Court of Massachusetts. And he had fairly earned the reputation of a fearless, enterprising, and successful trader and explorer among the Indians of the New England coast, and in the Connecticut Valley. Evidently, he was now sharing the better side of his nature. These were priceless qualities, which might have been of the greatest value to the several communities with whom, from time to time, he was identified in the planting of.[49]

In Watertown in the late fall of 1633, my father ran into Oldham, who at that time was finally viewed as a well-respected citizen of the Massachusetts Bay Colony. Oldham acquired church membership in Watertown with a grant of 500 acres. Through conversation Oldham led my father to believe that he knew much about the Indians.

My father discovered that Oldham had been influential in opening trade relations with the Narragansetts. Oldham also was one of the first Englishmen to venture into the Connecticut River Valley in 1633 with three other men. Following his visit in 1633 with the Indians, smallpox appeared and spread through the valley tribes, halting trade. The disease had spread among the Dutch trading houses along the Connecticut River in 1633 and then around the trading houses of the English in the same area. Soon the disease spread to Rhode Island and Massachusetts. Amongst the Narragansett, 700 had died. Oldham had traded with all of these tribes before the outbreak and the coastal tribes expressed to the River Indians along the

Connecticut that Oldham had been amongst them. Thus, some of the natives laid the blame for the outbreak of disease on Oldham, who had stayed at the different Indian villages.

Despite the Indian claims, the trip was productive for Oldham. During this visit to the Connecticut River Valley, he obtained some black lead, as well as hemp, which was much better than the English. Oldham followed a path that passed through Watertown through Waltham and Wayland into Farmington, and then southwest to the Connecticut River.

Oldham's stop in Watertown at the mill where my father was working is where the two recognized each other. Oldham told him about his expeditions into Connecticut and the promising trade goods he discovered available. He told my father that there would be settlements there in the near future and "he had to secure at least ten men to go with him the next year, but only in time to prepare the soil for the following year's crop." Those who came with Oldham to Pyquag, also known as Wethersfield, were from the Watertown church.[50]

My father later told me that at this time of his life he was ready to leave Watertown and acquire his own land. After his encounter with Oldham, he began to think about a more successful enterprise which he could lead for the well-being of his family. The rich land watered by the Connecticut River attracted many of the Massachusetts Bay settlers dissatisfied with their cramped land holdings and inability to work off the land. Such vast "numbers had come over from England, and planted themselves in the vicinity of Boston, that the people at Watertown, Dorchester, and Newtown, began to find themselves crowded into such close neighborhoods, that they had neither land enough fit for culture, nor pastures for their cattle. Especially they were in want of meadow lands."[51] Impressed by reports of the rewards within the Connecticut River valley, where meadows were said to be far more fertile than the stony soil of the bay, residents of Dorchester, Watertown, Roxbury, and Newtown looked toward Connecticut.[52]

In the fall of 1634, Oldham and eight or nine companions made another overland journey to the Connecticut valley, establishing a small trading post, putting up temporary houses, and spending the winter trading from that location. My father, my mother, and I were a part of this party that wintered in crude log huts and planted a small crop of winter wheat.

For the whole of that season, the Watertown settlers, in little parties of a few families, continued to make additions to the little company of pioneers at Wethersfield. Oldham settled Wethersfield in 1634 and in 1635, sixty to eighty more men, women, and children arrived from Massachusetts to settle.

John Oldham was the Bay agent who held peaceful trade with the Pequots in accordance with a treaty formed on November 7, 1634. He did a lot of trading during the year 1635 in the course of his tireless trading rounds. My father said Oldham never stayed long in Wethersfield and returned to the Connecticut from Boston in April 1636.[53].

Wethersfield was known as Pyquaug to the Indians, and at first went under the name Watertown by the planters but eventually became Wethersfield, Connecticut. It was a new experience for everyone but quickly turned difficult. By the first December famine began to set in with the cold. The father of the household measured out the bread and meat to his offspring, until both bread and meat were gone. Corn was bought in small quantities from the Indians, but these neighbors hadn't enough to spare[54]. Only a few hundred acres were cleared and the rest was forest. Many wondered how this land was to support them.

When my father arrived in Wethersfield it seemed his business enterprise would succeed through fur pelts. He began setting up expeditions with trustworthy river Indians to secure the fur trade along the Connecticut River. My father thought he was going to deal solely with the Massachusetts Bay Company, in which the Bay Colony in turn would ship out the goods directly to England as payment for colonial expenses. However, trade upriver to Springfield became my father's best route for a rewarding enterprise.

William Pynchon who was one of the founders of that city established the earliest fur trade operation in Springfield in 1636. Pynchon had been a prominent eastern Massachusetts figure who had held a number of positions in Massachusetts Bay government. In the 1630s he was one of the Bay's leading merchants whose commercial activities included fur trade in Massachusetts Bay and Maine. William Pynchon rapidly cornered the Connecticut River Valley fur trade market. [The Massachusetts Historic Commission][55]

My father became very successful in the fur trade after joining in a partnership with William Pynchon, especially with dad collecting fur from Wethersfield up to Windsor and simply shipping it up to Springfield. My father would travel to and from Springfield often and that is where all of his business dealings were. Springfield developed into the leading fur trade center in the Connecticut Valley.

The location of Springfield assured its rapid growth as a fur trade center. The adjacent Connecticut River and nearby Westfield River provided access to natives of the middle Connecticut River and Hudson River valleys, and the Bay Path assured contact with the colonial settlements of eastern Massachusetts, particularly Boston. Thus, by the mid 17th century, William Pynchon and his son John had established and maintained regular trade contacts with Agawam, Norwottuck and Pocumtuck hunter trappers and middlemen. These natives acquired furs and pelts either by hunting or trapping in the uplands.

From Springfield the native furs and pelts were transported to Boston by boat on the Connecticut River and along the Southern New England coast. These goods were then shipped on to England and Europe where they were prepared for sale in the European, English, and colonial markets. [The Massachusetts Historic Commission][56]

When the Indians first learned that the white men were willing to trade all sorts of wonderful items for a skin that was caught so easy as the beaver, they began to hunt and trap the animals with reckless abandon. There was an abundant supply of beaver at first, but the beaver population would quickly diminish. Beavers did not migrate and when the population within a wetland was all killed, they became extinct in that area.

My father's success in Wethersfield was great early on, but a few years after we settled anger would begin to develop. I suppose my father should have been more conscious of the tension cultivated in the wilderness between the settlers and Indians along the river.

My father should have listened closely to the opinion on the existing conflict in Connecticut from one settler in Watertown before we left. The ill opinion toward Connecticut Indians was shared the day of our departure to Wethersfield. A fellow worker on Mayhew's plantation told my father what he had heard of Connecticut Indians hours before we left for the Connecticut River Valley in 1634:

> Connecticut had been settled by several of the most warlike and numerous tribes ever known to New-England. Of these the Pequots, the Mohegans and the Podunks were most active and powerful. The southeasterly region was the seat of the Pequot dominion. The Mohegan possessed a portion within the eastern part. The Podunks had their seat of residence just east of what is now Hartford. The smaller tribes were scattered through the whole territory of that state. [Sanders][57]

With this counsel my father did not question our departure. Upon our arrival in Wethersfield, we were actually welcomed by the Wongunk tribe along the beautiful Connecticut River. The Confederacy of the Wongunks, also known as the Sequins, had many smaller bands related to them. The Wongunk's were a branch of the Mahicans or Mohegans of the upper Housatonic valley, who were pushed out of that region by the Mohawks. They moved into the Lower Connecticut Valley because the Nipmucks of the Massachusetts central hill country denied any entry into their country. The Pequots were also related to the Mohegans, but still oppressed the Wongunk's.

At one time the Mohegans, probably close relatives of the great Lenni Lenape, ranged from the Hudson River as far east as the Connecticut River, but by the time the white men encountered the Mohegans their numbers had diminished into groups around the Housatonic into Connecticut. According to one Indian account on the Mohegan tribal history, a description is written by Chandler Whipple:

> A great people came from the Northwest: crossed over the salt-waters, and after long and weary pilgrimages, planting many colonies on their track, took possession, and built their fires upon the Atlantic coast. (…) They became, in process of time, divided into different tribes and interests; all, however, speaking one common dialect. This great confederacy would comprise of Munsees, Mohegans, Narragansets, Pequots, Penobscots, and many others.[58]

The River Indians in the Wethersfield area were led by their sachem Sequeen or Sowheag, whose son Sequassen was sachem to the Hartford Indians known as the Suckiaug. The Suckiaug of Hartford, the Wongunks or Sequins of Wethersfield, the Matianucks of Windsor, the Hockinums living on the east side of the River, and the Podunks, spread throughout the area. The tribes stretched south of Hartford and into Wethersfield. They were willing to provide beaver skins, corn, and fertile land for the English settlers' new homes. In exchange, the settlers and their powerful guns could provide protection from the Pequots.

I came very knowledgeable of the local Indian activity because of my father's fur involvement with the river Indians spanning from Wethersfield to north of Springfield. He learned the bounds, conflicts, and lifestyle of several different tribes. He received great attention from many business partners located throughout all the colonies for his large inventory of pelts. Many men would stay over our house and I would listen to everything they would tell my father about where they were from and what tribes lived in that area. Many of these men slightly understood Indian dialect and I would listen to everything they shared during their visits to our house. I was not allowed contact with the Indians in Wethersfield, but I still became very interested. I suppose we crave what we are denied.

I learned a lot of the six river tribes who lived north of Connecticut in Massachusetts:

The southernmost of the six native tribes was that of the Agawams. They were located on the Connecticut River floodplains between Enfield Falls, Connecticut on the south and South Hadley on the north. At the time of first colonial settlement the Agawam tribe was occupied by a large native population, particularly on the West Springfield and Agawam floodplains. A palisaded village was situated on the eastern side of the Connecticut River in Springfield.

The second tribe mentioned was known as the Norwottucks dominated the mid portion of the Valley from South Hadley Falls to Sugarloaf Mountain. Norwottuck territory is claimed to have extended nine miles east and west of the Connecticut River into the uplands of Hampshire County. The Norwottuck tribe along with that of the Agawams was probably the most heavily populated of the area. Their village appears to have congregated in two areas, one on the Hadley peninsula and the other in Northampton.

Another area tribe's boundaries extended from Sugarloaf Mountain in southern Deerfield to the convergence of the Connecticut and Millers rivers. This was the homeland of the Pocumtucks. They were the dominant native group during this period, the Pocumtucks played an important role in native inter-regional politics, joining a Mohawk- Narragansett alliance opposing the Mahicans. The primary Pocumtuck settlement was situated in the Deerfield Valley in Deerfield.

The fourth, and northernmost, area tribe was that of the Squakheags. Their area encompassed Northfield. The Squakheags, in contrast to the other native tribes, were more closely tied to the northern interior tribes and the French in Canada than to the coast. Squakheag settlement concentrated in two villages in Northfield.

The fifth native tribe was that of the Woronocos located west of the Agawam tribe on the Westfield River floodplain. Only one possible village site has been reported.

The final tribe described was located in the southeastern corner. This was the home of the Quabaugs, a sub-tribe of the Nipmucs of central

Massachusetts. Quabaug territory appeared to be defined by the Chicopee River. Their limits are unclear, but appear to have extended into northern Connecticut. [The Massachusetts Historic Commission][59]

The men who stayed at our house from Massachusetts were known as sub-traders, just as my father was considered. They acquired furs from natives primarily from the villages of Norwottuck, Pocumtuck and Squakheag. Sub-traders from Southern Connecticut also stayed at our house often. They were my favorite guests because they knew of all the local history, especially that between the Pequots and the Wongunks.

Apparently prior to our move to Wethersfield, complications would arise within the Wongunks' domain. They were here in the area before the Pequots, but the strength of the Pequots forced a war and then much more conflict over land ensued with the arrival of Dutch and Englishmen.

"In 1626 a Pequot war party had defeated the Wongunk sachem Sequin (Sowheag), the leader of the loose alliance of River Indian bands, and finally after three defeats in battles with the Pequots, the Connecticut River Indians thereafter agreed to pay annual tribute to the Pequot Grand Sachem Tatobem and received in return a pledge of Pequot protection."[60]

After this Wongunk defeat European interest in land would grow increasingly along the Connecticut River and it was the Dutch who studied the land at first. They were the first to attempt settlement along the river in 1623 but lacked numbers for the vast territory they wished to cover. However, they again attempted fortification in 1632. In the summer Dutch agents bought large tracts of land from one of the Pequot Sachems, probably Tatobem.

The Dutch finally finished their fort, called The House of Good Hope, in June 1633. However, the Dutch were allies with the Mohawks of New York because of the Dutch settlement there, and that alliance conflicted with the Dutch providing the Mohegan Band of River Indians with firearms, though trade was not denied. Interestingly enough, the English actually had the first opportunity to settle in this land in 1628 and then in 1631 when the River Indians sent an envoy to Boston in hopes of receiving aid, but nothing came of the effort.

In 1628 this Podunk Sachem, Natawanute, had visited Winslow at Plymouth to encourage him to enter into trading relations, and Winslow himself had gone down and inspected the region. Notawanute had explained the use of wampum as a medium exchange. [Charles Burpee][61]

Sometime during the year 1631 an Indian Sachem visited the governors of the Massachusetts and Plymouth colonies in the appearance of a beggar. "He said his name was Wahquimacut. He described the country occupied by his own and kindred tribes as a rich, beautiful valley, plentiful in corn and game. The land was divided by a river called Connecticut, which he represented as superior to all other streams, as well in its size and in the purity of its waters, filled with a variety of the fish that swam in it, and the number of the otter and beaver that might be found along its banks." There

45

were a considerable number of Indians in Connecticut, a population probably around six thousand, with the mass of these tribes in the eastern half of the state.

Wahquimacut begged that each of the colonies would send Englishmen to make settlements in this valley. He even offered to give the new immigrants eighty beaver skins annually, and supply them with corn, all as encouragement to try the experiment. The river sachem proposed that two men should first be delegated to view the country, and make report to the governors, before any steps should be taken towards a removal there. The governor of Massachusetts declined to join in the enterprise.

Governor Winslow, of Plymouth, without directly agreeing to it, was unable to remove the idea from his mind, and soon after the encounter with Wahquimacut, went himself to spy out the riches of this Indian habitat. During his voyage in 1632, he found the river valley as a primitive paradise and thought the area would be a great fit for a trading post. "All that his eye rested on was wild and modest, as if no foot except that of the savage had stepped there since the dawn of creation." Thus Winslow named himself the discoverer of the river and the valley. He made a very favorable report of the country and during the following year other explorers from Plymouth searched the Connecticut River up and down.

Sometime in 1632, "the year before the Dutch began in the River," Governor Winslow, of Plymouth, and his associates "had a place given (and that place [Plymouth would] afterwards possess) in what is now Windsor. It seems the sachem Natawanute of the small band of Indians located in Windsor, who had been removed from that land by the Pequots, sold this land to the Plymouth government. Plymouth, in turn, reinstated the Indians within their homeland.

"In October, 1633, Captain Holmes, in a vessel sent by the Plymouth trading company holding a framed blockhouse ready for raising, "brought home [to Windsor] and restored the right Sachem of the 'place, called Natawanute.'" Natawanute (Grand Sachem of the Podunks) was the sachem who had been driven out by the Pequots. He was then brought home and restored by the Plymouth company, though almost all his band were swept away by the small-pox in the spring. [James Hammond Trumbull][62]

An argument formed between the Dutch and English concerning who had claim to the land. There were claims that the Dutch purchased land from the Pequots and the English from the Sequins, but the land conflict between the two European nations would not become a matter of any interest. The English population would grow so fast, and greatly outnumber the Dutch on the Connecticut River, that it would leave little room for Dutch success. But the Dutch would remain in their Hartford Fort of Good Hope for many years, as the English had little concern of them.

As the land sales began for the Massachusetts Bay settlers in Wethersfield with the Wongunks, qualified agents handled sales, and interpreters and witnesses for both parties were present. The sachem of the Wongunk tribe, Sowheag, added his mark if he agreed. At this time, the Indians felt they were getting the best of the bargain, and they usually retained rights to hunt and fish on the land.[63] For the Wongunks, alliance with the settlers had become more favorable an option than paying an annual tribute to the Pequots.

The Pequots had actually invaded Connecticut from the northwest between 1575 and 1614. They had settled between the Niantic nation, occupying a strip of approximately eighteen miles on the southeastern coast which divided the Niantics in two. They built and maintained large forts across the Mystic River to the east, from which they attempted to bring the Eastern Niantics under their control. They immediately had attached themselves with the Western Niantics.[64]

The Wongunks like other River tribes, had long resented the harsh domination that the Pequots held over them, and it was partly in hope of ending their subjection to the Pequots that the river valley tribes had welcomed the English. The English who settled Wethersfield, interestingly enough, left Massachusetts without a clergyman to lead them. Of all the towns belonging to Connecticut, Wethersfield seems from the first to have been most involved in difficulties, civil and ecclesiastical. The settlement had been commenced by a high-spirited and very excitable people, impatient of control, delighting in the most daring enterprises, and became stimulated rather than alarmed at the dangers that harassed them.[65]

During this early period of settlement, there had been some murders of sea traders. These men were caught adventuring along the coasts or rivers, and being not sufficiently manned, and lacking caution, they became the easy victims to the Indians. But these, after all, seemed to my father's associates as random cases in nature, isolated instances, having no special relation to one another, and therefore they did not arouse the fears of the Wethersfield community, who went on peacefully, planting their fields, raising their houses and getting to feel more and more at home in their New World surroundings.[66]

However civil the beginnings in Wethersfield seemed hostility soon arose. Sowheag learned that his new English neighbors were no better than the Pequots, his former overlords. Either the settlers at Wethersfield didn't seem to understand the terms of the purchase agreement or they simply chose to ignore the arrangement. The misunderstanding occurred when Sowheag set up a wigwam in Wethersfield in early 1637, and as a result, was then driven out by force. In frustration the Wongunk chief thus turned to his former enemies, the Pequots, for assistance in resolving the matter.[67] "At first Sowheag turned to the English for protection against Sassacus; now he turned to Sassacus for protection against the English."[68] Sowheag would become the one to plant the seed for open warfare upon a New England tribe: the Pequots.

By this time, the River Indians in the vicinity of the Wethersfield settlers— those Indians from whom the settlers had bought their land and with whom they were in daily contact—had so far proved friendly, and though recently there had been some disagreement with them, still there was no reason to consider them hostile. The southern Indians, however, especially the Pequots, had of late shown much restlessness and suspicion of the white man's presence among them. By a series of murders and attacks upon property, the Pequots had kept the neighboring

English settlements in a constant state of alarm, and no one in Wethersfield expected what was to occur.

On the morning of April 23, 1637 during the time of prosperous work, there fell, like lightning from a clear sky, a disaster so great that paralyzed the hearts and energies of the Wethersfield settlers. A party of Pequots, some say two hundred, came up the Connecticut River in canoes as far as The Island and, from that standpoint, watched through the forest for their opportunity to attack, probably in the early morning, upon the Wethersfield people who were at work in the meadows on the adjacent west bank of the river. The unfortunate settlers were clearing and preparing their lands there for the spring plowing, men and women being busy and unsuspicious of danger. They were suddenly surprised by the savages and in the quick disorder and struggle that ensued, six men and three women were killed and two maids were carried away.

Having done this, the savages left as fast as they had appeared. Thrilled with their performance, they attracted the attention of the garrison down the Connecticut River called Fort Saybrook, which they sailed past near the mouth of the River. They hoisted up poles in their canoes upon which they hung the clothes of their slain victims, mocking the sails of the white man's ships. There was nothing that could be done by the soldiers in the fort to rescue the two captive maidens, who could plainly be seen in the savage's canoes. Captain Lyon Gardiner in command of Fort Saybrook, did order a cannon to be discharged at the fleet of canoes, which came near putting the captives in even more danger than before.

I was told that the Dutch governor, in the most noble of all efforts, sent a sloop to Pequot to redeem the two English maidens, though it violated their peace with the Pequots. The sloop offered a lot for the maids' ransom, but nothing was accepted. Therefore the Dutch, who had many Pequots on board, kept six of them and with them, exchanged the Pequots for the two maids, who had no violence committed to them. [Adams and Stiles][69]

What occurred in Wethersfield is what we call the Wethersfield Massacre. I was eleven at the time and I can still remember all of our neighbors crying with the look of shock, especially in fear of the two girls who had been kidnapped.

Sowheag's revenge against the settlers through the Pequots' invasion would force the New England colonies into forceful action. It is a fact that the previous actions of the Pequot had Massachusetts Bay already preparing for war against that tribe prior to the massacre. Massachusetts had declared war two weeks before the Wethersfield Massacre, but her forces hadn't yet taken the field. Connecticut hadn't even made a formal commitment to war, but suddenly provoked by the disaster at Wethersfield, the general court of Connecticut on May 1st, 1637, voted for an offensive war against the Pequot.[70]

The Connecticut general court represented the little republic of less than three hundred. An excited session it was. It was filled with doubts and swarming with important considerations for the survival of the colony. There is little evidence that there was any fear within the General Court of the fifteen picked men, six magistrates and nine committee-men, who had the fate of Connecticut in their hands. The first written memorial of their doings is in the following words: "It is ordered that there shall be an offensive war against the Pequot, and there shall be ninety men levied out of the three plantations of Hartford, Wethersfield, and Windsor."[71]

It was as early as 1636 that the three river towns, Hartford, Windsor, and Wethersfield, had established a General Court. It is well that they did, for the Pequot raid on Wethersfield showed the need for a combined force. Under this General Court the first military conscription (enlistment), the first levy of taxes and the first declaration of war took place. Thus the first raising of a company to attack the Indians took place in Connecticut.[72]

In response to the Wethersfield attack, the Connecticut General Court, comprising two magistrates and three commissioners from each of the three river towns declared an offensive war against the Pequot Indians. Although the three towns together contained no more than 250 inhabitants, the court ordered the enlistment of an army of ninety men, with forty-two to come from Hartford, thirty from Windsor, and eighteen from Wethersfield. Each soldier was to provide himself with a pound of gunpowder, four pounds of shot, twenty bullets, and a musket for the trip downriver. A barrel of powder per man would be issued once the company reached the English Fort Saybrook. The planning for the invasion of the neighboring Pequot village was finalized by the enlisted colonial force at the mouth of the river in Fort Saybrook.

As mentioned above, the Massachusetts Bay Colony made preparations to wage war against the Pequots before Connecticut did. The Bay's General Court on April 18, 1637, had authorized a levy of 160 men, passing an emergency tax measure to raise 160 pounds to pay some of the anticipated costs. But the court directed the magistrates to enlist the help of the Plymouth Colony in bearing the burden. Plymouth, however, felt they had reasons to not endorse the cost of the war, possibly because of the Bay Colony's earlier refusal to aid Plymouth in its struggle with the French in Maine, where in 1633 Plymouth's prosperous fur trade become short lived as their Maine post fell to the French.[73]

To understand Massachusetts necessity to declare war upon the Pequots before the Wethersfield massacre I must explain a couple of important issues: Why was the declaration of war against the Pequots being called for by the Massachusetts government prior to the Wethersfield Massacre? Also, why was the Pequot Tribe so violent toward the Wethersfield Settlers? Might the assault have been part of a larger retaliation effort to obtain justice according to Indian custom? Was the invasion of the Pequot fort by the sanctioned Connecticut force, known as the Pequot War, necessary?

There were many factors, as with any war, which determined the invasion and destruction of the Pequot fort by the colonial force. The Wethersfield Massacre simply expressed to the Connecticut colony the necessity to eliminate the Pequots. To the north, the necessity to declare war upon the Pequots by Massachusetts Bay was, in part, a result of the actions by the Pequots in retaliation to the invasion of their village in 1636 by a force of Massachusetts Bay men led by John Endicott. This invasion was legally justifiable due to two previous murders committed by Indians, as well as the possible alliance between the Pequots and Narragansetts.

One of the murders was of my father's friend John Oldham, who was the only reason we lived in Wethersfield. The Block Island Indians killed him in 1636 and it was a great conflict to the Massachusetts Bay. However, there was a prior murder of a seaman which may have been committed by some Pequots. This murder received a much greater retribution than true justice called for. In 1633, the Pequots and Niantics killed a drunkard Englishman named John Stone, who was already unfavorable to the colonies.

John Stone may have been killed in retaliation for the murder of the Pequot Sachem Tatobem, who was killed by the Dutch on the Connecticut River. It is told that Sassacus's father, Tatobem, was lured aboard a Dutch vessel to trade, but was murdered. Thus Tatobem's son, Sassacus, sought revenge, and when the next trading vessel arrived he boarded it and found the Captain's cabin. The ship was English, not Dutch, but because the Indians could not tell the Dutch from the English, the Pequots consequently murdered all of the Englishmen onboard led by Stone.

Following these murders, a fear for the Pequot began to loom over Massachusetts Bay. In October 1636, after the murder of Oldham which was committed by a tribe not of the Pequots, a plan for invasion of a Pequot village was still being prepared by Massachusetts Bay with the purpose of a disciplinary expedition. The plan was to first strike the sub-tribe of Narragansett Indians on Block Island for their role in the murder of Oldham, and then the next blow was to be against the Pequots in their home territory on the coast eastward of the Niantic River. Apparently, this expedition sailed with the purpose to avenge the murders of the two traders.

This was unfortunate for the Pequots, as it seems to me they did not do much wrong. A different tribe had killed Oldham, and Captain Stone as you will see had already been banished from the Massachusetts Bay colony before his murder for ill conduct. Stone would become more valuable dead than alive to the Bay colony. Stone's murder had occurred with the increase of white men interested in the rich Connecticut River land.

The Indians committed Stone's murder in accordance with their retaliatory customs and not the way in which the white men would prosecute murder.

Those who held authority in the region were the Europeans consisting of the Dutch and the English, the Indians vying for supremacy consisted of the Pequots and the Narragansetts. It is not important to my purpose to discuss the claims for discovery, but one thing is certain: the English claimed, through right of discovery, grant from their monarch, and subsequent purchase of the Indians, the possession of most of the country, and have kept it ever since.[74] The Pequot Indians, on the other hand, who had claimed the valley earlier than the Europeans, claimed supremacy by right of conquest over the tribes living around the river whose right of discovery was best of all.

The Dutch briefly held settlement on the river before the English. They negotiated a commercial agreement with the Pequots concerning freedom of trade. "The territory purchased by the Dutch was to be freely used by Indians of all nations, and was to be a territory of peace. The hatchet was to be buried there. No warrior was to molest his enemy while within its bounds."[75] The Pequots bound themselves to respect the Dutch and allow all Indians, regardless of tribal affiliation, access to the Dutch trading post. The Dutch obviously sought Narragansett trade with their abundance of currency known as wampum. The Pequots quickly realized that their Narragansett rival, who was independent traders with the Dutch, could use the Europeans to drive the Pequots back out of Connecticut.[76]

The peace declared in the Dutch-Pequot Agreement of 1633 would be short-lived. The Pequots, who guarded the river tribes rights against both the Narragansetts and the Dutch, must have felt honorable in wanting to remove Narragansetts from their tributaries' land in order to control trade. The Pequots had great interest in eliminating the Narragansetts from encroaching on their territory.

The Pequots wouldn't allow a rival to challenge their livelihood upon the Connecticut. In the fall, a group of Pequot warriors ambushed and killed several Narragansetts or tributaries of that tribe, along the path toward the House of Good Hope, which had barely been completed. The victims were Narragansetts and the Dutch felt this act broke their peace agreement with the Pequots. When the Dutch negotiated with Pequot Sachem Tatobem the purchase of the site for their trading house, the Dutch supposed that the Pequots would permit other Indians to trade at the post.

The Pequots chose murder to show their dominance over the Narragansetts, and as a result, the Dutch retaliation was immediate and severe. When the Pequot principal sachem, Tatobem, boarded a Dutch vessel to trade, he was seized and held for ransom. The Dutch informed his tribe that they would never again see their leader if they didn't pay a bushel of wampum to his abductors. The Pequots immediately sent the payment to the House of Good Hope and demanded Tatobem's freedom. They received his corpse in return.

One large war party of the Pequots could have easily driven the Dutch from the Connecticut Valley following the murder of their sachem. Surprisingly though, Tatobem's murder didn't ignite a deadly assault on the tiny and exposed Dutch trading house. Despite the loss of a sachem, the Pequots didn't want to give up trade with the Europeans. They wanted to control trade, not end it.

In murder committed by someone outside their family, according to Pequot tradition, the tribe obtained retribution by killing the villain or someone of relation to justify the wrong. The act of retribution toward the Dutch for Tatobem's murder was committed through a band of Pequots accompanied by some western Niantics, but, regrettably, the Indians found victims who were to be English, not Dutch.

The Englishman, Captain John Stone, "having some chance occasion with the Dutch at the trading house up the river, got hold of some of the Indians. There were on the bark about twelve Indians, who had in all probability formerly plotted their bloody design; and waiting an opportunity when some of the English were on shore and Captain Stone asleep or drunk in his cabin, set upon them and cruelly murdered every one of them, plundered what they pleased and sank the bark."[77] Stone, his associate Captain Walter Norton, and all six crewmen perished in the raid.

Pequots who later described the circumstances of Stone's murder, during a visit for aid in Boston in 1634, reported that Stone had first abducted two Indians near the mouth of the Connecticut River in territory occupied by the western

Niantics and he forced his captives to guide him upriver and intended to kidnap them for ransom. After Stone's ship anchored for the night, a band of Indians had boarded Stone's ship, pretending to be interested in trade. While this Indian band diverted the crew above deck, the new Grand Sachem of the Pequots Sassacus, Tatobem's son, visited the captain in his cabin. Stone, an alcoholic, had drank himself into a stupor and collapsed to his bunk. The sachem split Stone's head with a hatchet and threw a blanket over his body. In the violence that followed, the Indians cornered the ship's crew in the kitchen, seized some loaded muskets, and fired into a supply of gunpowder, which exploded. They then killed the remainder of the crew, looted the cargo, and set the ship ablaze.

I don't think the Pequots thought anything would result due to their revenge because it fit in their customary defense of avenging murder. However, by the fall of 1634, Pequot control of the trade of the Connecticut valley was weakened. Their trade with the Dutch collapsed with the killings at the House of Good Hope of Narragansetts and the assault on Stone's trading ship. They faced not only the hostility of the Dutch, but the hostility of their Indian neighbors to the east, and now an Englishman had been murdered.

The murder of Tatobem, therefore, marked the beginning of disorder for the Pequots. Tatobem had withdrawn many of his Pequot allies and river tribe tributaries, and his son and successor, Sassacus, was unable to hold together even those who were supposedly Pequot. Uncas, a Pequot exile, was the great force that unified the white man and the red man to bring this Pequot dysfunction to an end.

Uncas became to be known as the sachem of the Mohegans. The Mohegans were something of a sub-tribe through intermarriage, and were also a tributary of the Pequots. The Mohegans were led by Uncas and succeeded with the help of the English. Thus Uncas formed a new political creature. Uncas was the classic example of a New England Indian who strived for political power and successfully used the help of those from a different continent to get it.[78]

Uncas, the man who would emerge in the mid-1630s as the leader of an expanding Mohegan tribe, was physically imposing, strong-willed, and a ruthless politician. Uncas had claimed by birth both Mohegan and Pequot sachemships. He had married a daughter of Tatobem. He had quarreled with his father-in-law and had continually spent time in exile among the Narragansetts. Begging and obtaining Tatobem's forgiveness, Uncas was allowed to return to his village in Mohegan country near what is now Norwich, Connecticut.

Following Tatobem's murder, Uncas saw a chance to succeed him as Pequot Grand Sachem. To become Grand Sachem, the candidate needed to be a member of one of a small number of prominent families. Hence Tatobem's son Sassacus was chosen after the murder. Uncas denied an acceptance for the Grand Sachem and sponsored the removal of Sassacus. His efforts didn't work, and once again Uncas fled to the Narragansetts. He didn't stay long. Uncas would return and humble himself to the Pequot sachem, as he wanted to live in his own country again. Sassacus granted his request on condition that Uncas would remain loyal. Uncas agreed but soon again broke his oath. His renewed crusade against Sassacus won few Indian supporters, and once again Uncas fled. Welcomed by the Narragansetts who held some form of relations with the Mohegans, Uncas again soon sent word of his insult toward Sassascus. The Grand Sachem once again accepted Uncas's renewed pledge of loyalty to the Pequots and allowed him to return to his village. Yet again though, Uncas would soon be at work provoking a new rebellion against Sassacus. Uncas would return to the Pequot tribe after obtaining pardons some five times.

One reason for Uncas's rebellious nature may have been the tribute the Pequots sought from the Mohegans. Pequot tributaries remained greatly distanced from the Pequots because of the tribute the Pequots sought. For example, it was Sassacus's challenge to Mohegan hunting grounds that eventually drove their members away, and through this splitting up from the Pequots, Uncas began winning over some of the River Indian Bands also unfavorable to the Pequots. All these factors helped Uncas position himself in a war that would enable him to take his place as Pequot Grand Sachem. Thus, the Pequots' destructive force threatening the colonies existence may have been part myth, as Pequot power was in decline.[79]

Stone's murder had begun the momentum against the Pequots, and Uncas' unconfirmed tales further strengthened the anger toward the Pequots. The decrease of Pequot dominance increased Uncas's power. His exaggerations strengthened colonial fear whether the statements were true or false, as the colonists accepted the statements from their faithful friend. The Pequots had, however, sought early intervention from the English.

In 1634, the Pequots sought Englishmen for aid from the Dutch and their Indian rivals. Sassacus turned to Boston for assistance in dealing with these issues. Shortly after Stone's murder, the Pequots sent a trading party to the House of Good Hope and within a short time, however, the Dutch killed a Pequot with a blast of cannon shot. Now, not only were the Pequots threatened by the Narragansetts, but they were no longer business partners with the Dutch. Aside from needing protection from the English in Boston, they were also becoming very dependent on foreign trade. The Pequots, though, didn't think anything of an English ill will toward their tribe after killing Stone and they sent a delegation to Boston in 1634. "The English, I intend to show, held themselves free from any peace with the Pequots as a people guilty of shedding English blood."[80]

In October of that year, a Pequot messenger presented himself before the governor at Boston, and made proposals for a treaty.

> The messenger brought a present for Deputy Governor Ludlow from his sachem. He laid down before the governor two bundles of sticks, indicative of the number of beaver and other skins which the Pequots would give the English, and promised also a large amount of wampum, and therefore requested a league between his people and the pale faces. Ludlow accepted the presents thus made to himself, and gave him in return a moose coat of equal value for the Pequot chieftain; but the governor kindly told the messenger, when he took leave of him, that Sassacus must show his respect for the English by sending deputies of greater quality than he was, and enough of them, before a treaty could be made with the colonies. [Robert Boodey Caverly][81]

"The messenger, rather humbled in being the bearer of his own disgrace at a foreign court, seems to have done his errand faithfully, for in due time two Pequot counselors appeared, carrying presents, and of character requested to the business in hand. Deputy Governor Ludlow said he was not against peace, but that there were some old scores to be settled between the two powers. "[82]

At Boston in 1634, the English signed a treaty with the Pequots and Sassacus's envoys made their marks: a bow and arrow and a hand on the document. The Pequot envoys did obtain a trade agreement, yet the English asked such a high price for trade and friendship that the Pequot ambassadors were not entitled to accept any tributary request. The English tributary request eventually failed acceptance when the Pequot Envoys presented the terms to their council upon their return home.

On the other hand, the Pequot envoys, while in Boston seeking aid, offered the Puritans handsome land concessions to encourage the English to settle in Connecticut, as the Pequots were losing control of the Connecticut River Valley. The Pequots, though, were not aware of the ill feelings toward them by the English because of Stone's death.[83]

The agreement reached at Boston would fall short of Pequot hopes and expectations. The magistrates, also, declined to pledge themselves to defend the Pequots, even with the conditions of the treaty agreed upon that provided the English to be sold as much land as they needed in the country of the Connecticut, provided they would make a settlement; and the Pequots were to give them all possible assistance in the settlement. Furthermore, the magistrates of Massachusetts Bay were already of the conclusion that they would not assist the Pequots in any future Indian trade war, as the Narragansetts not only were more powerful but were also closer to the Bay settlements. The Pequots thus failed to find a European military ally in Boston. However, through the treaty's terms, in 1635 more settlers came to Connecticut, "bringing their wives and children and the Indians received them with joy. The sachems of the Poquonnucs and Podunks, as well as Sowheag or Sequin of the Wangunks, willingly sold them all the land they could use. Sequassen, sachem of the Hartford Tribe, sold them Hartford and the whole region westward, including the territories of the Tunxis, as far as the country of the Mohawks. Nassecown of Windsor, was so taken in love with the coming of the English that, for some small matter, he turned over to them all the land on the eastern side of the Connecticut to which he laid claim."[84]

The Pequot envoys, for their interest, did get an apparent trade agreement, but the English asked for a substantial amount of tribute for their hand in trade and partnership. The colony would send no vessels for a long time to trade with the Pequots. Finally, the first evidence of the fulfillment of the 1634 treaty was when John Oldham traded with the Pequots along the Connecticut shore in 1636. Oldham finished his trade mission successfully, but would be killed when he stopped on Block Island thereafter for probably trading with the Pequots.

During the treaty occasion in November 1634, the Boston magistrates declared the gift offered by the Pequots of otter skin and beaver coats, and skins of wampum, inadequate. They informed their visitors that they would expect to receive four hundred fathoms of wampum, forty beaver skins, and thirty otter skins, which Sassacus would not fulfill. The magistrates wrote, "we should be at peace with them, and as friends to trade with them, but not to defend them. There was no intention by the Bay Colony for military assistance.[85]

Thus, at the home council of the Pequots, the treaty was denied. The treaty of Boston was denied because the gifts asked for were exceeding anything Sassacus was willing to part with. Ultimately, the gifts received by the English from the Pequot envoys in Boston would eventually be returned back to the Pequots at a later time, which was a show of great disrespect. However, the Pequot land concessions weren't to be returned.

The other major Puritan requirement for a treaty of peace and trade for the Pequots was even more troublesome. Bay Colony officials informed the envoys that because they killed an Englishman (Captain Stone) they must first deliver up those who were guilty of his death in order to receive any aid.

The Pequots answered that Captain Stone had been killed in reparation for the murder by the Dutch of Tatobem. His murderers, the envoys explained, hadn't known that he was English, not Dutch. The captain, the Pequots argued, had acted in an unrighteous manner by abducting two Indians at the mouth of the Connecticut River. They declared that, if the guilty Indians were worthy of death, they would move their sachem to have them delivered, but cautioned that given Stone's bad behavior they couldn't be certain that the sachem would agree to take action against Stone's killers. Boston, truly, had no reason to mourn or seek retribution for Stone's murder, as he was banished from the colony for unfavorable conduct, unless it was a necessity to discipline the Pequots.

Massachusetts came to realize Stone was worth more dead than alive. Stone's reported death at the time seemed to be petty retribution for the Pequots. He was an unfavorable character to the colony, and his death lay dormant with no punishment for two years.

The treaty request by the magistrates for the men who killed Stone and his crew was more than simple Puritan justice. Some of the murderers were not Pequots. The other Indians involved belonged to the Western Niantics, who were easily confused with the Pequots. As the Bay demands for the killers were part of the treaty, it formed a situation the Pequots weren't accustomed to. If the Pequots seized the persons of the Niantic tribe involved with the murder and delivered them to Massachusetts, it would have violated Indian custom and honor.

Thus, the Pequots refused to support decisions of which outside sachems hadn't been notified. The Pequots didn't threaten to stand in the way if Massachusetts should send its own men to do Puritan justice on the Western Niantics.

This treaty conference satisfied both the Bay magistrates and the Peqouts initially, though in time, the treaty would cause more harm than good. With the English migration into the middle Connecticut River Valley following the treaty, other areas along the River became of interest for the English, especially around the home of the Pequots near the mouth of the Connecticut River. Control by the English of a main entrance by water into and through central Connecticut and into Massachusetts became a subject of great importance. An English settlement on the mouth of the Connecticut River would have an effect on both the Dutch who held the region prior and the Pequots who considered the area of Saybrook home.

Saybrook, a fortification at the mouth of the Connecticut River, was first becoming a reality when two of the few Puritans in the English House of Lords, Saye and Sele and Brooke had constant reminders that they might soon need a haven abroad in order for safety outside of England. Thus they had granted to other Puritans a small tract of land around the Connecticut River. In the course of the year 1630, the famous Plymouth Company, the mother corporation that gave life to all the New England grants, granted the whole territory of what was subsequently called the colony of Connecticut, and much more, to Robert Rich, Earl of Warwick. The patent confirmed this grant to him from Charles I in that same year, and expressed the assignment to the proprietors with a description of the boundaries.

On the 19th of March of the year 1632, however, Robert Rich, Earl of Warwick and president of the Council for New England, executed under his hand and seal the grant since known as the old patent of Connecticut, wherein he granted the same territory to Saye and Sele, Brooke, and ten of their friends on March 19th, 1632. [86] The grantees seem to have done little about their rights until 1635, when at that time Lord Saye and Sele, Lord Brooke, and other associates, the patentees of Connecticut, commissioned John Winthrop, Jr., to be governor of that territory for a year. His commission included constructing a fort and settlement at the mouth of the river. [87]

Recruiters in England during 1635 recruited a company of men for making fortifications and for the building of houses at Saybrook. They were to construct a fort at the mouth of the Connecticut River. The fort construction also brought responsibility on the governor of the colony for securing at least 1,000 to 1,500 acres for the fort and for the residences. The other soldiers were to locate there for their own protection.

After being sent to England to recruit, the ship named Abigail returned on October 6, 1635, and arrived in Boston with John Winthrop Jr. The Abigail carried with her the commission from Lord Saye and Sele and Lord Brook, to begin a plantation in Connecticut, and make Winthrop Jr. governor there.

In March 1636, Lieutenant Lion Gardener arrived for his command at the mouth of the Connecticut, and would construct Fort Sayebrook. The placement of the two cannons on Fort Hill and a ten-foot-high mound within the palisade allowed Gardener command upon the treacherous, sand-clogged channel at the river's mouth. Within the fort grounds were a small freshwater pond and space for both a garden and an orchard. Gardener also erected a wooden hall subdivided into apartments, as well as a barracks and small storehouse. The settlement was named Saybrook in honor of the two prominent patentees, Lord Saye and Sele and Lord Brook.

Fort Saybrook lay upon the Connecticut River, "at the mouth of it, a place of a very good soil, good meadow, all sorts of good wood, timber, variety of fish of several kinds, fowl in abundance, geese, ducks, deer, and squirrels, which were as good as English rabbits. Its location was on a fair river, fit for harboring of ships, and bounds with rich and godly meadows. This lies thirty miles from the upper plantations on the river Connecticut." [88]

With all the development by the English, the ever-changing state of the Indian on the Connecticut River, and the resulting anger that intensified through actions unfamiliar to the Pequots, the whole region was in a most unstable state. Fort Saybrook, soon after its formation, was troubled by rumors of a Pequot attack. The Pequots, additionally, had made no intention to pay the full wampum tribute mandated in the treaty agreement at Boston in 1634, nor did they fulfill the English demands that they apprehend and deliver to Puritan justice the murderers of Captain John Stone and his crew.

When John Oldham pressed them on those matters, the Pequots replied that the tribal elders hadn't approved the treaty. Oldham thus declared them a very false people. There were numerous sources throughout the valley that intensified rumors of a Pequot uprising. English suspicions and anxieties about Pequot motives were steadily increasing, especially through reports from friendly Indians who warned of Pequot plans to destroy the English settlements in Connecticut.

A Plymouth Indian agent at Windsor named Jonathon Brewster sent a letter to John Winthrop Jr. (at that time Governor of the Connecticut Colony) reporting that Uncas told him that the murder of Stone had been planned in a Pequot council of war and that Sassacus orchestrated the affair:

To the worll John Withrop Govr at the mouth of the river Coniticutt (...)

Woncase (Uncas), sent me word that upon the 23rd of May of last, Sasocuse, chiefe sachem of the Pequents, with his brother, Sacowauein, and the old men held consultation one day, and most of one Night, about cutting off of our Plymouth Barke, being then in their harbor weakely manned, who resolving thereupon appointed 80 men in Armes before Day to surprise hir; but it pleased the over Rueling Power of god to hinder them, for as soone as these bloody executioners arose out of Ambush with their canoes, they discerned her under sayle with fayre winde returning home. (...)

I understand likewise by the same messenger (Uncas) that the Pequents have some mistrust that the English will shortly come against them, and therefore out of desperate madnesse doe (the Pequots) threaten shortly to sett both upon Indians, and English jointly. Further by the same Sachem, I am enformed that Sasocuse with his Brother, upon consultation with their own men, was an actor in the death of Stone, and these men being 5 of the principal actors alive, 3 living at Pequent, and 2 at Ma ham le cake...

Yours in all love and service
Jonathon Brewster.
Plimouth House in Cunitecutt:
This 18th of June 1636

In Uncas's statements it seemed to the colonists that the Pequots were certain of orchestrating an English attack. In reaction to the Pequot threat, the river town colonists began to hold training days and make powerful speeches. The colonists had sensed that there must be a state of preparedness, and to that end it was regulated in the first year's records, June 7th 1636, that every man must have ready for the constables' inspection once a month a gun, two pounds of powder, and twenty bullets, or be fined ten shillings, and there must be monthly training. No firearms should pass to natives under any circumstances. [The Pequot] could only rely on the knife and tomahawk, arrow, and ambush.[89]

Likewise, the Pequots were so alarmed by rumors of an impending English attack on them that they were now plotting a defensive war. The Pequots honored fully their promise concerning English occupation of Connecticut, but their failure to obey the more demanding provisions of the 1634 treaty developed deep suspicions that Indians were the devil's agents. "Indian diplomacy apparently did not require promptness in fulfillment."[90]

Finally, the Pequots were to be warned that, if they should persist in their refusal to surrender the murderers of Stone, the English would take revenge upon them. One of the Pequots that killed Stone and his crew apparently was their own sachem, and the three other murderers were living openly in the principal Pequot village. At first, the distance between Puritan and Pequot territory prevented immediate intercourse on the matter. Yet once English migration into Connecticut in 1635-1636 expanded, renewed efforts were made to secure Pequot agreement to Puritan demands. The interaction between the Puritan and Pequot would also lead to many more misunderstandings.

In the southern portion of Connecticut, one location during the migration where space between the Puritans and Pequots didn't exist was Saybrook. The rumors of the Pequot evil now planning an invasion against Fort Saybrook alarmed the authorities at Boston and John Winthrop Jr., the river governor, who took up residency at Saybrook.[91]

Winthrop would become informed of Governor Vane's ultimatum from the Massachusetts Bay. In early July 1636, Governor Vane notified John Winthrop, Jr., that he had been commissioned by the Bay Colony to investigate Pequot conduct and to secure both the surrender of the murderers of Stone and the full wampum payment discussed in 1634. Winthrop's instructions requested that he first begin by asking the Pequot's Principal Sachem in a friendly manner for a meeting to discuss central matters. Winthrop's instructions were to threaten war if he could not secure Pequot submission.[92] The Pequot, though, had no intention of paying the full wampum tribute requested in the treaty agreement in Boston in 1634, nor were they going to hand over the murderers of Stone.[93]

In Saybrook, Lieutenant Gardener was dismayed by the Massachusetts Governor's intentions to pressure the Pequots. He exclaimed to the commissioners from Boston, "I know you will keep yourselves safe in the Bay, but myself, with these few, you will leave at the stake to be roasted, or for hunger to be starved; we being so few in the River. They must consider that there were only twenty-four people at the fort, men women, boys and girls, and not food for more than two months, unless we saved our corn field, which could not possibly be if they came to war, for it is two miles from our home."

Gardener later claimed that Winthrop and his commissioners promised him that they would do their utmost to make an effort to persuade the Massachusetts authorities to resist from war for a year or two, till Saybrook could be better provided for it. That promise was not kept.

Sassacus wouldn't give in to any of the demands within the treaty's terms, and the colonial emissary's declaration to the tribe was to be that the Bay would have the Pequot's lives, not their presents. So the Pequot sachem was called for, to come to Saybrook. An unnamed Pequot representative spoke with Winthrop through an interpreter in July 1636, and the presents—otter skin coats, beaver, and skins of wampum—that were presented to the Boston magistrates in 1634 were returned sorely against Gardener's will. The return of the presents was practically a declaration of war by the English. Having placed Gardener and his garrison in jeopardy by provoking the Pequots, John Winthrop Jr. then left Saybrook, disregarding his promise to return promptly to his duties there.

I don't know much of the reaction from the Pequots from the returned items by the Saybrook Company. However, I've been told that Sassious, sachem of the western Niantics, who lived on the east bank of the river across from Saybrook, was present at the meeting in July 1636. Sassious, frightened by talk of avenging Stone and his crew's murder, sought to place himself and his people under the protection of the English and accordingly gave Winthrop Jr. a grant of land at the meeting in July 1636.

The Pequots thus became suspicious of Sassious, as violence was soon approaching inevitable. The Pequots, in turn, asked Gardener if the English would wage war on the western Niantics. Gardener replied that the Saybrook garrison couldn't tell one Indian from another and Gardener became troubled by the Pequot suspicion of Sassious. He began stalling for time in dealing with the Pequots, for he wanted to find any means that would bring temporarily peaceful relations with the Pequots, but, aware of rumors of Pequot plans to attack the English, he feared violence. With the prompt departure of Winthrop Jr., for Boston, Lieutenant Gardener was left to cope with whatever consequences might follow the returning of the gifts to the Pequots.

Several days after Winthrop's departure, an Indian named Cocommithus appeared at the gates of Fort Saybrook. In fluent English, he explained that he had once lived at Plymouth but had joined the Pequots and now came bearing a message from Sassacus that the Pequots held two of the English horses and wished for trade. The Grand Sachem, despite the ultimatum, wanted trade with Saybrook. Lion Gardener of Saybrook described his decision to proceed in trade with the Pequots:

> He desired that Mr. Steven Winthrop would go to Pequot with trucking cloth and all other trading ware, for they knew that we had a great cargo of goods of Mr. Pincheon's, and Mr. Steven Winthrop had the disposing of it. And he said that if he would come he might put off all his goods, and the Pequot Sachem would give him two horses that had been there a great while. So I sent the Shallop, with Mr. Steven Winthrop, Sergeant Tilly, and Thomas Hurlbut and three men more, charging them that they should ride in the middle of the river, and not go ashore until they had done all their trade, and that Mr. Steven Winthrop should stand in the hold of the boat, having their guns by them, and swords by their sides, the other four to be, two in the fore cuddie, and two in aft, being armed in like manner, that so the out of the loop-holes might clear the boat, if they were by the Pequots assaulted; and that they should let but one canoe come aboard at once, with no more but four Indians in her, and when she had traded than another, and that they should lie no longer there than one day, and at night to go out of the river,

two of them go ashore to help the horses in, and the rest stand ready with their guns in their hands, if need were, to defend them from the Pequots, for I durst not trust them. [Lion Gardener]

It seemed reasonable for those at Saybrook that Sassacus had taken in two English horses and would return them if the English would send a trading party to the Pequots, yet, upon their return to Saybrook after the trade expedition to the Pequots, Gardener was angered to learn that his men hadn't done what he ordered of them. With Saybrook's men sailing into the harbor, the Pequots didn't seem aggressive and were hesitant to board the shallop in the manner the English specified. They still had Tatobem's death aboard a Dutch ship and the threats of revenge for Stone's murder in mind and did not board the shallop. Two of the Englishmen therefore went ashore. One of the men entered the sachem's wigwam not far from the shore. Wincumbone, the sachem's wife, was present in the wigwam and made signs for the English to leave, for they would cut off his head; which, when the Englishman recognized this, he drew his sword and sprinted to the others, and got aboard, and then immediately out came the abundance of Indians to the water-side and called them to come ashore, but instead, the traders immediately set sail and returned to Saybrook. Upon Gardener hearing the result, he assumed the Pequots planned for Saybrook's destruction.

Soon thereafter, death would occur from the hands of the Indians upon an English trader, but the killers were not Pequots. Some time following the Saybrook interaction with the Pequots, John Oldham had returned to his trading post upriver at Wethersfield and in late July 1636, Oldham then visited Saybrook again, sold a few items to Lieutenant Gardener, and set sail for Block Island accompanied by two Narragansett Indians and two English boys.

On July 29, another trader, John Gallop, happened to be on a trade mission to Long Island in a small bark but was brought toward Block Island because of a change of wind. Near the island, he spotted a pinnace at anchor, which he knew was Oldham's. As Gallop came closer he saw that the deck was filled with fourteen Indians. He and his men pursued the scene and began firing with his only two muskets, two pistols, and some duck shot at the Indians on the deck. Gallop then rammed the pinnace, frightening the Indians so that six jumped out.

Gallop continued to damage Oldham's ship and five more Indians jumped off into the sea and drowned. With the fleeing of so many Indians, Gallop and his companions boarded Oldham's ship. One Indian appeared from a hatch and surrendered. He was tied up and thrown into the hold. Then another surrendered. Gallop, fearing their skill to untie themselves, had one of the two Indian captives thrown, still bound, into the sea. Gallop and his men then searched the ship. They found the body of Oldham hidden stark naked, his head cleft to the brains, and his hands and legs cut as if they had been cutting them off. The corpse was still warm. After burying Oldham at sea, Gallop then unloaded what remained of Oldham's cargo, took his sails, and tried to tow his ship. But with night coming and the wind rising, they let it go and the wind carried her to the Narragansett shore.

The murderers belonged to the Block Island Indians who were affiliated to the Eastern Niantics, who were themselves tributaries to the Narragansetts, not the Pequots. A short time after Oldham's murder, three Narragansetts appeared in Boston with a message from Canonicus, their head sachem. Two of these men had been with Oldham. The sachem, in the message written for him by Roger Williams denied that any member of his tribe had participated in the crime. From the one Narragansett who had not been with Oldham, however, the colony authorities got, either by force or willingly, a different story. He stated that the Narragansett sachems, except for Canonicus and Miantinomo, were aware [of] the murder, that they had plotted to kill Oldham because he was trading with the Pequots. The authorities sent messengers back to Canonicus, with the demand that the two white boys who had been with Oldham be returned, and that the guilty Block Islanders be punished for the crime. [Chandler Whipple][94]

The letter sent to Boston by Narragansett principal sachem Canonicus expressed that the Narragansetts were deeply grieved by Oldham's death and would take appropriate steps to avenge it. Canonicus reported that Miantonomi, the other principal sachem, had already left for Block Island at the head of a force of seventeen canoes with two hundred men to punish the Block Islanders. The Bay Colony officials, though, were suspicious and refused to accept the Narragansett claim that they had sent a force to avenge Oldham's murder.

It became understood that all sachems of the Narragansetts, except Canonicus and Miantonomi, were the arrangers of Oldham's death, yet somehow at this point, "the Massachusetts Bay Colony accused the Pequots of harboring Oldham's murderers, and of having participated in the crime. The only excuse they could possibly have had for this rash accusation was that the Pequots had harbored other killers, as was the case of Captain Stone."[95]

It was also alleged by the Narragansett envoy who visited Boston after Oldham's death that the two Narragansett Indians who sailed with Oldham, joined him in Boston. They were part of the conspiracy and had participated in the fatal assault on Oldham. The magistrates were enraged by that revelation but refrained from arresting the two presumed villains because they were sent as messengers from Canonicus and were therefore entitled to diplomatic immunity. The next day Governor Vane of Massachusetts Bay wrote to Canonicus. He informed the sachem that he suspected his Indian envoys of involvement in Oldham's murder and that he had refrained from arresting them because they were on a diplomatic mission, but that now he expected the Narragansetts to send them back to Boston for investigation.

After receiving the message, Miantonomi, seeking to deflect English wrath, suggested that Oldham's murderers had taken refuge with the Pequots. The Narragansetts also sent word that they had recovered and would return near one hundred fathoms of wampum and other goods of Mr. Oldham's. The Bay Colony discovered that three of the seven Indians that had drowned after participating in this grave crime were Narragansett sachems. While the Bay didn't hold Canonicus or Miantonomi responsible, the Narragansetts were to surrender all those who played a role in the murder.

Shortly after news of the death of Captain Oldham reached Boston, Bay Colony officials strongly took into account the Pequots' refusal to obey the renewed demand that the terms of the treaty of 1634 be honored by payment of wampum and surrender of the murderers of Stone. The magistrates interpreted both Oldham's murder and Pequot noncompliance as evidence of an Indian uprising. One of the greatest colonial follies now lay ahead.

Rather than waiting for any more Indian outbreaks of violence, the Puritans decided to eliminate the savages before they struck and threatened the new settlements. The Bay Colony believed that a preventative strike would secure their safety, and, thus, the Indians would become terrified into obedience by the example of violence towards those who had murdered Englishmen.

The governor and council of the Massachusetts Bay Colony consulted with the colony's clergy about doing justice upon the Indians for the death of Mr. Oldham. Assured that the Lord would smile upon a raid, the Bay Colony sent off a force of ninety men, under the command of John Endecott and Captain John Underhill, who then were the military trainers in the Colony, to Block Island. The military commission also called for the Pequots to surrender all who had a part in the Stone murder, the Oldham murder, and other murders during the recent past. They also intended to bring back women and children as slaves or hostages.

The relationship between Pequot and Puritan was no longer one of a mutual understanding through a treaty. Thus Endicott's orders in 1636 were to take possession of Block Island by force, kill all of its adult male inhabitants, and enslave their women and children. After punishing the Block Islanders, Endecott was to sail to the Pequot village near the mouth of the river, demand the surrender of the murderers of Capt. Stone and other English, exact from the Pequots a payment of damages to the colony of a thousand fathoms of wampum, and take some Pequot children as hostages to assure the tribe's future good behavior. If the Pequots refused to supply those children for shipment to Boston, they were to be taken by force.

Endicott's accompanying force consisted of ninety soldiers who were all volunteers. They served under the command of two captains, John Underhill and Nathaniel Turner. Accompanied by two Indian guides, Endecott's little army embarked in three pinnaces on August 22, 1636. Reaching Block Island just before dusk, the ships encountered high surf raised by a gale blowing out of the northeast. The landing proved difficult. An Indian walking by the Block Island shore saw the English party and the other warriors were hidden behind the embankment near the shore. Fifty or sixty able fighting men, with arrows notched, awaited the English landing.

As the men in the first detachment struggled through the pounding surf toward shore to hit the beach, the Block Islanders shot their arrows. The other detachments unable to land jumped overboard, waded through the shallow but rough waters to the beach and a few men were left behind to guard the boats. Once on firm ground, the Bay Company began firing at the Indians. As bullets flew over their heads, the warriors quickly fled and were not to be found during the two days Endicott's party remained on the island.

The island contained two Indian villages, which the war party found deserted. Thus, Endicott's men saw little action on Block Island. Although they spent the day on the island, putting cornfields and wigwams to the torch, Endicott's troops weren't able to kill and enslave Indians as ordered. The Block Islanders were hidden very well. Leaving the blazing village, Endecott and his men travelled through narrow and overgrown paths in search of the Block Islanders. The natives remained invisible. Finally, in anger, Endicott admitted he could not find them, and then gathered his forces at the close of the second day of the campaign.

They then sailed away from Block Island toward the mouth of the Connecticut River and stopped at the small Saybrook Fort, where they would stay four days because of poor weather. Endicott's force was now joined by the few men under the command of Gardener before the Bay company travelled to the second destination of this campaign: the Pequot village.

Following a brief stop at Saybrook fort Endicott and the force sailed eastward along the coast. They passed the domain of the Western Niantics, and the tribesmen shouted from the shore, "What cheer Englishmen? What do you come for?" When the Indians ashore got no answer, they became alarmed and now cried, "Are you angry, Englishmen? Will you kill us? Do you come to fight?"[96] The Indians, at first, hoped that they had come to trade. The English, however, remained silent and dropped their anchor in the mouth of the Thames (Pequot River), in the center of Pequot country. The Indian greetings met with no response and their welcoming mood changed. That evening, as the fleet remained anchored at the mouth of the Pequot River, the Pequots and their western Niantic allies stayed on the shore as lookout having made fire on both sides of the river, they feared the war party would land during the night.

Early in the morning after the all-night anchorage in Pequot River, an elder Pequot statesman paddled out to Endecott's shallop by canoe to inquire why the English remained in the Pequot River. Aboard Endicott's boat, the elder Pequot sagamore requested the reason for the visit. The Puritan officers informed him that the governors of the Bay sent them and demanded the heads of those persons who had killed Englishmen. To their surprise, the Pequot elder responded with a confession: The Pequots, he admitted, killed Stone. He told the English it was a just act of retribution, for Sassacus had intended to avenge the death of his own father. Even with Tatobem kidnapped by the Dutch and after his kinsmen had paid the ransom demanded for his life, the Europeans betrayed all decent custom and put the Grand Sachem to death. "Who," the Pequot elder cried, "could blame us for avenging so cruel a murder?"

The elder Pequot representative justified Stone's murder;

"We know not that any of ours have slain any English. True it is, saith he, we have slain such a number of men; but consider the ground of it. Not long before the coming of these English into the river, there was a certain vessel that came to us in way of trade. We used them well, and traded with them, and took them to be such as would not wrong us in the least matter. But our sachem or prince coming aboard, they laid a plot how they might destroy him; which plot discovereth itself by the event, as followeth. They keeping their boat aboard, and not desirous of our company, gave us leave to stand hallooing ashore, that they might work their mischievous plot. But as we stood they called to us, and demanded of us a bushel of wampam-peke. This they demanded for his ransom. This peal did ring terribly in our ears, to demand so much for the life of our prince, whom we thought was in the hands of honest men, and we had never wronged them. But we saw there was no remedy; their expectation must be granted, or else they would not send him ashore, which they promised they would do, if we would answer their desires. We sent them so much aboard, according to demand, and they, according to their promise, sent him ashore, but first slew him. This much exasperated our spirits, and made us vow a revenge. Suddenly after came these captains with a vessel into the river, and pretended to trade with us, as the former did. We did not discountenance them for the present, but took our opportunity and came aboard. The sachem's son, Sassacus, succeeding his father, was the man that came into the cabin of Captain Stone, and Captain Stone having drunkmore than did him good, fell backwards on the bed asleep. The sagamore took his opportunity, and having a little hatchet under his garment, therewith knocked him in the head." [John Underhill][97]

The English, however, objected, but the Pequot representative added that the Pequots thought that Stone was a partner in the murder of Tatobem, "for we distinguish not between the Dutch and the English, but took them to be one nation, and therefore we don't feel that we wronged you, for they slew our king, and thinking these captains to be of the same nation and people of those that slew him, made us choose this revenge."

The English commanders may have respected the elder for coming aboard, but they still accused him of being a liar. They argued the Pequots could easily tell an Englishman from a Dutchman, as they have experienced both nations. Increasing in anger, the Puritan commanders rejected the explanation, declaring that if they were not given immediately the heads of those persons that have slain their own, they would attack. The Pequot representative calmly responded, "Understanding the ground of your coming, I will entreat you to give me liberty to go ashore, and I shall inform the body of the people what your intent and resolution is, and if you will stay on board, I will bring you a sudden answer." The English did grant permission for the elder to go ashore. The Pequot also asked the English not to come ashore until a conference was held on the situation.

Endicott, wary of the elder Pequot's true intentions upon reaching shore, disregarded the request to stay offshore and immediately landed his forces in armor and in full battle array. At once, they were lined up in military order. The elder seeing the English land their forces, came pleading not to advance any closer, but stand in a valley. Suspecting an ambush, Endicott marched the soldiers up to a hill.

The English saw that between the lower point they had been and the Pequot encampment there stood a small hill which the Indians could use to their advantage. Instead, the English chose to use it for their advantage, and Endicott marched his troops to the higher ground. Soon after they had taken possession of the hill, the elder reappeared, joined by three hundred men who surrounded the English. However, most of the men were unarmed. Some of the Pequots recognized the Saybrook troops and conversed with them. The Pequots told them there was no one there to answer the war party's demands. The elder told them that neither of the princes were home because they had gone to Long Island, so no tribal business could be conducted.

The Pequots cleverly delayed any battle by means of conversation for an hour or so, while in the meantime, they managed to have their wives, children, and most of their belongings sent out of the plantation. Some Pequots were standing remotely off and did begin to laugh at the English for their patience. Endicott finally became impatient and he told the Indians, "Begone, Begone! You have dared the English to come and fight with you, and now we are ready." Thus the Indians retreated and were chased by Endicott who ordered his soldiers not to open fire. The Pequots, feeling secure, laughed and let arrows fly, but hit none. The whites opened fire and killed one, but the rest of the Pequots scattered out of range with their families and belongings secured. Endicott, on the other hand, was furious at being outsmarted by the Pequots.

Again, as with Block Island, Endicott found himself reduced to an infuriating hunt for fractional bands that took occasional potshots from rocks and thickets.[98] Marching into the village, Endicott and his men set fire to the wigwams and the corn harvest and dug up and destroyed the goods that the Pequots had buried.

Now the English had truly started a war with the invasion of the Pequot Village. The unlucky expedition of John Endicott was soon followed by months of violent events. The wolves were roused, and their bite deadly. The first attack was made upon the Saybrook Fort, to which place some of the corn taken from the Pequot village had been transported. "Perhaps the Pequots reasoned as the ministers and magistrates of Massachusetts had done with the murders of Stone and Oldham, that they who shared the plunder were responsible for the bloodshed."

The Connecticut plantation, understanding the disrespect of the enemy to now be so great, sent down a certain number of soldiers, under the conduct of Captain John Mason, to strengthen the [Saybrook] fort. The enemy had began hovering about the fort, continually took notice of the supplies that were come, and forebore drawing near it as before; and letters were immediately sent to the Bay, to that right worshipful gentleman, Master Henry Vane, for a speedy supply to strengthen the fort. For assuredly without supply suddenly came, in reason all would be lost, and fall into the hands of the enemy. This was the trouble and perplexity that lay upon the spirits of the poor garrison. Upon serious consideration, the governor and council sent forth in February the following year, Captain John Underhill, with twenty armed soldiers, to supply the necessity of those distressed persons, and to take the government of that place for the space of three months. [John Underhill][99]

Early in October 1636, following the failed invasion of August, as five men belonging to the Saybrook garrison were carrying home hay from the meadows, the Pequots concealed themselves in the tall grass, surrounded them, and took a man by the name of Butterfield prisoner. The rest escaped. Butterfield was roasted alive, with the most brutal tortures. Nothing could stop the activity of these Indians, now that they were provoked. They lurked in the lowlands that surrounded the fort. They stole up and down the river by night and day, watching for victims. A house had been built for the uses of the garrison about two miles from the fort, and six men were now sent to guard it. Three of them went out upon an errand, when one hundred Pequots rose against them and took two of them. Success finally made them so bold that they destroyed all the store-houses connected with the fort, burned up the haystacks, killed the cows, and ruined all the property belonging to the garrison that was not within the range of the garrison guns.

In February 1637, the Pequots killed some English at Saybrook. Thus, in that same month, the court met at Hartford, and ordered that letters should be sent to the governor of Massachusetts, denouncing the evils resulting from Endicott's expedition, and calling on the governor for men to help prosecute the war with vigor, in which Underhill and twenty armed soldiers were sent.

Lieutenant Gardiner went out one day in March, with about a dozen men, to burn the marshes. The Indians lay in wait for him, and as he passed a narrow neck of land, the Indians killed three of his men, and mortally wounded another. Gardiner himself was also wounded. The Pequots pursued him to the walls of the fort, and, surrounding it in great numbers, mocked the fugitives, imitating the dying groans and prayers of the English whom they had taken captive and tortured, and they also challenged the Saybrook men to leave the fort and come out and fight like men.

Soon after that incident, the Pequots in canoes would board a shallop as she was sailing down the river. She had three men on board. The Englishmen made a bold defense, but in vain. One of them was shot through the head with an arrow, and fell overboard. The Indians took the other two and killed them. They then split the bodies in twain, and suspended them all by their necks over the water, upon the branches of trees, hideous spectacles, to be gazed at by the English as they passed up and down the river.

In examining a major source of this Pequot rage, Endicott's foiled expedition, it appears the Bay magistrates failed to grasp for some time how dreadfully they had exposed their peers along the Connecticut River to Pequot revenge, as well as establishing the possibility for a united tribal formation against all the white colonies in New England. The Block Island Indians, who were tributaries to the Narragansetts, and the Pequots, were both invaded by Endicott's force. The Puritans had a trading house not only on the Connecticut but also at Sowams and various other points in Indian country and quickly perceived the ultimate threat to their colony.[100] The Bay Colony, though, blamed the Pequots for the warlike climate; this was believed because the Pequots didn't provide the requests desired by the English in terms of the treaty and their reaction of Endicott's invasion.

The river towns of Connecticut were furious by Endecott's actions, complaining their lives had been placed in danger. To make matters worse, the Pequots would send as a result a representative to the Narragansetts claiming that the English were minded to destroy all Indians. Rumors spread that the Pequots and Narragansetts had concluded a peace after four years of hostilities. Sources mentioned that Pequot ambassadors were already on Narragansett Bay urging Miantonomo to ally the Narragansetts with the Pequots and to form a numerically superior force with which to annihilate the barely four thousand English in all of New England.[101]

Fortunately for the English, the Narragansetts promoted neutrality with the colonists, since a Narragansett-Pequot alliance would be disastrous to New England as a whole. Instantly grasping the possible doom of Massachusetts in an alliance of the Pequots and Narragansetts, Governor Vane of Massachusetts and the Council rushed a frantic appeal to Roger Williams, who lived among the Narragansetts. Williams commission was to use his utmost and speediest endeavor to break and hinder the league labored by the Pequots and work for a league between the Narragansetts and English instead.[102]

Within a few days an embassy hurried from Boston to Canonicus' court, fourscore miles away by their own estimate. Roger Williams entertained the Massachusetts embassy at his house in Providence, sent word to Canonicus, then escorted the delegation as interpreter. An imposing assembly received the English at Narragansett, where proceedings opened with a feast of white chestnuts and cornmeal mush with blackberries mixed in. The parley took place afterward in a state-house. Canonicus, well stricken in years, lay on his side on a mat, his warriors sitting on the ground with their knees doubled up to their chins as they listened intently to Williams' translations.

Canonicus amazed the English by his wisdom and discreet answers. Miantonomo, though more forward in siding with the English, was struck as a very stern man, of a great stature, of a cruel nature, and with all his nobility, caused his attendance to tremble at his speech. The Bay emissaries actually believed at that time that the two Narragansett Grand Sachems could field thirty thousand fighting men. Though the number was nearer four thousand, that would still have been formidable for Massachusetts.

At the time of this meeting, Williams had already won Canonicus to pro-Bay neutrality but quickly transformed this neutrality to active alliance. He did it by working on Miantonomo more than Canonicus. Canonicus was always shy of the English. While he was a prudent and peaceable prince, he never cared to court the English, never feared them, and never acknowledged any precedence of their government over his own. In May 1637, furthermore, when Williams went to notify him of the Bay preparations against the Pequots, Canonicus was very sour, and accused the English and Williams of sending the plague amongst them, and threatening to kill him especially.

One way Williams sweetened Canonicus's spirit was by gifts of sugar, for which the sachem had a great fondness. Roger Williams wrote to Governor Winthrop: "Sir, if any thing be sent to the princes, I find Canonicus would gladly accept of a box of eight or ten pounds of sugar; and, indeed, he told me he would thank Mr. Governor for a box-full."[103]

Frequently he harassed Williams to ask Winthrop to send more. Canonicus must have been around seventy years old at this time, and he lived to be past eighty. In 1636, he had turned over the active administration of his government to Miantonomo, who had exercised equal authority since 1632. Not that Canonicus didn't have sons to inherit his sachemship, but the nephew Miantonomo appeared far more impressive; the arrangement seemed to be best for the tribe and entirely acceptable to the sons.[104]

The answer to the English Colonies' dilemma of the Pequots was to be found in the Narragansett-Mohegan-Connecticut-Massachusetts alliance and was one of the greatest feats of confederation in early New England.

"It wasn't the Pequots, though, who initially stirred up Narragansett vengeance. It is true that Canonicus gave an island to Mr. Oldham, by name Chibachuwese, upon condition, as it should seem, that he would dwell there near unto them."[105] "Oldham, however, traded with their enemies the Pequots and it is undoubtedly true that the plot at the murdering of Oldham was planned and perpetrated by Canonicus's Narragansetts, even though it was thought that the Pequots were the ones harboring the murderers of Oldham and that they also were guilty of partaking of guilt in his murder."[106]

Negotiations amongst the Massachusetts Bay delegation and the Narragansetts were a success and the Narragansett sachem, Miantonomi, spoke; he stated that they had always loved the English, and desired firm peace; that they would continue in war against the Pequots and their confederates until they were subdued. The following day, the Narragansetts joined an alliance with the English against the Pequots. Uncas, the Mohegan sachem, furthermore, wanted to contribute to an alliance that would force war with the Pequots.

There was a separate incident that sped up the declaration of war upon the Pequots. The attack on Wethersfield was the ultimate incident and brought the Connecticut River Valley and the Connecticut General Court into a state of war. The general court of Connecticut on May 1st, 1637, voted for an offensive war against the Pequot. Reverend Thomas Hooker and the leaders of Hartford Colony commissioned Captain John Mason and ninety-odd planters to take this fight to the enemy. They were civilians, not soldiers, yet they had been drilling as a trained band through the latest hostilities. In Hartford, through Mason's commission, the men crowded into ready boats. They glided down-river past struggling, war-wounded Wethersfield to the other English post on the Connecticut River, called Saybrook Fort.[107]

Thus, the little army of Connecticut commanded by John Mason, of Windsor, and Lieut. Robert Seeley, of Wethersfield, prepared an offensive invasion upon the largest Pequot fortifications, as the Pequots had murdered around thirty of the English. In the wake of the Wethersfield attack, as the forces gathered in Hartford to embark to Saybrook, Uncas "was at the Podunk fort across the Connecticut, where he was assembling a Mohegan contingent; he reported the joy of the Pequots over their success."[108] Seventy warriors would eventually accompany Uncas when his band would depart Hartford toward Saybrook. Most were Mohegans, but some of his followers must have been drawn from the neighboring River Indian villages. The English whom Uncas offered his assistance to had already begun preparing for war when the Mohegans arrived in Hartford.

The soldiers from the several towns rendezvoused at Hartford and after religious exercises their hearts were reinforced by a counsel from the Rev. Thomas Hooker, in the course of which he said to them, "although gold and silver be wanting to either of you, yet have you that to maintain which is far more precious, the lives, liberties and new purchased freedoms of the endeared servants of our Lord Jesus, and of your second selves, even your affectionate bosome-mates, together with the chief pledges of your love, the comforting contents of harmless prating and smiling babes."

It was on Wednesday, the 10th of May, that the army embarked at Hartford and set sail for the mouth of the river. The renowned John Mason was Captain of the army, and Samuel Stone, was its chaplain, or spiritual guide. As Connecticut's force formed following the massacre with a hundred sixty men, ninety English levied from the plantations and the Bay, and seventy Mohegan Indians, they set sail from Hartford in a fleet, of pink, pinnace and shallop, accompanied with many Indian canoes on their task of war.[109] "The fleet comprised of a pink or narrow-stern rowboat, a pinnace or eight-oar rowboat with probably a small sail, and a shallop or schooner-like craft."[110]

The water was so shallow at this season of the year that the vessels several times ran aground in dropping down the river. This delay was so irksome to the Indians, that they begged to be set ashore, to which Mason consented, on their promising to meet the English at Saybrook. "Despite suspicion, it became impossible to refuse the request of the Indians that they be landed and take the familiar trail where progress would be faster."[111]

The Dutchmen crowding at the mouth of the Little River witnessed the meager display of force with amusement and probably with doubts of success. It is noteworthy that all Dutchmen observed the strictest neutrality. There was kinship by color of skin, but there was also Dutch opportunity to gain dominance in colonization, though not without antagonizing England herself.[112]

It was not until the 15th of May that Mason and his men arrived at Saybrook, having spent five days in sailing about fifty miles "through adverse wind, sluggish current and inexpertness of oarsmen delayed the stronghearted little party."[113] Uncas eventually led his men overland as Mason and the English floated clumsily down river. "On the early arrival of Uncas at the fort, Gardiner put him to the test." Near Saybrook fort, six Pequots were lurking in a nearby cove. Uncas with twenty of his braves were obligated to bring them in, dead or alive. Four Pequots were killed, one escaped, and the sixth was made prisoner."[114] Uncas delivered the severed Pequot heads to the English at Saybrook. Upon hearing of this, Mason viewed the attack as a special Providence.

Captain John Underhill, who joined with Uncas when he reached the English troops, verified the report of this skirmish. Underhill, at Saybrook, also presented to Mason his services, with nineteen men, for the expedition, if Lieutenant Gardiner would consent it. Mason was delighted with this and resolved to send back twenty of his own troops to protect, during his absence, the almost defenseless towns upriver.[115]

> When Captain Underhill and Gardener had seen their commission in Saybrook, they both said they were not fitted for such a design, and they said to Major Mason they wondered he would venture himself, being no better fitted; and he said the magistrates could not or would not send better; then Gardener said that none of his men should go with them, neither should they go unless they, that were bred soldiers from their youth, could see some likelihood to do better than the Baymen with their strong commission last year. Then Gardener asked them how they trust the Mohegan Indians, who

had but that year come from the Pequots. They said they would trust them, for they could not well go without them for want of guides. Yea, said Gardener, but he will try them before a man of theirs shall go with you or them; and he called for Uncas and said unto him, you say you will help Major Mason, but Gardener wanted first to see it, therefore send you now twenty men to the Bass river, for there went yesternight six Indians in a canoe; fetch them now dead or alive, and then you shall go with Major Mason, else not. So he sent his men who killed four, brought one a traitor to Saybrook alive. And Gardener gave him fifteen yards of trading cloth on his own charge, to give unto his men according to their desert. And having stayed there five or six days before they could agree, at last the soldiers agreed about the way and act of the Mohegan, and took twenty insufficient men from the eighty that came from Hartford and sent them back up to Hartford in a shallop. [Gardener][116]

Mason reached Saybrook on a Wednesday and began discussion, at length, on how and what manner they should go forth into the Pequot's home, as they were unknowing of the country. They ultimately decided to sail for Narragansett Country and to then march through that country which bordered upon the enemy. The grounds and reasons of those actions are as follows:

First, the Pequots, the enemies, kept a continual guard upon the river night and day.

Secondly, their numbers far exceeded the English; the two Wethersfield captives who were taken by the Dutch and restored to Saybrook have mentioned the Pequots having sixteen guns with powder and shot.

Thirdly, the Pequot being on land and being swift on foot, might much impede a landing, and possibly dishearten the army; invasion was expected only by land, there being no other place on shore but in the river nearer than Narragansett.

Fourthly, with the landing in Narragansett the force should come upon their backs, and possibly surprise them unaware.[117]

Mason must have covered all this at a conference with Gardener at Saybrook upon arrival. They were stuck in five days of discussion at Saybrook. Mason invited Lieutenant Gardener to speak frankly, knowing that he refused a war for at least a year or two, till better provided for it. Gardener wanted to let fortification alone awhile. At last, even though Gardener knows the "war is best won away from home, contributed four of Saybrook's soldiers, but he refused to go."[118]

Underhill felt that they must form some alliance upon Uncas and the Indians. The question of whether to really trust these allied Indians was puzzling, all because they had had no experience of Mohegan fidelity. Underhill feared that the Indians in time of greatest trial might revolt and join with the Pequots.[119]

The English also may have been unaware that Uncas' power was rising as Sassacus' power was crumbling. Uncas had made at least five attempts to unseat his sachem, and always had been humbled for it in exile and then forgiven again; he couldn't have survived without friends. With Uncas's alliance growing upon the English, a Pequot became any person identified as such by a Mohegan. In this war, Native judgment decided who lived and who died. [120]

70

As trust had been developed, the English needed a well-orchestrated plan to invade the two main Pequot forts. Sassacus' Weinshauks Fort and Mamoho's Mystic Fort were the biggest palisaded villages in the region, and Sassacus at age seventy-seven also held twenty-six villages tributary to his influence. Native people as far away as Wethersfield turned to him in appeal, and we have seen he responded in force. His reputation in war had a terrifying power. In New England Indian warfare, strict rules existed against killing anybody but enemy braves. The Indian fort is where women, children and valuable stores were kept from being adopted by the enemy tribe. The braves would fight it out with little harm done.[121] For war against the English, however, the Indians would divide themselves into small bodies, so that the English were forced to change their usual stance. Thus the Indians would divide their force to answer the Indians' seperate forces.[122]

Mason urged the scheme of sailing past the Pequot country, as far as Narragansett Bay, and, there landing his army, he would then march through the Narragansett country under the protection of the old hereditary enemies of the Pequots, steal upon the Pequots in the night and crush them.[123]

Thus the decision was made to first set sail for Narragansett Bay as the starting point for invasion; they set sail Friday morning. These ships, with seventy-seven soldiers and some sixty Mohegan warriors aboard, sailed out of Saybrook Harbor bound for Narragansett Bay. At this time the Massachusetts men had been summoned for war. The Bay Colony voted to raise two hundred men, the Plymouth Colony fifty, to go to the aid of Connecticut. The Plymouth Colony never did raise its fifty men, but forty of the Bay Colony soldiers, under Captain Daniel Patrick, were sent at once to join the Narragansetts, where they could obtain canoes in which to visit Block Island. Rumor had it that the Pequots had moved their women and children there for safety. Once he had conquered a neighboring island, Patrick was to go back to the mainland and join up with the Connecticut troops against the Pequots.[124]

Upon arrival in Narragansett country they could not land until Tuesday at sunset because of severe wind, at which time Captain Mason landed and marched up to the residence of Miantonomo, the chief sachem of the Narragansetts. Mason told the sachem that he had not an opportunity to acquaint him beforehand of his coming armed into his country; yet he doubted he wouldn't approve the object. Thus the English had come to avenge the wrongs and injuries they had received from the common enemy, the Pequots, and march toward Pequot country from Narragansett. Miantonomo expressed himself pleased with the design of Mason, but thought his numbers were too few to deal with the enemy, who were, as he said, "very great captains, and men skillful in war."[125]

The first requirement for the attack on the two Pequot forts worked wonderfully as they were seen passing the forts by sail as if the company were leaving the region. Secondly, the force returned westward on land undetected and were planning to attack the forts at night. Respecting Miantonomo's stature, experience, and power in numbers of braves, Mason requested only free passage through his country.

That same evening a Narragansett runner arrived at the camp with a message from Captain Patrick. Marching overland, Patrick had gotten as far as Providence with his forty men, and he urged Mason to await his arrival before moving on. Helpful and necessary this added strength would prove, Mason decided against waiting, as such a delay was strongly opposed by his men, who had now been two weeks away from home and wanted to get back to their farms and families. In addition, the Narragansett and Pequot tribes were not now openly at war and there was some intercourse between them. Word might get through to Sassacus of the march of the colonists. [Chandler Whipple][126]

It was on Wednesday, the 24th of May, that the little army of seventy-seven Englishmen and sixty Mohegans and Connecticut River Indians began their march for the Pequot forts. The English force headed west with Uncas and his braves; the force received no promised guides or auxiliaries from Miantonomo's village. The trek started slow through the wilderness paths, and that day they journeyed twenty miles out of Narragansett country to the home of the Eastern Niantic. According to the captains, these Eastern Niantics offered no assistance to the inadequate force. The eastern Niantic was a country that bordered on the Pequot territory and it was the seat of one of the Narragansett sachems. But the sachem refused to treat with the English, or let them enter his palisades to pass the night.

Mason, upon questioning their conduct, felt these Indians were in a partnership with the Pequots. The Eastern Niantics set a strong guard about their fort, and would not allow one of their own to escape from it during the night. But the conduct of the Niantics was truly the result of fear, rather than an alliance with the Pequots. During the following morning, several of Miantonomo's men that he sent caught up to the column, the Narragansetts were smiling and now going to join the force in their expedition. For when the Niantics saw that the Narragansetts desired to assist the English, they took heart, and, forming a circle, declared that they too would fight the Pequots, and boasted how many they would kill. When Mason resumed his march on Thursday May 25th, he had about five hundred Indian warriors.[127] These new friends became loud with loyalty-oaths, signs and ceremonies that swore to their aggressive cooperation ahead.[128]

The force was now accompanied by 500 Indians, consisting of Mohegan and river Indians, Narragansett, and Eastern Niantic warriors. The massive force then headed west to the Pequot village. Wequash, a Pequot who defected to the Narragansett and became a Niantic Sagamore, revolting from Sassacus, guided the party toward his former tribe. He spoke that the Pequots mainly retired into two forts for security.

Along the trek westward toward the two forts, however, the force reached a shallow crossing and stopped on grounds where the Pequots would fish, groups upon groups of Narragansetts began to manifest great fear, and great numbers started deserting; returning home because of a great concern of Sassacus and the Pequot fort. They had now come into the country of Sassacus, and found that they were within a few miles of his principal fortress. The expedition seemed no longer to be pleasant for them, but a violent fate grew more and more realistic with every step that lessened the distance between the Narragansetts and the neighboring Pequot. Mason called Uncas to him, and asked him what he had to expect from the

Indians. The chief replied that the Narragansetts would all drop off and leave, but that he and his Mohegans would never leave the English. "For which expression and some other speeches of his," Mason said, "I shall never forget him."[129] Uncas's Mohegans stayed.[130]

After the reduced force refreshed themselves, they marched three miles and came to a field which had lately been planted with Indian corn and with this find they presumed they were very close to the enemy. The force was motivated to reach the forts, but understanding that one of them was so remote that they could not come up to it before midnight, they chose, with extreme heat exhaustion and want of necessaries, to invade the nearest of the two forts, the one to be known as the Mystic Fort.[131]

With the force unable to reach Weinshauks, Sassacus' fort, the fort they intended to attack, they simply resolved to attack the Mystic fort. In the morning of the 26th of May, 1637, they encamped in Groton, between two rocks. They were now so near the enemy, that the advanced lookout could distinctly hear the savages singing and dancing within their fort with great merriment.

The night prior to the attack proved to be comfortable, being clear with moonlight. The English appointed guards and placed sentinels at some distance; they heard the enemy singing at the fort, who continued on until midnight. The force was informed that as the Pequots saw the pinnaces sail by them some days before, it was concluded the English were afraid of them and were to not come near them; the message of their song was to that purpose.

In the morning, the force awoke and saw it very light. The men rose, commended themselves to God, and then thought immediately to move toward the assault. The allied Indians who remained showed a path and told the English it led directly to the fort. They held their march about two miles, wondering that they came not to the fort, and fearing they might be deceived, but seeing corn newly planted at the foot of a great hill, supposing the fort was not far off, a champion country being round about; then making a stand, Mason gave the word for some of the Indians to come up. Uncas and Wequash appeared. The English demanded of them, where was the fort? They answered it was on the top of that hill. Then the English demanded where were the rest of the allied Indians? They answered, behind, but afraid. The English told the Indians they should not fly, but stand and watch whether the English would now fight. Then Captain Underhill came up, who marched in the rear, and commending themselves to God, divided the men. There being two entrances into the fort, they intended to enter both at once.[132]

The attack was now set on this morning. Thus the seventy-seven Englishmen under Captains Mason and Underhill charged their long sought target, even though dogged and frustrated by cautious, fleeing Native allies. Improvising on a plan greatly changed, they failed to strike their target in the night, and were not able to set up the crippling ambush they planned.

Up and then along the flanks of the sloping wooded hill the English charged. Above in the trees they could see smoke from campfires inside Mystic fort, but not a living soul. Swords drawn, their muskets primed and fuse-matches struck alight, the armored English labored up through the trees and formed two files rushing to

73

surround the Mystic palisade. They did not bring along their Narragansett and Mohegan allies, but positioned them behind themselves encircling Mystic Fort.

The captains, leading the colonies in the first New England War, would determine the fate of Connecticut and southern New England, especially with the disappointments of Block Island and the first Pequot Village invasion.

Mason and Underhill waved Uncas, his Mohegans, and the remaining Narragansetts to the side, into an exterior circle. The Narragansetts were of very little service in the attack upon the Pequot fort, holding themselves distant.

The fate of Connecticut was now to be decided with Captain Mason leading his company up to the northeast side. The first real obstacles for the English at the Mystic fort were a dog within the fort barking and a Pequot lookout crying out, "Wanux! Wanux!" meaning, English! English! The English then commenced their assault on Mystic with a booming, all together volley into its massive palisade. The English fire and then the fort's silence then drew the English in. The captains each gathered half of the men and entered separate entrances.

The Pequot braves—"the amount will be forever unknown because truly only 'Pequots knew how many bodies were in Mystic'" [likely under 100][133] —stayed in the Mystic fort and lured their enemy in, as their people may have all escaped prior to the invasion.

The entrance near which Mason stood was blocked up with bushes about breast high. Over this petty obstruction he leaped, sword in hand, shouting to his men to follow him. But Seely, his lieutenant, found it easier to remove the bushes than to force the men over them. When he had done so, he also entered, followed by sixteen soldiers. It had been determined to destroy the enemy with the sword, and thus save the corn and other valuables that were stored in the wigwams. With this approach, the captain, seeing no Indians, entered one of these wigwams. Here he found many warriors who crowded hard upon him, and beset him with great violence; but they were so amazed at the strange spirit that had so suddenly thrust itself upon them, that they could make but a feeble resistance. "There, Mason is 'beset with many Indians,' of unspecified age and gender, in such close quarters that his gun and sword are little use. "'They, are many, yet they cannot prevail,' that's all Mason says about them, leaving us to assume he killed them all or they fled from the wigwam."[134] Mason was soon joined by William Hayden, who, as he entered the wigwam through the breach that had been made by his captain, stumbled against the dead body of a Pequot, whom Mason had slain.

Mason, still intent on destroying the Pequots, and at the same time saving their property, now left the wigwam, and passed down one of their streets, driving the crowd of Indians from one end of it to the other. The Mystic Fort had embraced a large area of about twenty acres and housed more than seventy houses in this space, with lanes or streets passing between them. "Mason claims to see many Indians in the lane or street; and he making towards them, they fled." At the lower extremity of this lane stood a little company of Englishmen, who, having effected an entrance from the west, met the Indians as they fled from Mason, and killed about half a dozen of them. The captain now faced about, and went back the whole length of the lane, to the spot where he had entered the fort. He was exhausted, and quite out of breath, and had become satisfied that this was not the way to exterminate the

74

Indians. Two of his soldiers stood near him, close to the palisades with their useless swords pointed to the ground. Their dejected faces told him that they felt as he did, that the task was a hopeless one.[135]

"We shall never kill them in this way," said the captain, and then added, "We must burn them!"

With these words the request of the council of war to save the prizes of the enemy was annulled.

Before the wigwams were ignited, the forty or so Englishmen inside with the captains searched around to see if they'd been mocked. With the unlikelihood of Natives sleeping in their lodges through the commotion, destruction manifested and the captains picked up firebrands from the Pequots' campfires. Almost in an instant, the little village was wrapped in flames, and the Pequot warriors fled in dismay from the homes that had just before sheltered them. The mat-roofed lodges of Mystic kindled so fast into flames that the English were forced back outside the fort.

Outside, facing the wooded hills now, the company found themselves in a situation where they became trapped between the two Pequot forts and many angered Pequot warriors. Immediately coming in from the west, the Pequots were now to be joined by their relatives from the other Pequot fort Weinshauks. The combined Pequots then charged upon the force with their prime men, and let fly their weapons, at which time Mason's force set forth to Pequot harbor. Underhill's men managed to volley, and they killed enough Pequots to break their first charge with bullets that outreached the arrows. But the real battle was just beginning. More and more warriors would attack the isolated English, exceeding their strength and ammunition. Around three hundred is the presumed amount of braves that had joined the conflict from the other Pequot Fort Weinshauks.[136] The English ships were a great distance from them and most of the Indians but Uncas, his men, and a few Narragansetts now deserted them.[137]

The English force also now became aware of Indian conduct in war. The Indians fell out amongst themselves, the Pequots, Narragansetts, and Mohegans were changing a few arrows together, and after such a manner, it seemed as if they fought seven years they would not kill seven men. They came not near one another, but shot remote, and not point-blank, as the English do with bullets, but at rovers, and then they gazed up in the sky to see where the arrow fell, and not until it is fallen do they shoot again. But spending a little time this way, the English were forced to cast their eyes upon their poor maimed soldiers, many of them lying upon the ground, wanting food and such nourishable things as might refresh them in this faint state. But the English were not supplied with any things to help them, but only were able to look up to God.

The English-allied Indians, who had stood close to them, fell into confusion, and were determined to leave the English in a land they knew not which way to get out. Suddenly fifty of the Narragansett Indians fell off from the rest, returning home. The Pequots spying them, pursued after them. Then came some of the other Narragansetts to Captain Mason and Underhill, crying, oh help us now, or our men will be all slain. The Captains answered, how dare you crave aid of us, when you are leaving of us in this distressed condition, not knowing which way to march out of the country? But yet you shall see it is not the nature of Englishmen to deal like heathens, to use evil against evil, and the English aided them. Underhill pushing on with thirty men, in the space of an hour rescued their men, and in the English retreat to the body, slew and wounded above a hundred Pequots, all fighting men, that charged the rear and flanks.[138]

The English somehow survived the hundreds of braves from the other Pequot fort Weinshauks, who drove the English into the lower ground off the western side of Mystic Hill. The English survived the Pequot world of war. More braves poured into the fight, hundreds shot arrows with the English panic growing, yet there were not many casualties.[139]

Mason's and Underhill's outnumbered English bled with their backs to the sea, when the boats fortunately were spotted as the Captain on the boat eyed the smoke from the burning of Mystic Fort.[140] While debating what measures should be adopted, it was with delight that Mason saw his little vessels, their sails filled with the welcome gale that blew from the north-east, gliding into Pequot harbor. The fainting soldiers hailed them with joy, as if they had been angels sent to deliver them.[141]

The end of the colonial retreat was somewhere along the Mystic shore where they met their ships. The Pequots were playing upon the English flanks, and one Sergeant Davis, a strong soldier, spying something black upon the top of a rock, stepped forth from the body with a carbine of three feet long, and, at a venture, gave fire, supposing it to be an Indian's head, turning him over with his heels upward. The Indians observed this, and greatly admired that a man should shoot so directly. The Pequots were much daunted at the shot and refrained approaching so near upon the English. Coming forth to the Pequot River the English met with Captain Patrick, who under his command had forty able soldiers who were ready to begin a second attempt. But many of the existing soldiers being maimed and much wearied, the English refrained that night, and put their wounded and some others of their men aboard as Underhill set sail for Saybrook fort. Captain Mason and Captain Patrick marching over land, as they could not desert their Indian allies in Indian country, burned and spoiled the country between the Pequot and Connecticut River, where Saybrook received them. The Pequots received such a terrible blow and destruction unreparable.[142]

Mason, with twenty of his men, and Patrick with his forty, set out to Saybrook fort by land, while Underhill with the wounded and the remainder of the Connecticut troops went by water. The whole company, when received, was royally entertained by Lieutenant Gardener at the fort.[143] "This victory, believed-in, but riddled with doubt, is the birth of the Puritan colonies' confidence in themselves as here to stay."[144] This was a decisive victory, and the Pequots were assumed ruined. Many were taken captive and many more were to be destroyed.[145]

Many others, following the invasion of Mystic Fort, felt the Pequots were left in utter confusion. Many of the tribe's leaders blamed Sassacus for the defeat, and only special pleading by his councilors persuaded them to spare his life. Most of the Pequots agreed, however, that safety only existed in flight. The majority headed west for Mohawk country, where they hoped to find asylum, while others sought refuge with neighboring tribes.[146]

Among those who fled west was Sassacus. Sassacus, however, fleeing to the Mohawks of New York for shelter, was slain and his skin and hair were brought to Boston.[147] So ended the great Pequot sachem.

The return of the colonists to their colony now granted "rights of conquest" to Connecticut within the Pequot bounds, and also, the safe return brought relief and inspiration for other Puritan colonists. Thus, when the little army returned home, victorious beyond their hopes, it was a natural thing for the friendly Indians, in their gratitude over the destruction of their enemies, to surrender to the English the site of their village, and divide it among the soldiers, and themselves remove, as we know they did about this time. The River Indians ceded vast tracts of their land. Hence the Pequot War folklore was created.[148]

It may be said that the annihilation of the Pequots can be condemned only by those who read history so incorrectly as to suppose that savages, whose business it is to torture and slay, can always be dealt with according to the methods in use between civilized peoples. New England, with their virtues was bound to treat the red man with true justice and avoid cruelty in punishing his misbehavior. But if the founders of Connecticut, in confronting a danger which threatened their very existence, struck with savage fierceness, we cannot blame them. The world is so made that it is only in that way that the higher races have been able to preserve themselves and carry on their progressive work. (John Fiske)[149]

On arrival at Suckiaug or Hartford, Mason said, "we were entertained with great triumph and rejoicing and praising God for his goodness to us in crowning us with success and restoring of us with so little loss. It was the Lord's doings, and it is marvelous in our eyes."[150]

Thus the enemies that had escaped scattered, and the Pequots now were a prey to all Indians. Happy were those that could bring in their heads to the English, of which there came almost daily to Windsor, or Hartford. The Pequots, though, growing weary of this, sent some of the chiefs that survived to mediate with the English. They offered that if they might but enjoy their lives, they would become the English Vassals, and to use them as they pleased, which was granted them. At which point, Uncas and Miantonomo were sent for, who with the Pequots met at Hartford. The Pequots were being demanded, how many of them were then living? It was answered, about one hundred and eighty, or two hundred. They were then given to Uncas, Sachem of Mohegan eighty; to Miantonomo, Sachem of Narragansett, eighty; and to Ninnigret of the Niantics, twenty. The Pequots were then bound by covenant, that none should inhabit their native country, nor should any of them be called Pequots any more, but Mohegan and Narragansetts forever. [John Mason][151]

The Mohegans and Narragnsetts were compensated accordingly for their efforts. A three-way treaty would be negotiated in hopes of a perpetual peace between the English, Narragansetts, and Mohegans. The Treaty of Hartford in 1638 resulted from the Pequot demise. Its purpose was to settle the scattered Pequots and arrange a system to advance Indian conduct within the colonies. On the 21st of September, Uncas and Miantonomo, with the remaining Pequots, met the magistrates of Connecticut at Hartford. With about two hundred of the vanquished tribe still surviving, a treaty was entered into between Connecticut, the Mohegans, and the Narragansetts.

The Narragansett and Mohegan sachems agreed to capture and execute any Pequots guilty of disobedience. The English also gained, after the Hartford treaty, most of eastern Connecticut, as Uncas ceded most of his land, aside from villages and fields, for political strength. The treaty also forced the Narragansetts and the Mohegans to inform the Colony of any intentions of war against a rival tribe.[152]

The Treaty of Hartford, 21 September 1638 reads as follows:
ARTICLES BETWEEN THE INGLISH IN CONNECTICUT AND THE INDIAN SACHEMS

A Covenant and Agreement between the English Inhabiting the Jurisdiction of the River of Connecticut of the one part, and Miantinomy the chief Sachem of the Narragansetts in the behalf of himself and the other Sachems there; and Poquim or Uncas the chief Sachim of the Indians called the Mohegans in the behalf of himself and the Sachims under him, as Followeth, at Hartford the 21st of September, 1638.

Imp'r. There is a peace and a Familiarity made between the sd Miantinome and Narragansett Indians and the sd Poquim and Mohegan Indians, and all former Injuryes and wrongs offered each to other Remitted and Burryed and never to be renued any more from henceforth.

2. It is agreed there fall out Injuryes and wrongs for fuetur to be done or committed Each to other or their men, they shall not presently Revenge it But they are to appeal to the English and they are to decide the same, and the determination of the English to stand And they are each to do as is by the English sett down and if the one or the other shall Refuse to do, it shall be lawfull for the English to Compel him and to side and take part if they see cause, against the obstinate or Refusing party.

3. It is agreed and a conclusion of peace and friendship made between the sd Miantinome and sd Narragansetts and the sd Poquim and the sd Mohegans as long as they carry themselves orderly and give no just cause of offence and that they nor either of them do shelter any that may be Enemyes to the English that shall or formerly have had hand in murdering or killing any English man or woman or consented thereunto, They or either of them shall as soon as they can either bring the chief Sachem of our late enemies the Peaquots that had the chief hand in killing the English, to the sd English, or take of their heads, As also for those murderers that are now agreed upon amongst us that are living they shall as soon as they can possibly take off their heads, if they may be in their custody or Else whensoever they or any of them shall come Amongst them or to their wigwams or any where if they can by any means come by them.

4. And whereas there be or is reported for to be by the sd Narragansetts and Mohegans 200 Peaquots living that are men besides

squawes and paposes. The English do give unto Miantinome and the Narragansetts to make up the number of Eighty with the Eleven they have already, and to oquime his number, and that after they the Peaquots shall be divided as abovesd, shall no more be called Peaquots but Narragansetts and Mohegans and as their men and either of them are to pay for every Sanop one fathom of wampome peage and for every youth half so much- and for every Sanop papoose one hand to be paid at Killing time of Corn at Connecticut yearly and shall not suffer them for to live in the country that was formerly theirs but is now the Englishes by conquest neither shall the Narragansetts nor Mohegans possess any part of the Peaquot country without leave from the English And it is always expected that the English Captives are forthwith to be delivered to the English, such as belong to the Connecticut to the Sachems there, And such as belong to the Massachusetts; the sd agreements are to be kept invoylably by the parties abovesd and if any make breach of them the other two may joyn and make warr upon such as shall break the same, unless satisfaction be made being Reasonbly Required

    The Mark of MIANTINOMMY
    The Marks of POQUIAM alias UNKAS
        JOHN HAINES
        ROG'R LUDLOW
        EDW'RD HOPKINS.[153]

And so perished the great Pequot nation and Sassacus. The refugees without any tribal affiliation scattered here and there, and only Uncas keenly accepted and adopted several of them into his tribe of Mohegans. Miantonomo believed Uncas was using his share of the Pequot prisoners to increase his own power. In October a feud between Miantonomo and Uncas became apparent, denying any possible peace between the two.

In Hartford, Miantonomo, at a private conference, gave the Council the names of all the remaining members of the Pequot tribe who had been guilty of killing Englishmen. A list of these names was read to Uncas who admitted that it was correct. Miantonomo then said that of the remnants of the Pequot tribe, Canonicus had few. Canonicus had ten or eleven out of the seventy who had submitted to him, the others never having come in, or having returned to their old hunting grounds after coming in. The rest were either with the Mohegans or in their ancient territory, which was the same thing, as the Pequot territory naturally became Mohegan territory.[154] "Uncas became furious with Miantinomo for having informed the English colonists of secretly harboring Pequot refugees. Uncas then spread the rumor that Sequassen had conspired with Miantinomo to make Miantinomo the Grand Sachem of all the New England tribes, and to declare war upon the whites. Hearing this rumor, the magistrates summoned Miantinomo to Boston to answer accusations."[155]

Miantonomo and his Narragansetts were considered favorable to the English during the Pequot invasion, however that relationship would quickly change. After performing this good service of sharing his men for the Pequot invasion, he later would become insulted, threatened with bodily harm, and murdered as a result of

79

colonial consent. "The reader must consider that the Mohegans under Uncas fought with the Connecticut troops in this war; and it seems to be probable that as the Mohegans, and Uncas, were on very friendly terms with Captain Mason, the commander of the expedition, and may have received some recognition or consideration at the hands of the whites; that recognition, however, was not extended to the Narragansetts and their chief, who also were on the United Colonies side."[156]

Interestingly enough, the division of the remaining Pequots made the Mohegans under Uncas the most deadly enemies of the Narragansetts, even with the elimination of the Pequots, the Narragansett greatest former threat. The combination of Pequots and Mohegans, thus, became the dominant tribe in old Pequot.

The destruction of the Pequot people strengthened the hand of Uncas thus giving him authority over most of the surrounding tribes, with the exception of the Narragansetts. He now declared to be Sachem of the Mohegans, and all the tribes formerly subject to the Pequots. This included the River Tribes, whose sachems were Sequassen and Sohweag.[157]

Even with the Pequot destruction the colonists had still continued to fear an Indian insurrection. Similarly to the colonists, the Indians also formed a grim perception of their permanent neighbors; the lingering memory of the Pequot destruction made New England Indians wary to engage in conflict with the colonists. Any conflict for Indians now existed only between rival tribes vying for English protection and allegiance; hence the Mohegans against the Narragansetts.

Sowheag (Sequeen), who greatly provoked the Pequot uprising in Wethersfield, was a problem for the Puritan authority following the Pequot war. The Wethersfield settlers wanted justice, but Sowheag argued he had acted against the colonial injustice. The Wethersfield colonists did feel they did a minor wrong to Sowheag by not allowing him to settle within the jurisdiction of his own town, yet he still was presumed responsible for causing the Wethersfield Massacre. Endicott's failed raid upon the Pequot tribe in August 1636 brought no consideration for Pequot retaliation on Wethersfield in April 1637.

The leaders of the River colonies had to write to the Massachusetts magistrates for assistance on how to handle Sowheag. The Massachusetts magistrates' answer was Sowheag was the receiver of the first wrong and had been justified by his act. The size of his vengeance was not relevant.

The case fell out to be this: Sowheag gave the English land there, upon contract that he might sit down by them, and be protected. When he came to Wethersfield and had set down his wigwam, they drove him away by force. Whereupon, he not being of strength to repair this injury by open force, he secretly draws in the Pequots.

Such of the magistrates and elders as could meet on the sudden, returned this answer: That, if the cause were thus, Sowheag might, upon this injury first offered by them, right himself either by force or fraud; and that by the law of nations, and though the damage he had done them had been one hundred times more than what he sustained from them; yet that is not considerable in point of a just war; neither was he bound to seek satisfaction in a peaceable way; it was enough that he had complained of it as an injury and breach of covenant. In accordance with this guidance the Wethersfield people proceeded and made a new agreement with the Indians of the river.[158]

A deal was made favorable to both sides and a few years following went without injuries, and Sowheag eventually moved to Middletown. However, worry did begin to show as the settlers were unwilling to place confidence in a chief who indirectly caused the massacre.

While I lived in Wethersfield at this time, there was a growing suspicion of Sowheag's alliance to the settlers. Rumors ran rampant of Indian conspiracies in the 1640s and brought about investigation after investigation of tribal actions.[159]

Indians in the Connecticut River Valley, in hopes of protection and stability, would continue to offer land as collateral for English goods received on credit with future payment in fur. However, as the supply of furs eventually dwindled, Indians could not make their payments and lost their land. From the English view, trade with the Indians became unnecessary to support their material needs. English colonists therefore solely wanted Indian land, rather than trade goods or honor, as time progressed.

This helped calm the colonies and at the same time threatened the long-term livelihood of many Indian communities. Private property in land became the foundation that allowed the New England colonies to thrive and also to eliminate the Indian.

Part III: 1643

Another event of considerable weight that influenced the decision to become a praying or preying Indian was the murder of Narragansett Sachem Miantonomo in 1643. With the Mohegan-Connecticut alliance strengthening following the overthrow of the Pequots, Narragansett sachem Miantonomo may have justly deserved more benefit than he had received for the Narragansett participation in the Pequot War. Conflict arose when Indians related to Miantonomo hunted in what was considered former Pequot lands, but Connecticut and the Mohegans didn't accept it. The Narragansett tributaries were quickly challenged with force. Uncas was the Indian representative for Connecticut's Indian force and Uncas's men consequently fell upon the Narragansett hunters in the Pequot lands.

Miantonomo took to Massachusetts for permission to use his force in retaliation of the Mohegans' acts on the hunting grounds. Boston told him to sit still and await developments. Connecticut all the while backed Uncas and winked at his reestablishment of the old Pequot tribe under his guidance. Tension between the two tribes also increased because of the scramble for wampum. One reason for Connecticut's behavior toward Uncas was his willingness to pay large quantities of the shell currency for Pequot refugees. The method was simple and plain: as more Pequots found their way under Uncas, more wampum tribute was sent to Connecticut.

Between Connecticut and Massachusetts there was no mention of any commitment to the Indians. However, Connecticut's dislike for the Narragansetts remained, while Massachusetts' protection was conditioned on the Narragansetts' serving as subjects, yet, those Indians were unwilling to take that position. The Mohegans were Connecticut's allies, but not Massachusetts'. In five years' time after the Hartford treaty of 1638, the Puritans finally settled their own colony's differences and formed a united colonial confederation. The spirit of that union of the colonies became know as the United Colonies. The necessity to unite the

83

colonies possibly began when an accusation of war occurred in 1642. Several Indians, presumably Uncas and his tribe, approached Connecticut leaders with warnings that the Indians all over the country had combined to get rid of all the English after the harvest. Connecticut, consequently, advised Massachusetts that troops of militia should be sent from both colonies to join at Fort Saybrook.

Boston's response was panic. The Massachusetts magistrates determined to strike some fear into the Indians. All the Indians who could be reached within their bounds were disarmed, and the Massachueset sachem Cutshamoquin found himself in Boston's jail.

Additional investigation raised questions, however. The Boston magistrates became convinced that none of the Indians of Massachusetts had been plotting. When the General Court assembled on September 8th, it advised caution. There was a belief that this all came from the hostility between Miantonomo and Uncas, who continually sought to dishonor each other with the English. Reports had been raised every year.

One example I learned of Uncas' false accusations was when he claimed he had been wounded by a Pequot warrior, who had become a subject of his after the defeat of the Pequots. When questioned, this Pequot fled to the Narragansetts. Uncas reported the incident to the Massachusetts authorities, charging that Miantonomo somehow had been responsible for this attempt to kill him. To clear himself, the Narragansett Sachem journeyed to Boston with the Pequot, and denied any knowledge of the affair. The Pequot explained that Uncas had inflicted the wound on his own arm in order to accuse Miantonomo. Miantonomo agreed to hand the supposed Pequot over to Uncas, but instead of so doing killed him soon after leaving Boston.[160]

Miantonomo would soon feel the wrath of Uncas' constructed accusations as well. An order went forth to Miantonomo to come to Boston to explain the rumors of the conspiracy and disloyalty in regards to the speculation of war by the combined Indian force.

> It was a widespread belief that he was planning a general conspiracy. Clothed in his robes of state, he made his defense before the grim elders of New England so successfully that Governor Winthrop wrote of him as having shown good understanding and principles of justice and equity, and to have accommodated himself to their understanding. Most of the charges against the Narragansett were preferred by Connecticut, and this reflects the clever touch of Uncas turning his influence with the Connecticut authorities to good account. The Massachusetts authorities were not blinded and they refused to agree with the request of Connecticut that war be declared against Miantonomo. [Ellis and Morris][161]

Upon Miantonomo's arrival in Boston, he appeared with great pride to order that he be faced with his accusers. The magistrates didn't know who the accusers were, because Connecticut hadn't provided evidence. Miantonomo had his own ideas. He wanted to meet Uncas at Boston for a confrontation and demanded that his accusers be punished, as he had no sense of guilt. In Boston that was quite an act.

The magistrates were so overcome that they allowed Miantonomo to dine at the lower end of their own table [162]

Consequently, with this paranoia of Indian attacks, the English force formed the "Union of the Colonies of Massachusetts Bay, Plymouth, New Haven and Connecticut, [which] was formed (1643) under the title of the united colonies of New England. This was the famous league. The object was a common protection against the Indians, and the encroachments of the Dutch and French settlers."[163] No war was to be commenced by any colonial member without approval of the United Colonies. The united force's intentions may also have been for obtaining Indian land.

There became no doubt that the 1638 Hartford treaty would not insure any peace for Miantonomo. Anything he did to Uncas or the United Colonies would bring destruction upon himself. He may have angered the colonies most severely, on a subject not covered by the treaty, when he ceded valuable Narragansett land for payment to Englishmen not of the Puritan theology. Massachusetts wasn't pleased, jurisdiction of the land would cause problems in ensuing years, and those who bought the land within Rhode Island bounds were highly unfavorable to the Bay Colony. Furthermore, the allowance for the settling of Providence Plantation was through the Narragansetts who gave refuge to the persecuted Quakers from Massachusetts Bay. It was to Narragansett that Roger Williams fled when he was banished from Salem in 1636 and it was among them that Williams lived.

After the Narragansett allowance for Williams to settle Providence Plantation, it was there that a non-Puritan named Samuel Gorton fled with his increasing band of freethinkers when they were banished from Plymouth. Even in Providence, Gorton stirred controversy to such an extent that four of the town's freemen willingly subjected themselves and their lands to the government of Massachusetts to bring a formal complaint against Gorton and his associates. Gorton, meanwhile, had moved to Pawtuxet in 1642, and in 1643 he moved once again, this time to an area south of Pawtuxet along the Narragansett Bay. There he purchased a tract of land at Shawomet from the Narragansett Sachems including Miantonomo. Pomham was the local sachem who held the land and signed the deed under compulsion, but he would then flee to Massachusetts and submit all his land to the colony. Hence, Massachusetts now had to remove the unwanted squatters who dwelt in Massachusetts bounds upon the objections of the Shawomet chief Pomham and the Cowesset chieftain Soconococo.[164] With Massachusetts angered by the Narragansett management of land, they would ultimately deny Miantonomo the help he would legally need to keep his life.

Miantonomo, "by selling the Shawomet peninsula to Samuel Gorton, who the Puritans viewed as a spirit struck dumb with blasphemies and insolences, now involved himself in the quarrel between Massachusetts and the Gortonists. Massachusetts, then engaged in drawing "in the last of those parts who now live under another government, but grow very offensive." Simply, Massachusetts greatly desired the acquisition of the territory of Narragansett Bay. Urged by the enemies of Gorton, the Massachusetts authorities, it was Pumhan, the local sachem, who laid claim to the ownership of Shawomet and pleaded the inability of Miantonomo and Canonicus to give valid title to the lands they had sold. This scheme was successful, and a group composed of citizens of Rhode Island, standing ready to purchase the land in question as it was conveyed to them by Pumham and Saconomoco, offered their allegiance to the Massachusetts colony.

Miantonomo was again summoned to Boston, and could not prove, in the opinion of the authorities, his authority over Pumham and Saconomoco, despite the declaration of Roger Williams, that the authority of the Narragansett sachems over the lands and chiefs in question, had existed as far back as the settlement in Plymouth." Miantonomo on his return home, learning that one of his friends, Sequassen, had been roughly handled by Uncas, took up the quarrel and complained to Connecticut, who answered that "the English had no hand in it."

Miantinomo, still, felt the Connecticut white men were to believe anything Uncas told them. It seems Sequassen may have first chose acts of violence toward Uncas to eliminate the influential Mohegan chief. Sequassen was related to Miantinomo by blood, as well as by alliance to the Narragansetts, and Sequassen's acts would be considered part of Miantonomo's conspiracy. One important Mohegan was assassinated by Sequassen's band and attempts were made to kill Uncas.

> Uncas and a small party of Mohegans were attacked and one was killed by followers of Sequassen. On Uncas' appeal to the magistrates in Hartford he was told that it was wisest for the clans to reach some understanding. Thereupon Uncas attacked the Sequin village in Hartford's South Meadows, and killed seven and burned wigwams.
>
> This brought Miantonomo to the Hartford authorities who assured him that they could take no part for or against the Mohegans and matters must be settled peacefully amongst themselves. [Charles Burpee][165]

Uncas did not accept receiving insignificant revenge for his lost Mohegan and thus invaded the River Tribes home, killing seven and wounding around twenty men, burning wigwams, and carrying away great plunder. This act against Miantinomo's relatives occurred in the early summer of 1643 somewhere between Hartford and Wethersfield and made Miantinomo furious, and now he was the one to seek revenge, which would, ultimately, cost him his life.[166]

So, the Narragansett chief decided to retaliate first in accordance with the Hartford Treaty of 1638 and sought colonial consent. Miantonomo received what seemed to be colonial acceptance by Winthrop. "Miantonomo turned to Massachusetts and was desirous to know if they would not be offended if he made war upon Uncas. To which Winthrop replied: "If Uncas had done him or his friends harm and would not give satisfaction, we shall leave him to take his own course." [167] Thus the year sixteen hundred and forty-three was the year Miantinomo invaded Uncas's fort.

Miantonomo gathered a huge force of six or seven hundred warriors and marched into the home of the Mohegan around Norwich, Connecticut. Uncas heard of the invading force from outlooks stationed in the direction of the Narragansetts. Uncas learned from a scout that Miantonomi's force outnumbered his, yet he still chose to prepare his warriors. The Mohegan force left Shantok, the largest Mohegan settlement, with four hundred warriors. They met Miantonomo at the Great Plain, four miles from Shantok. There Uncas would use trickery to compensate for being so greatly outnumbered.[168]

As the two forces met, Uncas first called a conference and went out to meet Miantonomo. At the meeting between Uncas and Miantonomo the two faced each other between the two opposing forces. Uncas suggested the two settle this matter in one on one battle, and the winner would gain control of the loser's warriors. Miantinomo, however, would not accept it. Miantonomo refused, saying, "my men came to fight and they shall fight." Uncas, at that time, gave a signal and fell to the ground, hence, a surprise shower of arrows from three hundred Mohegan bows flew against their unprepared enemies who were within easy shot and unsuspicious of any such act.

The shower of arrows fell upon the helpless Narragansetts and Uncas sprang up, and with his warriors yelling their battle cry and holding their tomahawks, rushed upon the astonished enemy.[169] The Narragansetts fled panic-stricken. As Miantonomo's men broke and ran, the Mohegans pursued them through tangled thickets. Thirty Narragansetts died and many more were wounded in route. Miantonomo was wearing an English corselet which delayed his flight, and some pursuing Mohegans satisfied themselves with getting in his way, in order that Uncas himself, who was not in the front ranks of the pursuers, had the honor of taking him.[170] Uncas brought Miantonomo back to Shantok.

The Narragansetts hoped a truce could be formed between the two warring tribes, as the Narragansetts quickly collected forty pounds worth of wampum for the return of Miantonomo from the Mohegan tribe. The wampum packages were sent to Uncas, some to Uncas's wife, and some to his favorite counselors; but Uncas would not free his captive, and while Miantonomo was held prisoner, the two sachems spoke at length.

Miantonomo supposedly proposed that Uncas join him in an alliance against the newcomers. However, in accordance with Indian custom Miantonomo's life was forfeited upon capture, but Uncas, could not have been sure of how Connecticut and Massachusetts would regard the murder of Miantonomo. Uncas was also puzzled by the threat of Samuel Gorton who forbid Uncas to injure his captive as Gorton sent a messenger to Uncas, threatening dire vengeance if harm were done to his ally, furthermore, Uncas did not want to enter a war against the Narragansetts without colonial support,[171] as he did not want to remove himself from the good graces of the white man.

In the end Uncas took his prisoner to Hartford, which was a show of the respect Uncas held for English law. The English held him prisoner at Hartford, and his case was put at the top of the schedule of the first business meeting of the Commissioners of the United Colonies on September 7, 1643. Many things were set in motion with this meeting: the character for future colonial policy on Indian affairs, the ability to gain success through deceit and preferential treatment as Uncas had, and the conduct of policy makers driven by land and greed. Those distinguished men of the United Colonies legally decided to have Miantonomo murdered at the hands of Uncas.

The sentence of Miantonomo is one of the most unjust decisions that stand recorded by the Colonial Courts. He had shown many acts of kindness towards the whites; in all his intercourse with them he had demonstrated a noble spirit, and only six years before his death had assisted Mason and his little band of soldiers from Hartford in their conquest against the Pequots.[172]

I wonder why the English intervened in the affair at all. The only answer could be that they sought to make an example of Miantonomo to terrify the natives. The people of Rhode Island, who lived near Miantonomo, and whom he had often befriended, took sides with him while he was a prisoner, believing him to be in the right. Uncas and his constituents, on the other hand, brought up another piece of evidence as to why Miantonomo should sustain colonial punishment. They told the authorities at Hartford that Miantonomo had engaged the Mohawks to join him and that they were then encamped within a day's journey of the frontier, and were awaiting Miantonomo's release.

The authorities apparently believed this, without making any attempt to verify it, and used it as a piece of evidence. However, the main justification for the punishment of Miantonomo was because he was a treaty violator. They revived the Hartford treaty of 1638 with its stipulation that neither Uncas nor Miantonomo should war against the other until they had first protested, and that the English had heard their grievances. The language of the treaty may have been viewed as, "The English of Connecticut are to decide," not those of Massachusetts who Miantonomo received council with in regards to a retaliation against Uncas, for his acts against Sequassen and his men.

The unfortunate Miantonomo had brought himself to his own doom. The hatred between the rival sachems, Uncas and Miantonomo, was deep and finally turned deadly for one of the two sachems. Surprisingly though, Miantonomo's fate was to be determined by the clergy of the United Colonies Commissioners, because the commissioners were confused. According to English law there was no good reason for putting Miantonomo to death. The question was whether they should interfere with the Indian custom by which his life was already forfeit to his captor. The magistrates, however, suspected the Narragansetts of hostile intentions and in their time of confusion the commissioners sought spiritual guidance. A council of forty or fifty clergymen, from all parts of New England, were in session at Boston, and the question was referred to a committee of five of their number. Thus the question of life or death was left to five men who were willing to be made the scapegoats. "These same men belonged to the profession that showed itself to be made up of the most bloodthirsty of all the English, and even more so than any of those whom they delighted in calling savages."[173]

As the day came when the question was discussed whether Miantonomo should be put to death, the charges ultimately brought forward against him were these: that he had killed a Pequot who had testified against him in reference to his treatment of Uncas; that he had again and again tried to take the life of Uncas by assassination and poison; that he had broken his league in making war upon the Mohegans without taking his appeal to the English; and lastly, that he had conceived the horrible design of cutting off the whole English population, and had hired Mohawks and Indians of other tribes to assist him in its execution.

Thus Uncas imposed upon the commissioners by acting upon their fears in this delicate matter, and that several of these charges were sustained by the most wicked perjury, I can't doubt. The several accusations in most of their details, I believe to have been a Mohegan fabrication and backed up by the testimony of Mohegan witnesses. It seems that the commissioners questioned its truth, and hesitated to act upon it. At last it was referred to five principal clergymen of the several colonies, who, after a solemn, and I doubt not an honest debate, advised that sentence of death should be passed upon the accused. The commissioners followed this unfortunate advice, and assigned Uncas to execute the sentence. [Hollister][174]

The commissioners directed that Uncas should bring his captive "Into the next part of his government, and there put him to death, provided that some discreet and faithful person of the English accompany them and see the execution, for our more full satisfaction."

The decision was prompt and the sentence was authorized that Miantonomo must die. Roger Williams was at this time in England and unable to speak in behalf of the Narragansett Sachem. Thus Uncas promptly obeyed the directions given, taking with him two Hartford men as witnesses. Uncas took Miantonomo down between Hartford and Windsor, and it was Uncas's brother, following after Miantonomo, who clave his head with a hatchet.[175]

The decision made by the United Colonies commissioners displayed that there was only one path for Indian leaders to follow for self-preservation, as Uncas displayed. Others increasingly followed after Miantonomo's death to obey English rules. Certain Indians transformed toward the English culture to further preserve their own and their group's lives, even going so far as to submit their land directly to a colony or to the king of England in order to receive the same rights as the colonists.

After the Massachusetts, Connecticut, Plymouth, and New Haven colonies agreed in 1643 to form the United Colonies and executed Miantonomo, the major Narragansett sachems in Rhode Island sought a way to preserve their independence and to protect themselves. Probably having observed Rhode Island residents' success in appealing to a distant royal authority for protection, and in consideration with the decision of Miantonomo's fate, the Narragansett leadership chose to deal directly with the King of England.

The land issue that arose from Gorton's purchase from Miantonomi, and the submission of Pomham for the same land, led Gorton and the grieving Narragansetts into direct conflict with colonial leaders. As a result of the land issue, the Massachusetts authorities sent an armed force to remove the Gortonists. With no backing, as Rhode Island was not a member of the United Colonies, Gorton sailed across the Atlantic to London to discuss matters with the King, concerning himself and the Narragansett struggles. Thus in 1644 a previous minor land dispute now blossomed into an affair to be dealt with by royal authority. In a letter delivered on April 19, 1644, the Narragansetts, seeking relief for all their pain and grief, willingly decided, and most humbly, to submit, subject, and give over themselves, peoples, lands, rights, inheritances, and possessions unto the protection, care and government of that worthy and royal Prince, Charles, King of Great Britain and

Ireland. This effort was in large part because the Narragansetts held just cause of suspicion of some of His Majesty's pretended subjects.

The written act of submission made it clear as to what the Narragansetts hoped to gain; it stated that allegiance depended upon condition of his Majesties' royal protection, including protection against any of the natives in these parts. More importantly, however, they realized that submission to the king legally protected them from other subjects of the king living in the colonies: "Nor can we yield over ourselves unto any, that are subjects themselves in any case." The sachems understood they now employed the English empire in hopes of gaining advantages in their local struggles with the colonial authorities and other Indians. The Narragansetts wished to continue as friends not subjects to the United Colonies.

There were other Indians who had formed an allegiance with Massachusetts Bay, contrary to the Narragansetts' and the compact they had formed with the King. On June 22, 1643, as abovementioned, Indians within Rhode Island considered tributaries of the Narragansetts, Pomham and Socononoco, had journeyed to Boston and submitted themselves and their lands to the government of Massachusetts, ignoring any reference to the king. Massachusetts Bay then laid claim to Shawomet, but requested Miantonomo, prior to his death, to appear before the authorities to decide the ownership of these lands and to prove his claim of authority over the other two sachems who claimed the land theirs, as Pomham was sachem of Shawomet, and Sacononoco sachem of Patuxet.

The Narragansett land at issue was thinly settled by a colony of unchartered squatters, some of whom had made purchase from Miantonomo. In Massachusetts's view, many of these purchasers were undesirables for several reasons. All of them were establishing independent title to land that Boston wanted, and a majority of the squatters disregarded certain religious practices.

As Samuel Gorton and his associates were these independent residents at Shawomet, it would seem that Boston became very angry at that transaction and predicted that Miantonomo would lose his head for it.[176]

Before the certainty of the prediction by Boston, Miantonomo promptly appeared in Boston, and being demanded in open court, whether he had any interest in the said two sachems as his subjects, he could prove none. The two Indians of Rhode Island, Pomham and Socononoco, sought protection against the Narragansett, protecting their interest against Gorton, who had taken away their land in agreement with Miantonomo. The two submitting sachems were forced to appear before the governor of Massachusetts and sign a form, which they did and then departed joyful and well satisfied. This instance gave encouragement to many Indians to come in and submit to the Massachusetts government, in expectation of the like protection and benefit. Governor Winthrop considered the submission of Pomham and Socononoco, "a fruit of our prayers and the first fruit of our hopes that the example would bring in others."[177]

Before Pumham and Socononoco submitted land, there already existed great confusion by the fragmentation of lands in Rhode Island. The settlers planned and struggled against each other, and some chose to scheme with other Puritan colonies.[178] As Governor Winthrop explained, Massachusetts' interest had been partly to rescue these men [of Rhode Island] "from unjust violence and partly to draw in the rest in those parts either under ourselves or Plymouth, who now lived under no government but grew very offensive; and the place was likely to be of use to us, especially if we should have occasion of sending out against any Indians of Narragansett and likewise for an outlet into Narragansett Bay; and seeing it came without our seeking and would be no charge to us."

After Miantonomo's murder, the Narragansetts became very cautious with any Englishman. During the brief span after their Sachem's death, "the Narragansetts had by no means remained quiet under the loss of their sachem, but were continually harassing the Mohegans with their war parties. Miantinomo's authority was inherited, at least to some degree, by his brother, a young man of about twenty, named Pessicus. Within a month after the death of Miantinomo, and also in the following March, Pessicus sent presents to Boston, with messages that he wished peace with the English, but was still determined to make war upon Uncas. His presents were refused; unfriendly answers were returned to him, and he was told that the English would stand by Uncas whenever he should be attacked. These replies, however, produced little effect, for threats alone could not restrain the hatred and desire of vengeance, which was felt by the Narragansetts.

Twelve or fourteen Englishmen, sent by Hartford to protect Uncas, probably had enough and more than enough to do, all summer, in keeping watch, and running about from this point to that, to chase away the intruders. Things finally became so troublesome, that the Commissioners determined, [September, 1644,] that both parties should be summoned to Hartford, and plead their case before the Court.

Notwithstanding the restrictions which the English had been continually putting upon the Indians since their settlement of the country, the independent spirit of the Narragansett sachems was not quelled in any degree. Whatever externals of submission might have been apparent, underneath was a current of unrest and a harboring of revenge. [Herbert Milton Sylvester]¹⁷⁹

"In the years following, various regulations were adopted by the Connecticut government by which the intercourse between the Indians and the whites was to become more limited. The Indians were not allowed to live within a quarter of a mile of any English settlement; and if they brought their guns into the settlement they were to be confiscated. One tribe was not allowed to entertain wandering members of other tribes; and in no case was a strange Indian to be admitted to the settlements, unless fleeing from his enemy. Drunkenness prevailed among the savages, and the settlements were at times disturbed by their attempts to obtain liquor, and all Indians were forbidden to walk about the streets after nightfall, under penalty of a fine or flogging. The English were not allowed to take the property of an Indian for debt without consent, or upon legal warrant; and later it was enacted that such as trusted an Indian with goods were deprived of all right to appeal to law for the recovering of the same. It was during these years that the efforts for the Christianizing of the Indians were going on under the auspices of the Society for Propagating the Gospel in New England; and it is noted that at this time the Mohegans, as well as the other Connecticut tribes, had little if any knowledge of Christianity, and were still to be regarded as among the heathen." [Herbert Milton Sylvester][180]

The event of Miantonomo's death was so momentous for the colonies' development. What happened to him proved why Indians should not dissent against any portion of the English power: they would end up dead as Miantonomo. He was punished even after bringing his intentions of war against Uncas to the authorities— in other words, he had followed the rules. The legal effort by Massachusetts for the acquisition of some Narragansett land may have been the main factor of his fate, and ironically, the results initiated the first steps for the missionary program on the mainland. The death of the great Narragansett sachem signified the diminished protection a sachem provided for the tribe, and forced the Indian to depend on another form of authority outside the tribe for leadership. As easy as it was for this sachem to be destroyed, the scattered Indians now had to find protection in a new source and they had no problem in giving up their land for it.

His punishment set the stage for the submission of lands by the Massachusetts Sachems and their affiliates in 1644. These submissions opened the possibility of praying Indian villages sanctioned by the court, which came fifteen years after John Winthrop first proclaimed the missionary purpose. Miantonomo's death finally initiated the conversion of Indians toward the Gospel. Following the submission of Massachusetts sachem Cutshamekin and four others to colonial authority in March 1644, the General Court directed the county courts to instruct the Indians in knowledge and worship of God and to take care that the Indians should be civilized.

Christian practices became necessary for Massachusetts tribes when they ceded their land in 1644. This submission inevitably opened the door for the development of a new Indian society with religion leading those living within the bounds of the Massachusetts Bay colony. The Puritans believed that their government extended to all within the colony's borders and that the Christian Indians, who had submitted themselves to the Massachusetts Bay government in 1644, were lawfully to obey and be protected by the same laws that governed English settlers. Christian practices for the Indians within the Bay then became part of their colonial requirement. There existed a parallel between Rhode Island land submission to the king and Massachusetts Indians submitting themselves to Christianity: both submissions were mostly for order and protection.

The submission of the Massachusetts Tribe in 1644, which the several Indians signed, is as follows:

Wee haue & by these presents do voluntarily, & without any constraint or pswasion, but, of or owne free motion, put orselues, or subiects, lands, & estates under the government & jurisdiction of the Maisachusets, to bee governed & ptected by them, according to their just laws & orders, so farr as wee shalbee made capable of understanding; & wee do pmise for orselues, & all or subiects, & all or posterity, to bee true & faithfull to the said government, & ayding to the maintenance thereof, to our best ability, & from time to time to give speedy notice of any conspiracy,

92

attempt, or evill intension of any which wee shall know or heare of against the same; & wee do pmise to bee willing from time to time to bee instructed in the knowledg & worship of God. In witnes whereof wee have hereunto put or hands, 1643-1644.

> "Cutshamache,
> Nashowanon,
> Wossamegon,
> Maskanomett,
> Squa Sachem."

Before this submission was allowed to be accepted by them, the Indians were examined as to their religious belief and moral attitude. This examination was as follows:

"F. To worship ye onely true God, who made heaven & earth, & not to blaspheme him.

Answer: We do desire to revrence ye God of ye English, & to speake well of him, because wee see hee doth better to *ye* English than othr gods do to others.

2. Not to swear falcely.

An: They say they know not wl swering is among ym.

3. Not to do any unnecessary worke on ye Saboth day.

An: It is easy to ym ; they have not to do on any day, & they can well take their ease on yl day.

4 To hono' their parents & all their superiors.

"An: It is their custome to do so, for the inseriors to honor their superiors.

5. To kill no man without just cause & just authority.

An: This is good, & they desire to do so.

6. To comit no unclean lust, or fornication, adultery, incest, rape, sodomy, buggery, or beastiality.

An: Though sometime some of ym do it, yet they count that naught, & do not alow it.

7. Not to steale.

An: They say to you as to ye 6th query.

To suffer their children to learn to reade Gods word, yl they may learn to know God aright, & worship him in his owne way.

They say, as oportunity will serve, & English live among ym, they desire so to do.

That they should not bee idle."

To these statements the Indians consented, acknowledging them to be good. The authorities were satisfied with the result of the examination and accepted their allegiance. The general court ordered the colonial treasurer to give each of the Indians a coat of red cloth—two yards of material in each, and a pot full of wine. The Indians presented the members of the court with twenty-six fathom of wampum.[181]

It must be told that the Indians did not recognize that they were paying for the construction of the colonies with their highly valuable wampum in return for colonial acceptance. The reader must also keep in mind that the Pequots and Narragansetts had used payments of wampum more than any other tribes, as it was mostly made and kept in Southern New England among them. Ironically, the two richest tribes were the most harassed.

Part VI: The Praying Indians

A feeling of uneasiness within the Connecticut River Valley was felt in the mid 1640s. The worry was the result of so many various problems that have been previously addressed. One issue that my father had faced was the decline in his fur enterprise. There was such a great depletion of furs in the area since my father arrived in Wethersfield that it was no longer a profitable trade in 1645. Interaction with the River Indian also diminished greatly, which did not allow my father to be of any value to the Pynchon Springfield fur enterprise as it rapidly outdistanced the other competing posts of Connecticut in Windsor and Wethersfield.

> The Indian wampum soon became a too uncertain quantity except in dealings with the natives themselves. This resulted in the early spread of warehouses. In 1645 each town had two fairs a year in addition to its public market on meetinghouse square. At these there was exchange of all manner of commodities that should be brought in, for cattle or any merchandize whatever. In the earliest days this was the custom in Hartford. Standards were fixed by the court and it was a duty of the town clerk to see that they were kept constant and observed. [Charles Burpee][182]

It so happened in February 1645 that my father had met with a man who had ventured to Martha's Vineyard, an area known as Capawock to the natives. It was discussed between the two as to what was happening on the Island. Once again, in a time of uncertainty for my father, the name Thomas Mayhew came up and as soon as my father heard of Mayhew's involvement in a new venture, he instantly began to consider pursuing his great friend's enterprises.

> His abode was at Watertown, where he had good accommodations of land, and built an excellent profitable mill there, which in those first times brought him in great profit. But it pleased God to frown upon him in his outward estate: so hat he sold what he had in the Massachusetts, to clear himself from debts and engagements; and about the year 1642, transplanted himself to Martha's Vineyard, with his family. [Daniel Gookin][183]

Apparently, the first island settlement produced through Thomas Mayhew was established in 1642 and it took place on the island of Martha's Vineyard. A small band of planters under the leadership of Thomas Mayhew at Great Harbor, Martha's Vineyard, were the first settlers. With word of all this my father immediately made a decision to leave for Great Harbor, and my mother and myself joined him. My father was taken aback when we arrived, because it was not the elder Thomas Mayhew who had been responsible for the settlement in Martha's Vineyard, but his son Thomas Mayhew, Jr., whom he quickly acknowledged to be as distinguished as his father.

The beginnings of Great Harbor, Martha's Vineyard, date back to 1641 through a meeting in Boston by an emissary to the Right Honorable Earl of Stirling, who came in contact with Thomas Mayhew. The emissary, with authority from the Earl of Stirling, was granted to dispose of lands for the colonization of Long Island and parts adjacent, and was encouraged to further his master's interests and to further the colonization of his lands, negotiations were opened with the Puritan merchant Mayhew to accept a grant of one or more of the unsettled islands of Martha's Vineyard, Nantucket, and those adjacent, eastward of Long Island.[184] Thus, in a meeting in Watertown, Thomas Mayhew Sr. and Thomas Mayhew Jr. granted unto five of their neighbors a patent for the establishment of a large town upon the Vineyard with equal power in town government. A town proprietary was divided into shares. At Great Harbor, newcomers were admitted into the proprietary from time to time, either by an increase in the number of shares, or the sale of a share or fraction of a share by an individual proprietor.[185]

My father had made a lot of money in Wethersfield, but he did not feel there was much more to be gained through fur. At this time, new settlement must have brought fresh excitement to my father as he was looking for new means for work. He took my mother with him. He asked me if I wanted to come and at first I wasn't sure. I had a good job at a wood mill in Wethersfield, but I didn't want to do that forever. I felt I had a higher calling and hadn't yet found it. Therefore, in 1645, around the age of twenty, I boarded a small ship with my parents and decided to go with them to Martha's Vineyard in search of myself not knowing what the future held.

When we arrived at Great Harbor in Martha's Vineyard there wasn't much to the settlement, as was the case when we first arrived in Wethersfield. The economy and structure weren't much developed. Roads, paths, and bridges had to be built where nature held precedence. There was a lot of work for my father and me, on the bright side. An agreement for my father was made with the town proprietors that if he improved the land he would receive a share as an individual proprietor.

Felling trees with rough tools, sawing lumber, building homes and a mill and public buildings, laying out roads and paths, removing rocks and stumps from the land, planting crops of corn and vegetables, pasturing horned cattle and sheep, and fishing were tasks that required creativity and hard work. In accordance with the practice in New England the home lots of Great Harbor were grouped together in village style in order to coordinate military protection against possible Indian raids, and to grant the residents the advantages of public life from a compact settlement. At all times, though, we were watched by lurking savages, who remained at a cautious distance and refused, at first, to hold much intercourse with the foreign race.[186]

There was one Indian named Hiacoomes, however, who was the first willing to assist Mayhew in Martha's Vineyard. Hiacoomes was considered to be of the lowest kind of Indian in the Wampanoag Confederacy, who held no important role. The Wampanoags considered Hiacoomes as a useless man, yet when he began wandering around the new settlement at Great Harbor, Mayhew welcomed him.

In contrast to our paranoia of the natives, as time passed in Martha's Vineyard with the assistance of Hiacoomes, it was there that anyone first witnessed the Praying Indians. Contrary to the Pequots' loss of land and rights taken by the settlers, Martha's Vineyard Indian rights were faithfully preserved. On the island, certainly, no effort was made to crowd the Indian out of his possessions. The Indians who lived in Martha's Vineyard were the Pawkunnawkutts. There were nine separate tribes holding membership in this confederation, each governed by its own petty sachem, but all subject to the Great Sachem Massasoit of the Wamponoags, the dominant tribe of the confederation.[187]

Every foot of territory within the bounds of Mayhew's patent, settled by a white man, was purchased from its lawful Indian proprietor. Although Mayhew held an English title that professed acceptance from the crown, he chose to consider that title as granting him merely the exclusive right among Europeans to purchase lands from the aboriginal occupants. He held no control or ownership of any tract of land remaining in Indian ownership. When Mayhew sold land to a settler which he himself hadn't purchased of the natives, he sold merely a right to the settler to perfect the title from the proper Indian sachem.

It was the general consensus of opinion in New England that a patent of land derived from the crown awarded upon the grantee the English title subject to the Indian right of occupancy. It was the right of occupancy which the English purchased from the Indians, as the Indians had no conception of acquiring the title for a fee.

No man in New England was fairer to the Indians than Mayhew. He established churches, courts, and civil governments among them. It was the total opposite of the hostility felt in Wethersfield, where men felt justified in land purchases for beads and other trinkets, while the Indians thought they were just signing over the right for the settlers to share the use of the land. I can't lay too much blame on the white man for giving the Indian what he wanted. Beads were desired by the Indians as articles of ornament. Also, axes, firearms, and similar items of hardware were wanted just as the white man needed them.

Land titles were never understood by the Indians. They didn't understand that one man could become entitled to an estate so as to prevent others from using it. Land to the Indian was as free as the water or the air. Nobody could have the private right to it. So, when the European came and obtained deeds from the sachems, it was merely the admission of the new settlers to share the land with the Indians on equal terms. It wasn't that the Indian had ceased to have the right to enjoy the land but that another had become his co-occupant.

I think, aside from a new beginning, the main reason my father decided to move his family to Martha's Vineyard was because of how he remembered Thomas Mayhew Sr. in Watertown and Medford for his ability to succeed in whatever enterprise he took up and also in his fairness. He didn't realize, though, the son of Mayhew with the same name, born about the year 1620-21, was the Mayhew who had first settled Martha's Vineyard and his father later followed. It didn't bother my father of any sort, because he greatly trusted the Mayhew name and the son was of the same nature as the father. Shortly after we arrived in the early spring of 1645, however, Thomas Mayhew Sr. arrived from Watertown thereafter. It was a pleasant surprise for my father and Mayhew Sr. to start over at another location again.

Surprisingly, Thomas Mayhew Jr. was not much older than I was. I would come to find out that he practiced endless labor as a missionary among the native people, whom he could also communicate with in their language. I became envious when I saw him talking with the Indians in their dialect, especially because my father would never let me interact with the Indians in Wethersfield. My father solely dealt with them on his fur expeditions.

Mayhew Jr. told me the task of the native language was tedious and laborious. Few English teachers existed among the Indians, for most of the educated English young men did not endeavor to learn the Indian language. All in all, I only learned a handful of words after living on the island for more than ten years. It was a disheartening work that had to be mastered at the outset, before much else could be done. Few of the English were able to speak it. The speech was a language which greatly used the compounding of words. The Indian language, as well, offered no books.

Worst of all there was no aid by which the language could be learned, no grammar, no written specimens from which word sounds could be studied, for the language was an unwritten one. The only procedure open to one who sought to learn it was to strain one's ears in an effort to catch its sense in fragmentary bits from Indian companions, who knew little or no English. The only way I could join the missionary work was to have an interpreter along with my tours of villages.[188]

Unfortunately though, I didn't have enough time to work one on one with a friendly Indian. It took me about a year alone of clearing to have land to build a home for our family. My family stayed on the island the first year and in someone else's dwelling. My father and I also spent the first year clearing land for planters, and helping with roads in Great Harbor. This is the time when I realized Mayhew Jr. was not only developing an untouched Island for his own benefit, but more so for the improvement of the Indian. This is when I realized I chose the right destination.

Thomas Mayhew, Jr. was sympathetic to the Indian. Every action was for improving the Indian's material and spiritual life. I admired everything about him. In my opinion, the great achievement of his life was not the great accomplishment of settlement upon the island. In forming the Vineyard he was very successful, but his peaceful development of the Indian toward civilized conduct was his greatest accomplishment. His devotion toward civilizing and Christianizing the Indian inhabitants made him known to the Indian as a father, counselor, and sachem.[189]

There was no necessity for the missionary work at Martha's Vineyard to begin through force or fear. It was formed through the divinity of Thomas Mayhew whose spirit traveled through the heart and mind. By exhibiting this righteous living and teaching, he shared with the Indians the Christian God and a knowledge of civilized living. He taught them many forms of the religion: love, salvation and everlasting life. Through years under Mayhew's direction many Indians would pray to God. Their church would be the open field. The stage for Mayhew's sermon would simply be a nearby stone. Indian Heaven was the heaven also shared by all righteous men.

The successes of Thomas Mayhew Jr., as a missionary to the Indians first developed through his first convert, Hiacoomes. This Indian held an interest in the Christian faith and desired to learn to read. At first, Hiacoomes felt the ridicule of his fellow-tribesmen, who mocked Hiacoomes as he read while walking through the wilderness. Laughter arose toward the new religion that only worshipped one God, while those first in opposition to Hiacoomes worshipped thirty-seven principal gods.

Hiacoomes would continue to gain knowledge on the faith through the lessons taught to him on Sunday in the minister's house at Great Harbor, which I attended. The Indians slowly began to admire that Hiacoomes, who was considered of little importance among them, was now gathering information unaware to all.

The decision by other Indians to consider following Mayhew's efforts with Hiacoomes began when masses of the Indians within Martha's Vineyard caught the plague, probably beginning in the year following Mayhew's arrival in 1642. Mayhew's party was most likely the carriers of the germs and missionary Mayhew witnessed the strange disease spread amongst them. To cure the plague, the Indians would run up and down till they could no longer, they made their faces as black as night, gathered every weapon, spoke powerful words, but none of this worked and they were punished by the ailment. The Indians blamed all their sickness and death on breaking away from tradition. It was only Hiacoomes who denied the Indian certainty that Christianity was the cause of all the illness.

In 1646, the continually inflicting sickness swept over Martha's Vineyard, but by this time it became obvious to other Indians that Hiacoomes, who had followed the missionary, didn't suffer the plague. They mocked him as an imitation Englishman at first, but he was somehow still able to escape the severe wrath of the plague, while the traditional Indians who depended on mystical powwows were stricken. A small number of leading Indians of the island, who had once excluded Hiacoomes when he was of their belief, slowly began to follow him as a Christian teacher.

Hiacoomes told the Indians that he didn't fear the thirty-seven Indian gods. He explained that he was preserved through the great illness because of his fear of the great God only. Hiacoomes would come to share to them many of the sins that the Indian commits, such as having many gods and going to the powwows. The Indians would become aware through Hiacoomes that they were sinners.

Soon after Hiacoomes avoided the widespread illness, Mr. Mayhew was invited to give a public meeting, to make known to the other Indians the word of God. Mayhew did understand though that most of the Indians were held back because of the powwows witchcraft. It was also believed by the natives that the introduction of Christianity lessened the strength of the powwows and sachems.

Powwows are what the Indian priest and medicine men were called. Their great concern was that they would lose all their power if their tribe would convert. These powwows influenced all the stages of life, religion, peace, war, and health. The powwows were the most dominating position within the Indian's life. They upheld a strange and powerful influence over their superstitious fellow tribes-men. Among exorcism and charms, they were also recognized with the ability to relinquish many problems. One is reported to have made water burn, rocks move, and trees dance.

The powwows demonstrated their gift by physical harm, mental pain, torture, or even distraction of mind. Their greatest influence was psychological. The superstitious Indian lived in such great fear of the powwow's power that once told by a powwow he was cursed the most terrible mental pains and bodily symptoms would occur.[190]

On the side of conversion, the humbled Indian would learn from the white man some of the self-governing laws of man. In Martha's Vineyard the Indian no longer wanted to live in a subject state to a single dominating ruler. The Indian was willing to pay tribute to Mayhew, and was encouraged to do so by Mayhew, but he insisted that the tribute or tax should be put into reasonable ventures.

Mayhew Jr.'s selfless labor continued to win the attention of an ever-increasing amount of the islands Indians. He did not mind spending so much of his time on the uncivilized. He persisted through wet and cold and lodged in their houses. He expected no rewards. There were many obstacles that first obstructed the progress of the mission, but there would be three things that brought most of the Indians toward conversion. They wanted to know what wealth they would obtain by becoming Christians; if the sachems would approve of it; and what the powwows would do. Of these, the greatest concern came from the power of the powwows, who cursed enemies and unbelievers.

Christian meetings would continue with the Indians and in the year 1648 a great convention was held. At this meeting there was both Christian Indians and those who were in doubt. At this conference the dangerous power of the powwows was debated, many felt their power could kill. Others inquired as to who doesn't fear them?

Some replied there isn't a man that doesn't.

It was only Hiacoomes who rose to his feet, faced the large room, and challenged the powwows, "though the powwows might hurt those that feared them, yet I believed and trusted in the Great God of Heaven and Earth, and therefore all the Powwows could do me no harm, and I feared them not."[191]

The crowd then awaited the wrath of the thirty-seven Indian gods to punish Hiacoomes. Minutes passed, but nothing happened. Thus the Indians began to question everything they believed. The power of the powwows weakened and many Indians stepped forward to profess belief in the white man's God. They asked Hiacoomes to explain what his great God wished of them. Hiacoomes would then share around forty-five to fifty sins committed by the Indians. Committing so many amazed and touched their consciences and by the end of the meeting twenty-two unchristianized Indians became converts.

When Hiacoomes' disrespect of the powwows reached those not in attendance of the conference, the entire island powwow population became enraged. They then threatened the destruction of Hiacoomes. One powwow interrupted a meeting one Sunday where Hiacoomes was preaching and challenged the converts.

The powwow called three of them by name and the angered powwow told them they were deceived, for the powwows could kill any Christian Indian if they set the effort forth. Hiacoomes responded that he could stand in the center of all the powwows on the island safe and without fear and they could do him no harm.

For a significant amount of time Hiacoomes was the sole object of the curses of the powwows. They used every trick in their effort to ruin him, but all to no avail. Hiacoomes was immune to the psychological warfare of the heathen priests. One powwow would later confess of using one of his own gods in the form of a snake to kill Hiacoomes. His efforts proved worthless and in time chose to worship the Englishman's God with Hiacoomes.

As a result of this movement, Rev. Mayhew was quick to enhance the mission with the advantages gained by the downfall of the powwows. He increased his services, sparing neither health nor fatigue as he traveled many times about the island to preach at various Indian locations. He allowed me to come along whenever I pleased. In smoky wigwams at night, by the flickering light of a tent fire, he would relate to a crowd of primitive children the ancient stories of the Bible, and the Indians listened in wonder. Christian meetings went on to the joy of some Indians, and the envy of the rest.[192]

The efforts of Thomas Mayhew, Jr., on the Vineyard and John Eliot, a fellow missionary on the mainland of Massachusetts, began to interest persons of wealth in England. These men would ultimately foster money for the propagation of the gospel among the Indians in the New World. Interest in England had been inspired by letters written November, 18, 1647 by Mayhew describing the missionary work. Something moved the "hearts of some godly Christians in England to advance a considerable sum for encouraging the propagating and preaching of the gospel to the Indians within New England"[193].

At first donations were from individual sources, but as reports brought positive news, it was decided to unite their charities and thus the Long Parliament, July 27, 1649, passed an act establishing a corporation for the propagation of the gospel in New England, consisting of a president, treasurer, and fourteen assistants, called "the President and Society for the Propagation of the Gospel in New England;" later to be known as the New England Company. Oliver Cromwell led a general fund amounting to thousands of pounds that was gathered throughout England and Wales for this corporation, and then invested in real estate.

The corporation was the only Protestant missionary society in the world. The New England Commissioners of the United Colonies, who were the local agents in the management of the corporation's affairs and distribution of funds also supervised it.

Thomas Mayhew, Jr., performed his missionary labors with no financial compensation up to that point. Co-proprietary of sixteen islands, and son of an English governor, he could easily have bought and sold tracts of land. Instead he chose to help the uncivilized and live a modest life.

His modesty prevented mentioning his own circumstances, in which he established the first permanent English mission to the Indians of New England, and during the early years of his missionary efforts he had been overlooked by the English merchants, who had been so generous with money upon the Indians along the mainland coast. I also believe there may have been ulterior motives, such as real estate of new regions for the planters involved with the Society for the Propagation of the Gospel in New England. Mayhew and his father were the proprietor's of Martha's Vineyard just an island which may be why much less attention was on them rather than John Eliot on the mainland, wherein laid the abundance of western Massachusetts Nipmuck land which was unclaimed.

The Indians on Martha's Vineyard, however, were in good hands. Mayhew, Jr. formed a covenant in the Indian language, which he read and made understandable to the Indians, who consented with it, and promised to follow it faithfully.

The covenant was as follows:

We the distressed Indians of the Vineyard that beyond all memory have been without the True God, without a Teacher, and without law, the very servants of sin and satan, and without peace, for God did justly vex us for our sins; having lately through his mercy heard of the name of the true god, the name of his son Jesus Christ, with the holy ghost the comforter, three persons, but one most glorious god, whose name is Jehovah: We do praise his glorious greatness, and in the sorrow of our hearts, and shame of our faces, we do acknowledge and renounce our great and many sins, that we and our Fathers have lived in, do run unto him for mercy, and pardon for Christ Jesus sake; and we do this day through the blessing of God upon us, and trusting to his gracious help, give up ourselves in this covenant, we, our wives, and children, to serve Jehovah: and we do this day choose Jehovah to be our God himself, and to trust in him alone for salvation, both of soul and body, in this present life, and the everlasting life to come, through his mercy in Christ Jesus our Savior, and redeemer, and by the might of his holy spirit; to whom with the father and son, be all glory everlasting. Amen.[194]

In choosing rulers under these guidelines, the Indians chose those with goodness and those most likely to remove wickedness. This set in motion the Indian church at Martha's Vineyard, which the senior Mayhew was to fully organize with Indian officers and a pastor eighteen years later. There were 282 converts at Martha's Vineyard, not including children. Eight of these were powwows.

The work of the Vineyard mission was growing every year. With John Eliot asking for assistance and the publication of Mayhew's letter of 1647 to the Society for the Propagation of the Gospel the two would finally obtain financial support. Thomas Mayhew Jr., became a salaried missionary of England around 1654. During the years before financial recognition the mission by Mayhew had been supported entirely from the private funds of the Mayhew's.

During a yearly meeting of the commissioners of the United Colonies held in September of 1654 it was voted to allow Thomas Mayhew, Jr., for his labor this year the sum of forty pounds, and for a schoolmaster to the Indians and other employees the sum of ten pounds apiece per annum.

Finally, in 1654 Mayhew told me he could modestly support me if I were to join him as I always mentioned I would if it were able. I was going to start with building the meetinghouse for the Indians that was appropriated by the commissioners.

Circumstances for Mayhew had changed. Instead of depending upon his family's private purse, which was not enough to support the work, Thomas Mayhew, Jr., was now receiving an annual salary from the society. In 1656 the Vineyard mission had been in existence fourteen years, and it was becoming well improved. Mayhew Jr., felt he could now leave for a short trip to England, where the estate of his wife and her brother commanded his attention.

Thomas Mayhew, Jr., in 1656, asked the commissioners for permission to make the trip to England, but they felt that the mission would decline by his leave and they advised him to send someone else. Permission, however, would be given the following year, the trip would also give Mayhew the chance to show the English people a proper understanding of the positive missionary work in New England than he could do in letter. It would allow him to gain instruments for the further advancement of Indian conversion. The mission on the Vineyard created six small villages, containing about a hundred and fifty five families, and about eight hundred souls. Each of these villages held an Indian preacher.[195]

Prior to his departure, Thomas Mayhew, Jr., organized a farewell meeting with his native worshippers. He brought them to a distant location. There a service was performed and he asked all to be dedicated in their practices during his absence. His followers, didn't want to leave him, they followed him during his travel to the east end of the island for his departure by ship. The numbers grew at each meeting place until they reached the Old Mill Path. "Here a great combined service was held, and the simple children of this flock heard their beloved Shepard give a blessing to them and say the last sad farewells to them individually and as a congregation. It was a sad occasion, long held in memory by all of us who participated."[196]

It was the final ceremony the Indians heard from Thomas Mayhew, Jr. The ship would make its final departure from Boston and headed for Old England with Thomas, his brother-in-law, and an Indian convert aboard it. However, word quickly came to the Vineyard that Master Garrett and his ship was missing and no one heard or saw any type of disaster that would have took the ship Mayhew was on. "Weeks passed into months. Hope in time gave way to fear."[197] Thomas Mayhew Jr., was never to be heard of again.

Mayhew's father took full responsibility for the Indian mission while everyone waited praying for Thomas' return that never came. Thomas Mayhew Sr., was an amazing man as his son, yet, he was much older and my father's friend. Thomas Jr. was my age and we became great friends. I greatly admired all his sacrifice toward the natives and I didn't have the bond with the Indians as Thomas. I felt alone on the island with his loss.

My parents saw my pain and told me I should follow Mayhew's career and become a Reverend. I thought about it long and hard and after overhearing that the missionary effort was expanding in Massachusetts, I decided to leave the Great Harbor immediately. I decided to board a boat traveling up the Connecticut River passing my old home of Wethersfield, landing in Springfield, where it was the bark's destination for trade purposes. I wanted to continue what Mayhew started at Martha's Vineyard and attempt it in Western Massachusetts if it was possible. I heard so many stories of Springfield when I lived in Wethersfield and it was one of the most important of the pioneering settlements along the Connecticut River, as Springfields busy mills and bulging barns were a result of the valley soil.[198] Springfield was above the navigable waters of the Connecticut River, with hundreds of inhabitants, its location at the junction of the Valley Trail and the Bay Path gave it importance in the valley second only to Hartford.[199]

I didn't know exactly where to go in 1657 but I needed a change. I didn't want to live on an island for the rest of my life and I thought Springfield was close to Connecticut and also it was along the great river. I also heard the town had been settled for about twenty years. It seemed like a fit.

At this point in time, Springfield established itself as the commercial, political and social hub. As early as the late 1630s, agricultural produce, meat products and furs from Springfield were being shipped out from William Pynchon's Windsor, Connecticut warehouse to Boston. By the 1650's, Springfield had its own active trade contacts with Hartford and Boston. In addition, Springfield functioned as the primary distribution point for goods moving into or out of the mid and upper portions of the Connecticut River Valley. [The Massachusetts Historic Commission][200]

I figured in 1657 that when I arrived in the town of Springfield I would find my way toward missionaries similar to Mayhew. However, as I have realized nothing goes according to plan; and I would soon discover the gospel made little headway among the Mohegans and their northern neighbors in the Connecticut River Valley.[201]

When I first arrived in Springfield off the bark at the small waterfront shipping district located west of the Main Street my first thought was how developed Springfield was compared to any other place I had lived. My first stop was in the meeting-house which was located in the small civic district, an area which also consisted of a county courthouse and jail, all located on Main Street.

I met the town selectman Thomas Cooper there and I told him I needed some work and a place to stay. He told me a gentleman named John Pynchon set out on a pork-raising speculation and I was more than welcome to join him. I had no problem with that and I chose to experiment with swine as it was the first opportunity for work presented to me. It wasn't a job I would continue after the one attempt, however, it allowed me to form a bond with the very prominent, John Pynchon, who recognized my name because of his father's previous fur dealings with my father.

Working side by side with John Pynchon I learned all about his father, William, who had created a much greater fur enterprise further upstream than my father had in Wethersfield.

> After the late 1650s, however, Pynchon's operation underwent a relatively steady decline. (...) Particularly damaging to the fur trade was the abandonment and destruction of the primary Squakheag and Pocumtuck villages between 1663 and 1665. The region's fur traders thus lost two of their three most important sources of furs. This loss, combined with the declining beaver population and decreased market value for beaver pelts, signaled the demise of the fur trade in the middle Connecticut Valley by the early 1670s. [The Massachusetts Historic Commission][202]

John Pynchon was a good man and did a lot of trade with the Indians, and was as good a man to them as Mayhew, Jr. He educated me on the tribes along the river. He told me tribes existed in small communities along the banks of the Connecticut. He told me Uncas and his Mohegan tribe were also very active in the area and apparently the Puritan officials weren't happy with the reports of his activity. From his outpost at Springfield, John Pynchon told John Winthrop Jr. that peace couldn't occur as long as Uncas couldn't control himself. Uncas wouldn't permit the Podunk Indians to return to their dwellings and live in peace and safety, without molestation from him or his, unless they paid him tribute. In the spring of 1657, Tontonimo the Podunk sachem appealed for help, calling upon the Pocumtucks and Narragansetts to protect him from the Mohegan sachem. The Podunk sachem also called upon the Connecticut English, and may have offered at this time to cede a portion of his lands around Hartford to the River Colony in exchange for their services. As I stayed in Springfield, I heard more and more about the River Indians from Pynchon and others from Springfield.

Pynchon became a major figure in the Connecticut River Valley and was a man of tremendous importance in the village of Springfield, but also in the colony of Massachusetts, where he served as a magistrate. He held strong ties with local English and nearby Indians. It was required in English colonies for oaths of allegiance by freemen and residents and similar oaths were sought from Indians. However, Pynchon did not serve as a missionary.

John Pynchon called the Agawam, Pocumtuck, Pojassic, Wissantinnewag, and Nalwottog Indian tribes "Our Indians", meaning they were aligned with the English. Pynchon's Indians worked to enforce English trade laws with other Indians—especially of guns, liquor, furs, and foodstuffs—to maintain authority in the region.
[203]

Failing to find any missionary efforts to convert Indians in the Springfield area, I decided to enter into the blacksmith's trade because it was a very important trade, as his work was needed by everyone who was tilling the earth and clearing the forest. I began to realize as I lived in Springfield that my intention to become a missionary was not going to become a reality. The missionary effort on the mainland seemed to me to be a bit fabricated compared to what I experienced in Martha's Vineyard. Missionary practices actually seemed to be a component of New England's conquest for land, as Indians unfavorable toward Christian conversion were becoming segregated from the general public. The converts, however, were negatively affected as well by a form of segregation. As their land was submitted, the praying Indians were then placed in colonial-sanctioned praying villages. In theses villages the Indians were to follow English customs, labor, and religion.

The only thing different from when I lived in Wethersfield was that the tribe of hostility was no longer the Pequots, it was now the Narragansetts, and later to join the "hostile" Narragansetts in 1675 were the Nipmucs and Wampanoags.

It was also a much different atmosphere when I arrived in Springfield, Massachusetts than what I had heard of the mainland when I lived in Martha's Vineyard. What had been transpiring on the mainland was far different than the great progress in Martha's Vineyard. I understood that according to the royal patent of Massachusetts, the principal end of this plantation was to win and incite the natives of the country to the knowledge and obedience of the only true god and savior of mankind and the Christian faith. However, the more I experienced the main land it seemed the primary function of the mission was to make an impression in England. The mainland was such a vast wilderness that taming an entire wild species that roamed through it seemed near impossible. Conversion seemed likely for certain Indian tribes disbanded by disease, but there were many proud tribes that still had no intentions of aligning to colonial religion or order.

It was claimed that if England was to tolerate the unchristianized Narragansetts, it would hinder the work of John Eliot, as he had preached to the Massachusetts Indians in their own language. He was a man true to the mission and held a great hope in expanding conversions. The Indians of Rhode Island, though, were different from the Indians participating in Eliot's mission according to the claim of the agent overlooking the Massachusetts Bay and Plymouth interest in England, Edward Winslow. The Bay Colony's newly appointed agent in England, first arrived in London to challenge the Gortonists' title to Shawomet. [204] It was said of Edward Winslow that no one took better care of English children oversees than he. Once in England, Winslow would never return to New England. Through his stay in England because of public affairs, he was also instrumental in making it part of his business to solicit the parliament of lords and commons in producing the incorporation of the "Society for the propagation of the Gospel among the Indians of New England," meeting the needs which the labor of Eliot and Mayhew had required.[205]

The former governor of Plymouth was sent to London and began to share his favor of the mission to offset complaints of Rhode Islanders to Parliament, and he intended to make it appear as if all Indians intended to convert. This would make the true missionary purposes very meaningful and powerful, which would gain more financial support for the mission.

The Massachusetts Bay Colony was disappointed that in England the overseeing Warwick commission had awarded Roger Williams a charter and confirmed Gorton's title. Thus, the commission's decision to side with two heterodox Rhode Islanders convinced the Bay Colony that it needed to restore its reputation in England.

In May 1646, Gorton won his case before the Warwick Commission, as he argued that in September 1643 the Massachusetts Bay General Court sent an expeditionary force to Shawomet to arrest Gorton and his disciples, who according to the results of the hearing, resided within the jurisdiction of Massachusetts Bay because of Pomham and Sacononoco's submission. In October, the Gortonists were tried and convicted for blasphemy and contempt for civil authority, and were sentenced to perform manual labor, in leg irons, in various towns around Boston. Some six months later, the court, convinced that the Gortonists were seducing others to their views, changed the sentence to banishment from the colony, including Shawomet, on pain of death. The Gortonists then returned to Shawomet to test the Bay Colony. After receiving a threatening letter from Winthrop, they moved to Aquidneck Island, where they planned their next course of action. Thus, in June 1644, Gorton and two associates traveled overland to New Amsterdam and boarded a ship for England, where they hoped to secure clear title to Shawomet.

The situation in Rhode Island played such an important role in the birth of John Eliot's mission, and it is why I make such an emphasis on this great event. The Bay Colony's expansionist designs for the Narragansett Country satisfied the submission of Pomham and Sacononoco, which set a precedent soon followed by powerful sachems within the Massachusetts colony's charted bounds. A similar course led Williams and Gorton to travel to London to seek parliamentary protection against Massachusetts Bay.

Several months after Gorton won the Warwick Commission, one of Gorton's associates sailed back to Boston with a warrant from the commission that authorized him to proceed unmolested to Shawomet. Gorton chose to remain in London in the event that Massachusetts Bay renewed its quarrel with him.

The men who were guiding the affairs of Massachusetts recognized that the orders from a higher power were necessary to continue growth in New England, and Winslow whom they could trust would not neglect Puritan interests. Those guiding Massachusetts acknowledged that the authorities of the Bay Colony received money collected by their agents from English churches from which they had already borrowed money. Yet the agents would eventually not return to the churches from which they borrowed. Answers were sought toward the continuous gossip that argued the money given for New England had never been accounted for. It thus became a public service in England to alleviate the impending financial crisis in Massachusetts. Thus an agent was chosen in England to see what could be done to get help for the New England colonists.

In 1649 Parliament selected an agent whom they could trust not to neglect their interests following the execution of the King, which were weeks filled with nervous tension. Winslow was to "Act for the promoting and propagating the Gospel of Jesus Christ in New England."

The organization was completed by providing "That the Commissioners of the United Colonies of New England in New England for the time being, by themselves or such as they shall appoint, shall have hereby

107

Power and Authority to receive and dispose of the moneys brought in and paid to the said Treasurer for the time being, or any other moneys, goods and commodities, acquired and delivered by the care of the said Corporation at any time; ... which said Commissioners are hereby ordered and appointed to dispose of the said moneys in such manner as shall best and principally conduce to the preaching and propagating of the Gospel of Jesus Christ amongst the Natives; and also for maintaining of Schools and Nurseries of Learning, for the better education of the children of the Natives.

The Corporation within mentioned, desire all men to take notice, That all such whom God shall stir up to contribute to help forward this great worke, may repaire to Coopers Hall in London, where the said Corporation sitt, and there if they please at any time may have the sight of their bookes, how the Moneys collected and received for the use above-said, are from time to time disposed and improved, according to the true intent and meaning of the said Act. [Publications of the Prince Society, 1920][206]

However, some were to say the work of the Company was but a plain cheat and that there was no such thing as Gospel Conversion amongst the Indians presently.[207]

In England, Edward Winslow sadly disguised all persons and places, regarding the mission in New England. In particular, he disguised the labors of Thomas Mayhew, Jr., as if they were done by Eliot. Winslow exploited Mayhew's work to benefit Eliot's mission. On one occasion, Eliot even enhanced his own reputation at Mayhew, Jr.'s expense. In November 1648, the Apostle told Edward Winslow in a letter published, "Our Cutshamekin (the Massachusetts sachem) has some subjects on Martha's Vineyard, and they hearing of his praying to God, some of them do the like there, with some other ingenious Indians, and I have entreated Mr. Mayhew, who preaches to the English there, to teach them; and he does take pains with their language, and teaches them not without success." This letter formed a false idea that Eliot had formed the Vineyard mission, which had truly began three years before his own.[208]

Winslow also left out the fact that wampum tribute extracted by Massachusetts from various Indian tribes would have financed a considerable portion of the missionary effort. Winslow, however, represented the colony as too poor, and he made it appear that the Bay struggled to be able to support Eliot's work without English help. He also left out the statement by Eliot himself calling the Indians the dregs and ruins of mankind.[209]

Eliot may not have been influential in sharing with the majority of Indians he dealt with a proper Christian life for many reasons. Eliot and the local men of importance held a value for Indian converts as a tool for expansion. Since Eliot was the voice of divinity to his converts, whatever judgment he held was correct in their eyes. He sent leading converts as messengers to the Nipmucs and other non-converted tribes and the Christian Indians were used as instruments repeatedly. They were supplied with powder and shot for their defense in times of danger in the remote parts of the country where Eliot was trying to alter the souls of the morally dark. [210] Eliot wrote in his narrative, "I find a blessing, when our Church of Natick doth send forth fit Persons unto some remoter places, to teach them the fear of the Lord."[211]

It is hard to understand the mission Indians of the mainland, because different bands stood for different sides and some changed their stance. It also is just as hard to understand what intentions the settlers had for the New England Indians overall. The magistrates favored praying villages, yet the township's residence wanted all neighboring Indians banished. Thus Indian conversion seemed to be the validation for conquering Southern New England. Some colonists even accused the Indians of being ungrateful for not getting down on their knees to thank the English for bringing them the Word.

During the beginning of the Massachusetts Bay settlement, survival and then development held the Bay Company officials to lay off plans for the conversion of the natives. Nothing came to be for a decade and a half after settlement until it became a strong possibility for Puritan leaders. It wasn't an easy matter to propagate the Gospel among natives on the mainland for there were many issues as to why it took so long:

To begin, there was no leadership within the New England Puritan Church to direct the missionary program or be held accountable.

Another factor was that there were not enough resources, most importantly money and manpower, as there weren't enough ministers in the new towns.

Also, the difference of dialect was a hindrance toward spreading religion upon the natives. The few Indians who knew the English language weren't always dependable. There was no way for Englishmen to know if messages were translated correctly.

The opposition from the sachems and powwows was also another great problem. They saw that religion would take away many followers and remove their honor and tribute.

Another challenge for converting the aborigines into praying Indians was the process conducted to reach proper Christianity. The Puritan church mandated more than symbolic awareness or consistent attendance at church for conversion. It was necessary for each forthcoming candidate to take part in and fulfill a number of requirements in order to obtain complete church membership. Completion of church membership was an intense and extended program of instruction and study. After completing this conversion process, the candidate was required to show, in front of church elders and leaders, a deep Bible understanding and a complete knowledge of the Puritan creed. The majority of settlers, ironically, didn't even achieve this feat, let alone Indians who didn't know any of the dialect.

Throughout the 1630s and into the 1640s there had been no plan to convert the natives, but what unintentionally brought the conversion for the Indian into reality was the voluntary submission of weaker tribes of Rhode Island, tributaries to the Narragansetts. Thus the submission toward Massachusetts Bay by Sacononoco and Pumhan in 1643, who requested Massachusetts troops be sent against Gorton, brought neighboring tribes to the same end. Even though, there was no mention of conversion between Sacononoco and Pumhan, officials within the Bay colony were quick to identify the importance of this uncommon event and took full advantage of other submissions in the year to follow.

It must be understood that the submissions in 1643 and 1644 still didn't form a converted Indian. It was simply a beginning for government officials and religious leaders to begin to pressure the Massachusetts General Court into mandating their own laws upon the Indians. The Puritans decided that before any effort was made to convert natives, they were first to change the Indians into civilized men. The Indians were expected to change their means of life and develop a civilized conduct. The necessary changes included living in permanent towns, cutting hair, dressing in the manner of the English, and working some type of meaningful employment.[212]

Many magistrates did feel that faith be formed by the word, not the sword. The Indians weren't to be forced to worship the white man's god, but by law they could worship no other. If convicted of worshipping another, they would be fined. If the fine was not paid, they would be sent to prison for a period of time. These restrictions would eventually cause anger in some proud Indians.

For these laws to work they had to be consistently prosecuted, so officials set up a council to maintain order. The Massachusetts authority elected officials such as Gookin to travel from village to village to consider criminal cases and to also educate the Indians on laws, ethics, justice, and equity. It was the sachem's responsibility to enforce fines for smaller crimes. The fees collected were successfully used for the education of the Indian children, building public meeting-houses, or other community tasks.

Many Indians of the Bay area had shone an interest in the knowledge of the white man's god, but were prohibited from Christian instruction by the five ruling sachems of the Massachusetts tribe until those sachems sought submission in 1644. John Eliot felt that if they were gathered at a neutral location, out from under the control of their leaders and the threats of violence, he would be able to influence the majority and convert them.

One of Eliot's first religious services upon the Indians took place on October 28, 1646, when he conducted a service in Indian tongue at Nonantum, what we call Newton, under the leadership of Waban, who wasn't a sachem. Eliot credited Waban with leading the renewed Massachusetts interest in the Puritan faith. Waban actually went against his sachem Cutshamekin's opposition toward the Massachusetts conversion. Waban's people organized their efforts toward a place of worship in the town at Nonantum by means of English order. The town was located near the Watertown mill my father had worked on.

Eliot wanted Waban to bring his friends, in which Waban summoned the people of the village to gather at his wigwam. After they assembled, he introduced the minister and the other members of his company to the gathering. Eliot greeted them as friends and opened the meeting with prayer in English. After the prayer, Eliot began with a reading of the Ten Commandments. Each Commandment was presented first in English and then in Algonquian, followed by a brief explanation. He asked if they understood him and a loud positive group responded.

> His manner of teaching them was, first to begin with prayer, and then
> to preach briefly upon a suitable portion of scripture; afterwards to admit the
> Indians to propound questions;-and divers of them had a faculty to frame
> hard and difficult questions, touching something then spoken, or some other

110

matter in religion, tending to their illumination;-which questions Mr. Eliot, in a grave and Christian manner, did endeavor to resolve and answer to their satisfaction.[213] [Daniel Gookin]

Within a short time of these first attempts many Indians began to meet together to hear Eliot's services. Most Indians attended regularly at Nonantum because of curiosity, not faith. However, with each visit they became more trustful. In Neponset and Nonantum Eliot preached these two lectures for several years with good success, which were locations within four miles near Eliot's Watertown home.

Besides his preaching to them, he framed two catechisms in the Indian tongue, containing the principles of the christian religion; a lesser for children, and a larger for older persons. These also he communicated unto the Indians gradually, a few questions at a time, according unto their capacity to receive them. The questions he propounded one lecture day, were answered the next lecture day. His manner was, after he had begun the meeting with prayer, then first to catechize the children; and they would readily answer well for the generality. Then would he encourage them with some small gift, as an apple, or a small biscuit, which he caused to be bought for that purpose. And by this prudence and winning practice, the children were induced with delight, to get into their memories the principles of the Christian religion. After he had done the children, then would he take the answers of the catechetical questions of the elder persons; and they did generally answer judiciously. When the catechizing was past, he would preach to them upon some portion of scripture, for about three quarters of an hour; and then give liberty to the Indians to propound questions (...) and in the close, finish all with prayer.[214] [Daniel Gookin]

Thanks to Eliot these praying Indians discovered and used Christian principles that thousands of Englishmen do not understand. They also discovered education. Eliot "took great care, that schools should be planted among the praying Indians; and he taught some himself to read, that they might be capable to teach others; and by his procurement, some of the choice Indian youths were put to school with English schoolmasters."[215] However, "if any should sinfully neglect Schooling their Youth, it is a transgression liable to censure under both Orders, Civil and Ecclesiastical, the offence being against both."[216]

In the spring and summer of 1650, Eliot and several Indians began to search for a site for a central settlement. The settlement would have to be remote from the English, but close enough for Eliot to visit regularly and practice the word and other elements of the Christian lifestyle. The possibility of Eliot's vision first truly became real in 1649 when Parliament formed the Propagation of the Gospel in New England foundation.

By October 1650, they had selected Natick, an unimproved area along the Charles River. That same month, the General Court assigned Natick 2,000 acres of land to the north of the river. The first town of praying Indians was thus in Massachusetts known as Natick. The name meant a place of hills. It was located upon the Charles river, eighteen miles south west from Boston. The land was granted to the Indians, through the action of Mr. Eliot, by the general court of

Massachusetts and in the year 1651, a number of the converts united and formed this town. As soon as the Indians had built up their settlement, Mr. Eliot formed a civil government and on the sixth of August, about one hundred of them met together, and chose one ruler of a hundred, two rulers of fifties, and ten rulers of tens. This place has become the greatest name among the Indians, and also where their chief courts are held.[217]

The Nonantum Indians were pleased with the location and Eliot was pleased with their conduct. The Praying Indians were far away enough from the English, ironically, to learn the Puritan way. They conformed to English gender roles: the men tilled the fields and raised the livestock, and the women learned to spin and weave once the men had grown enough hemp for the purpose in the mid-1650s.[218]

The site had everything for a successful community: fertile fields, woodland, large river, and enough vacant land in which to grow without hindering other towns. With the vision of an improved life compared to the life spent in a wandering band, many would-be converts came to Natick. Other villages would also become developed with the success of Natick. Large numbers of Nipmucks would come to hear Eliot preach on a consistent basis once the town was functioning. It was practically a self-sustaining community working for the common good to avoid dependence on outside sources.

The Indian town was increasing in audiences. Indians traveled a long way to hear him. Chiefs invited him to their villages to preach. During the following years, Eliot went into the interior of Massachusetts to visit the Nipmuck tribes and converted many of them. The increase of the great distance traveled by Indians because of interest in conversion made Eliot come up with the solution for more Christian Indian towns where those who wished to convert could go and live.

As the converts increased in numbers, the natural resources within Natick could not support the population. Eliot felt additional towns were necessary, and as long as Indian leaders accepted management and daily maintenance, new towns could have succeeded as Natick had. Thus, the creation of Natick set a precedent for the establishment of other praying towns. In October 1652, the General Court ruled that "if upon good experience, there shall be a competent number of the Indians brought on to civility, so as to be capable of a township, upon request to the General Court, they shall have grant of lands undisposed of for a plantation, as the English have."   The formation of the Praying towns also served to steer clear of any disagreement between Indians and colonists over boundaries, as well as, to separate an area where the Indians were to live.[219]

In 1654, Okammakamesit was another praying town that was established. In May of that year, the General Court asked to award land, free from any challenge of an English interest, for the Nipmuck Indians of Okommakamesit. The Court's grant to the Indians through Mr. Eliot in 1654 was prior to the land grant made to the English on land that would be called Marlborough. The English, however, found to their disappointment that the Indian land granted, was to be in the same location of a portion of their own grant. Yet, the praying town was to be respected by the settlers if they wished to stay in Marlborough. This is a great example of fairness shown by the Massachusetts Council, as their members were humane in their position with the friendly Indians. These Indians were a branch of the Wamesit tribe, and had submitted to the Massachusetts Colony as early as 1643, and had received assurance of its protection of their rights. They were self-supporting, peaceable, and were becoming industrious and thrifty, yet were still not trusted by many of the neighboring English, who resented their grant of six thousand acres.[220]

This surrounding English community known as Marlborough was developed in 1656 and became incorporated as Marlborough around this Indian village called Okommakamesit. Marlborough was a growth off of Sudbury, one of the first frontier townships. The court blindly awarded to Marlborough some land already occupied by the Okommakamesit Indians. The Indians didn't expect the population of the English town to grow so fast, nor did the Indians realize the legal papers they signed would later be used to remove them from their tribal lands.[221]

Another praying town was proposed in 1657 for Punkapaog in the town of Canton, fourteen miles south of Boston, because "our poor Indians are much molested in most places." The name is taken from a spring that arises from red earth. The Indians that settled in Punkapaog were removed from Neponsitt mill and Ahawton was their ruler. The grant Eliot requested was approved by the General Court for six thousand acres. Within those couple years, four additional praying towns were added to the growing list: Wamesit (twenty-five hundred acres); Nashoba (ten thousand acres); Okammakamesit (six thousand acres), and Hassanamesit (ten thousand acres). Hassanamesit was the first praying town in the Nipmuck country.

The Indian praying towns had no sooner expanded when Eliot put future missionary work on hold. His Roxbury parish was rapidly growing with white men and he had to spend more time on church matters. More importantly, members of the Propagation of the Gospel in New England were hesitant to give more funds because Eliot didn't keep accurate records and provide them with accounting of costs and expenses. The purpose was to make certain that existing sources of funding didn't disappear and ensure that further income from donations would continue.

There was a disguised effort to combine the Christian and non-Christian groups among the Indian population records. If a sachem promised himself and his people to pray to God, which he was mandated to do under the treaties of submission signed in 1644, the entire tribe would be considered as praying Indians. Indians subjected under the submitting sachem could now be considered converts toward the gospel. For that reason, the estimates of converts are misleading.

Obviously this manipulation occurred because Eliot and Superintendent of Indian affairs Daniel Gookin knew that with the greater the image of the mission, the greater the continuing support of the missionary program. Their main cause may not have been the Indian's well being as Mayhew's was, as their greatest effort may have been toward making certain that funding did not stop. Most importantly, if they could increase their funding, both at home and in England, the mission would not become jeopardized. So Eliot and Gookin failed to document that a large number of the natives did not want to become Christians, while others held non-Christian feelings. It was imperative to not present the mission in a negative way and interfere with all the invested labor.[222] There was no reason to show negativity, because all of Eliot's work may have been foiled. Without the necessary funds to continue with the expansion of the praying towns, Eliot turned his attention to a full Indian translation of the Holy Bible.

This great work of translating the bible into the Indian language was encouraged by the honorable corporation for propagating the gospel in New England, residing in London. "Out of the revenues belonging to that flock, which then was more considerable than now it is, did pay for the printing thereof."[223]

Following the year 1654, when the people of Hassanamesit received a grant from the Massachusetts General Court for a tract of land four miles square, no new praying towns were settled for more than ten years. Eliot finished printing the Bible in 1663, and throughout this time he used his energy on the education and training of Indian preachers and teachers at Natick. With a number of trainees within the program in the mid 1660s and the accumulation of funds assigned during the Bible project, the corporation for promoting the gospel was again willing to give money. Numerous members of the Massachusetts tribe had become involved, and Eliot now looked west to the Indians of the Nipmuck country for converters.

After the first Indian Church was formed in 1646, and removed to Natick in 1651. The next one organized was at Hassanamesit (Grafton) in 1652. John Eliot wrote in 1654, Hassanamesit had become the central point of civilization and Christianity to the whole Nipmuck country. School was established and the Bible was read and studied in the Indian language. Young men were here educated and sent into the neighboring towns to preach the gospel. A regular government was created, and the forms of law were strictly observed. [The Nipmuc Indians][224]

The praying towns had thus fostered the Indians to a transformation in lifestyle. Aside from adapting to a foreign religion, there were other factors that changed the Indian lifestyle. Most obviously, the deterioration of the population of tribes increased the acquiring of land by the settlers, which did not please many natives. This increase of settlers had its most dramatic effect on the Indians of central Massachusetts, between the Boston area and the Connecticut River. The Indians of this region, mostly considered Nipmucks, had been isolated from the land pressures of the English, because most of the English migrants came to the Boston coastal area between 1630 and 1640. The children in these families did not seek land independently of their parents until the 1660s when they were of age to seek land and they pursued these new bounds in great numbers. Hence, the Nipmucks had to face a sudden invasion that provided them little time to adapt.[225]

There was a change for the Indian from a life of agriculture, hunting, and fishing, to one of expanded agriculture and animal husbandry. New crops such as wheat and other grains were used, and orchards were planted. Food production also increased because of the use of modern tools. The natives raised cattle and swine and they fenced their fields to prevent damage from wild animals.

At the older praying village of Wamesitt John Eliot would visit once a year in the beginning of May, the visit was not only toward the inhabitants of the village but also to take an opportunity to spread the gospel to the visiting strangers, who came in considerable numbers that time of season. They were greatly persuaded by the preaching of Eliot. Settlement was moving toward Western Massachusetts after the successful praying Indian villages of Natick, Punkapaog, and Wamesit. The Indians associated with the Nipmuc tribe throughout western Massachusetts, of whom many were considered peaceful and likely to convert, were now also becoming consolidated into praying villages. There developed seven new praying towns and the Indians of some of these towns began to open up to the gospel.

In July, 1673, Mr. Eliot and Daniel Gookin made a journey to visit some of them, and to encourage their growth toward the ways of God. Then again on September 14th, 1674, the two sent out toward the new praying villages with five or six godly persons, who were to be presented unto the new praying villages for ministers. The visit's "design was to travel further among them, and to confirm their souls in the Christian religion, and to settle teachers in every town, and to establish civil government among them, as in other praying towns."[226]

The party traveled west over the Connecticut Path. Their first destination was Hassanamesit and the teacher of that village was named Solomon. The village was about thirty-eight miles southwest from Boston; and is about two miles eastward of Nipmuck River. The name Hassanamesit meant a place of small stones. The town's population was not above twelve families, or about sixty people altogether.

Eliot and his group left Hassanamesit and journeyed to the town of Manchage, which fell west of the Nipmuck River. In terms of population, Manchage was around the same size as Hassanamesit. When the group arrived, Eliot found most of the inhabitants away. Eliot spoke with those present and informed them that they were assigning a young man, Wabesktamin, as minister for the town. At the time of this visit, there was yet any land granted by the general court for this or any of the new praying villages.

The next stop was Chabanakongkomun. This town was a new plantation; the Indians had gathered there about two years earlier and now numbered about nine families, or about forty-five souls. A man named Joseph is one from the church of Hassanamesit, who spoke English well, and was the founder and teacher of the town. His brother Sampson was the teacher at Wabaquasset, a village in Connecticut. Joseph and Sampson were the sons of Petavit, alias Robin, who was a ruler of Hassanamesit, who died three days before Eliot came. There was much respect held for Petavit. He was an Indian known for God and religion. He blocked the anger and disrespect of wicked Indians in order to praise the Christian religion when it was not popular, as he would stand by religion amongst sagamores who refused it. Petavit was possibly the strongest Indian influence for the progress of Christianity among the Nipmucks.[227]

Another visit for the missionary group was in Northeastern Connecticut at Wabaquasset. Eliot and his group took up quarters in the house of the chief sachem. Wabaquasset was by far the largest of the praying towns in terms of population; it was inhabited by one hundred and fifty souls.[228]

> Upon the 16th day of September, being as Wabquissit, as soon as the people were come together, Mr. Eliot first prayed, and then preached to them in their own language. Then Daniel Gookin "published a warrant or order, that he had prepared, empowering the constable to suppress drunkenness,

Sabbath breaking, especially powwowing and idolatry. And after warning given, to apprehend all delinquents, and bring them before authority, to answer for their misdoings; the smaller faults to bring before Wattasacompanum, ruler of Nipmuc country ; for idolatry and powwowing to bring them before me. [Daniel Gookin][229]

A number of Indian counselors came to the sachem's wigwam and joined in the religious practices. As this ceremony occurred, there sat a man at the end of the long-house, watching everything. The man, at the conclusion, spoke and informed Eliot and his party that he was an agent for Uncas. He said that Uncas had authority over the people of Wabaquasset. He protested that "Unkas is not well pleased, that the English should pass over Mohegan river, to call his Indians to pray to God."[230]

Eliot told the Indian to tell Uncas that Wabaquasset was within the jurisdiction of the colony of Massachusetts and that the government of Massachusetts intended to share the good available to all people within their bounds, most importantly Christianity. In response to Uncas' rule over the people of Wabaquasset, it was not Eliot's purpose to eliminate the Indian sachems' ancient entitlement over the Indians. The design of the English was to share with them the knowledge of Jesus and to eliminate their sins.

The party then traveled to Pachackoog, which was about forty-four miles from Boston in what is now the southwest corner of Worcester. The town consisted of a population of about one hundred persons or twenty families. James Speen of the Natick church had been performing sermons there for about two years. Horowanninit (alias John) and Woonanaskochu (Solomon) were the chief sachems of the village. Eliot's party first repaired to Sagamore John's house. With the arrival of Eliot and the missionaries, the sachems then grouped their people within the village for a religious service, in which Eliot gave the brief sermon. When the service was over, the first Indian court of any type in the area took place September, 28, 1674 and was held for the purpose of selecting civil and religious leaders. The two sachems (John and Solomon) were appointed civil rulers of the town and James Speen was to continue as their minister for another year. Concluding the court appointments, a man named Mattoonus, who was described as a grave and sober Indian, was to be elected as officer for the town. Then Gookin "gave the rulers, teacher, constable, and people, their respective charges, to be diligent and faithful for God, zealous against sin, and careful in sanctifying the Sabbath."[231] Ironically, Mattoonus would lead the first invasion against the English by the Nipmucks during the beginning months of King Phillip's War.[232]

By 1674, there were many developing praying towns. There are two other Indian towns, Weshakim and Quabaug, which were beginning to receive the gospel; making around nine praying villages in the Nimpuck country. However, Weshakim and Quabaaug were not fully settled and were omitted from the magistrate's consideration.

It was understood that most of the unconverted Indians were unhappy with the formation of praying towns, and their anger developed toward both the English and the converts. There came only two choices for the Indian: accept or deny the white man's religion.

For the twenty-five-plus years of the mainland mission not much had changed for the unchristianized Indians. However, in the early 1670s, Eliot and his adversaries let all participating Indians know that the colony would begin to heavily enforce civil and criminal laws of the colonial government and Puritan religion.

Foul behavior wouldn't be tolerated and there was to be strict enforcement of the policies. The Christian converts were to put themselves, lands, and estates under the government and jurisdiction of the Massachusetts, to be governed and protected by them, according to their just laws and orders, so far as they should be made capable of understanding them. Thus, the Praying Indians were expected to uphold the law and carry out minor legal issues which were more angering issues for the non-converts.

"Care was taken by the general court of the Massachusetts, at the motion of Mr. Eliot, to appoint some of the most prudent and pious Indians, in every Indian village that had received the gospel, to be rulers and magistrates among them, to order their affairs both civil and criminal, and of a more ordinary and inferior nature. These rulers were chosen by themselves, but approved by a superior authority." [Daniel Gookin][233]

The land situation became an unfavorable situation, for all Indians, Christian or not. The Court of Massachusetts had bounded, stated, and settled several townships and plantations of land for these praying Indians. The amount of land allotted to the Praying towns was connected with the size of the group. Land for settlement was only allowed to those who chose the Christian faith. As more converted, the court would consider increasing their petition for land. The non-Christian Nipmucks would grow to be not in favor of this and felt excluded.

The Massachusetts Court justified this by claiming rights to the land in the colony of Massachusetts by patent from their King. Second, the English had a grant for most of the land within this jurisdiction, either by purchase or the submission from the Indian sachems in 1644. The colonial government felt the only land the Indians were entitled to was the area granted to them by the court.

The court felt the treaties the tribes had formed with Massachusetts between 1643 and 1644 forfeited the Massachusetts Indian land. Once the Indians had voluntarily submitted, it appears that the colonial government prepared a standardized statement of loyalty, for on separate occasions the statement was worded identically. The Indians agreed "to be governed and protected by Massachusetts, according to their just laws and order, so far as we shall be made capable of understanding them." Unlike the Indians living in Rhode Island, the Indians in Massachusetts seemed to be willing to be instructed in the knowledge and worship of God.[234]

"Whereas one end in planting these parts was to propagate the true religion unto the Indians; and that divers of them are become subject to the English, and have engaged themselves to be willing and ready to understand the law of God: it is therefore ordered, that such necessary and wholesome laws, which are in force, and may be made from time to time, to reduce them to civility of life, shall be once a year, if the times be safe, made known to them, by such fit persons as the general court shall appoint." [Daniel Gookin][235]

The power within the treaties was that they automatically transferred the ancestral rights of tribal lands to the Massachusetts government. Therefore, the only way an Indian could claim property was by a grant from the general court.

Another factor in land rights was the Land Rights Law of 1652 stating that all land within the area of the Massachustts Patent was under the authority of the Massachusetts court, even if the land was granted or not. The Indians thus only held the title to land they worked or lived on. The law reflected the Puritan leaders' interpretation of the Old Testament, which read, "Heaven, even the heavens, are the Lord's: but the earth hath he given to the children of men." This understanding opened the door for Puritan land claims and enabled all Indian rights of ownership in Massachusetts to be observed and governed by the General Court's law. The Puritan theory of vacuum domicilium states free land is classified as open dominion, defined by Govenor John Winthrop as, "all land not actually in the possession of the natives; land which lies in common and hath never been replenished or subdued."

In the settlers eyes, Indian hunting grounds, the most important land to gather meat for the Indian family, was land considered vacant and awaiting occupation by those who would put it to good use. Under this opinion, the majority of Puritan leaders felt the English had a legal right to take possession of all the open or unoccupied lands within their jurisdiction. As the natives made no improvements to the territory, especially hunting grounds, the Puritans were of the opinion that they possessed natural right. Thus, private property was created from common land when labor was put forth on vacant soil or hunting grounds. [236]

The expectation of the Massachusetts government was to have all the Indians live within the sanctioned praying towns, thus, eliminating tribes from using their unoccupied and unimproved lands for future use. Ultimately, this creation would confine the Indians to specific locations and provide the English the authority to civilize and control Indian behavior without the Indians getting in the way of expansion. Massachusetts' Indians, therefore, became a separate body from the same Puritan government that represented them. Indians couldn't comprehend the consequences of signing the treaties. They simply thought they were going to share the land, not become segregated. If they had known it was a complete takeover, I doubt they would have agreed.

The Indians began to associate the religious movement in the colony with the system used by the Puritan leaders to seize all unoccupied or unimproved lands. Therefore, the Indians would have no use of their own ancestral territory. The Indians would eventually have to take up residence in one of the government-sanctioned praying towns or be pushed out of their ancestral lands. The execution of these regulations caused anger in the non-Christian Indians, and it was slowly fostering violent rage toward the Puritan government, which erupted in 1675.[237]

During King Philip's War, the dissenters toward the Puritan mission among the Nipmucks finally released their once-contained rage. They felt their rights to customary lands had been violated.[238] The anger of losing homeland not only angered the non-converted Nipmucks, but it also would begin to anger the converts. A number of Christian Indians, as well as missionary Indian members, joined the colonial enemy as they believed what was happening was wrong. The anti-Puritan movement was beginning to climax, and many of the Nipmucks eventually joined with King Phillip. [239]

Massasoit's son, Phillip or Metacomet, told some Rhode Islanders that he had a "great fear to have any of their Indians should be called or forced to be Christian Indians."

It should have become apparent to the reader that the intentions of the Massachusetts Bay Company to Christianize the Heathens always stood second to obtaining freedom to practice their own form of Christianity.[240]

Praying Villages:
Natick: 145
Punkapaog: 60
Hassanamesitt: 60
Okommakamesit: 50
Wamesit: 75
Nashobah: 50
Magunkaquog: 55
Manchage: 60
Chabanakongkomun: 45
Maanexit: 100
Quantisset: 100
Wabquissit: 150
Pachackoog: 100
Wacuntug: 50
Total population: 1,100[241]

THE
PRESENT STATE

OF

New - England,

With Respect to the

INDIAN WAR:

Wherein is an Account of the true Reason thereof,
(as far as can be Judged by Men.)

Together with most of the Remarkable Passages that have happened from the 20th of *June*, till the 10th of *November*, 1675.

Faithfully Composed by a Merchant of *Boston*, and Communicated
to his Friend in *LONDON*.

Licensed *Decemb.* 13. 1675. *Roger L'Estrange.*

LONDON.
Printed for *Dorman Newman*, at the Kings-Arms in the *Poultry*, and at the
Ship and Anchor at the *Bridg*-foot on *Southwark* side. 1675.

London, for Dorman Newman, 1675

Part V: The Final Puritan Conquest of New England

All the events I have previously mentioned culminated into the final war between the New England Indians and White men. I have pieced together many of these important events through various accounts. This final war which greatly shaped the New England settlements and shattered the Southern New England Indian was the conflict known as King Phillip's War of 1675. I feel this war permanently removed the existence of Indian tradition throughout Southern New England.

In this Indian War, the praying Indians participated on both sides. Some praying Indians during the outbreak of war were already against the colony as hostile Indians, while others that prayed fought on behalf of the colonists, joining colonial companies to help achieve victory. Some Praying Indians would change sides and become hostile to the colonies throughout the war.

The praying Indians that fought for the colonies throughout were the most reliable soldiers. The true standing of any particular Indian tribe's alliance at the time of the Indian War of 1675 is very difficult to identify, as many smaller Indian bands shifted sides. The Pakanahats or Pokanokets, the home tribe of which Phillip was sachem, as well as the Narragansetts and Nipmucs, were three tribes that became known as the colonial enemy. Though, the Narragansetts did not stir up any violence at the beginning of the war and were considered neutral until their tribe was invaded similar to the Pequot. The Pokanoket [Wampanoag Confederacy] and

Narragansett tribes held an opposition to the offers of the Gospel and their chief Sachems strongly rejected and opposed it.[242]

The war had begun within the Plymouth colony and some would argue the war also ended there. Two powerful tribes, as viewed by the colonists, lived within the bounds of Plymouth or near its border. The two great chiefs, Philip of the Wampanoags and Canonchet of the Narragansetts, were the head sachems of these powerful tribes.[243]

The Nipmucs, though, were from within the mainland of Massachusetts, yet they may have committed the most frequent hostile acts during the first months of war. Certain Nipmuc Indians living in praying towns joined into hostility against the English and also sent messages to the Christian Indians that the English planned to destroy them all, or send them out of the country as slaves.[244]

At the time of Philip's war, there were branches of the Nipmucs throughout the interior and each branch had their specific sachem. The Quabaug Indians, for instance, lived in the territory about the town of Brookfield, and the Nashaways held their chief village at Lancaster. [245] Of the Nipmuc tribes, one member, especially, in the beginning of the war, had a potent influence for the rebellion against the colonies. Mattoonus, who lived in the praying village of Pachackoog, had been made an officer for the town by Superintendent of Indian Affairs Daniel Gookin. Mattonus, however, would revolt and lead the first invasion against the English by the Nipmucks on the town of Mendon, Massachusetts, in July 1675.[246]

There are a number of possibilities that would explain Matoonas's assault on Mendon. One reason for his revolt may be that he had to revenge the death of his son at the hands of the English. Another option is that Philip's agents may have recruited him to get the Nipmucks to join in a rebellion against the colony as Matoonas' held such anger toward the English, and Philip may have felt Matoonas would bring other Nipmuck leaders to the side of the Wampanoags. Possibly, Matoonas' sachems may have told him to attack, because they didn't want to change.[247] Whatever the case, as Daniel Gookin put it, "The Indians here do not much rejoice under the English men's shadow; who do so overtop them in their number of people, stocks of cattle, &c. that the Indians do not greatly flourish, or delight in their station at present."

The second Puritan conquest has been named King Phillip's War or even the Narragansett War by some colonists; however, the war was a collection of various conflicts involving different New England tribes. One overall fact for the Southern New England Indian was that their strength had continued unraveling in the 1670s and the Indian population of Southern New England was around 20,000, about half of what the number of English settlers in the area was; about 4,000 were Narragansetts, about 3,000 were Nipmucks, over 1,000 were Wampanoags, while the rest were Mohegans, Pequots, Pocumtucks, Massachusets, River Tribes, and other bands.[248] In terms of man power at hand for the United Colonies commissioners, it was decided while in session all summer that a thousand men respond in reaction to the first sign of an outbreak of war—by quotas, Massachusetts, 527; Connecticut, 315; Plymouth, 158. However, three times that number was to be needed."[249]

Speculation made it seem as Philip was calling all the shots for the Indians, wherein fact, it may have been a generational gap that led some younger Indians to become hostile and some older Indians to seek peace. The Wampanoag Confederacy's sachem Philip was the great Massasoit's son, and Philip would become known as the great igniter of this grave New England war, yet he may simply have lost control of the younger Indians. Massasoit would be the first to open the gates that would welcome in swarms of Englishmen to settle in the New England Indians land. Yet, now about fifteen years after his death, his son was being accused of putting efforts forth to destroy the colonial settlements through a united Indian force of all the surrounding tribes. There were, also, other chiefs of other tribes who were important actors in the war.

Another tribe that must receive attention for their role in the war aside from Phillip's Wampanoags and the Nipmucks are the Narragansetts. Miantonomo's son Canonchet held the sachemship at the time of war. The relations on behalf of the colonies with the Narragansetts before the war was of arrogance, intolerance, and selfishness as the agreement between the King and the Narragansetts of 1644 held no binding amongst the surrounding colonies. At the beginning of King Philip's War, Canonchet, an able and brave chief, received constant hatred and falsehood from the now elder Uncas. Yet, the Narragansett sachem had still been able to maintain neutrality with the English, always keeping in mind what happened to his father. In 1675 he was by far the most powerful chief in New England, his fighting force being estimated at over a thousand.[250] Because of their strength, it was of most importance for the United Colonies to form a peace treaty with the Narragansetts immediately following the outbreak of war in 1675. The Wampanoags, led by Philip, were another issue. Chandler Whipple wrote:

> It was in 1647 when Canonicus died, a very old man. At some point thereafter Canonchet, son of Miantinomo, assumed his position as sachem of the Narraganset. In 1655 Edward Winslow of the Plymouth Colony, old and true friend to Massasoit, died. Massasoit realized that he was losing all his old friends among the English. He ordered his two eldest sons, Mooanam or Wamsutta and Metacomet or Pometacom, to go to Plymouth and adopt English names. It would appear that he thought of this as a means of protection, of making it easier for them to take their places in the English scheme of things. At any rate, the magistrates were much impressed with the noble manner of these two handsome young men. They gave them names of Greek History: Alexander, for the elder, Philip for the younger. Then in 1661, Massasoit abdicated his sachemship, left his base at Mount Hope and moved in with his old friends and allies, the Nipmucs. This somewhat scattered tribe ranged from areas around Worcester as far down as northeastern Connecticut. This put Massasoit in territory very close to that claimed by Uncas, as the Mohegan sachem now concentrated on land further beyond the almost altogether conquered river tribes. The power and territorial claims of Uncas continued to expand as his influence with the colonists had. He would attack the Nipmucs.
>
> Massasoit tried to mediate with the English, hoping they would force Uncas to make restitution for the damage he had caused. This attempt

124

resulted in partial failure. It appears that Uncas received no punishment. Uncas was a newer and more valuable friend than the old Wampanoag Sachem Massasoit. Massasoit would soon die thereafter. [Chandler Whipple][251]

Apparently before the war broke out in 1675, Phillip was planning a coordinated attack with other Indian nations for some time. The River Indians attacking the settlements along the Connecticut River, the Nipmucks attacking the interior towns, and the Narragansetts and Wampanoags attacking from Boston to Providence, all simultaneously, would have driven out most of the colonists from New England.[252] However, no united Indian force attack took place and it was actually the death of a Praying Indian named John Sassamon and the trial of his murderers that began the Indian war.

To understand the war I must take the reader to previous years:

Massasoit died around 1661 at the age of eighty-one. He was succeeded by his son Wamsutta (Alexander). The known children of Massasoit were Wamsutta, Pometacom or Metacomet or Phillip, Sunconehew, Amie, and possibly another daughter. Wamsutta was first known as Mooanam.[253]

Alexander was suspected of selling land to outsiders and there were rumors that he was trying to stir up trouble and to organize a general uprising. It was a noticeable fact indeed that Wamsutta had been selling lands for several years prior to the date of his father's death. Some of the English settlers at Boston, having visited the Narragansetts, wrote to Mr. Prince, then governor of Plymouth Colony, informing him that Wamsutta had sought the Narragansett tribe to engage with him in a war against the English. Captain Thomas Willet was sent as messenger to Wamsutta, living in Mount Hope. Captain Willet informed the chief of the ill story concerning him, at which Wamsutta seemed to take no offence, but remarked that the Narragansetts were the enemies of himself and his people, and that this was an effort of theirs to put an abuse upon him, and involve him in difficulty with the English.[254]

He was ordered to Plymouth immediately to acknowledge his loyalty. On July 7, 1662 a letter written to Josiah Winslow, Major Commandant of Plymouth Colony Militia, describes the colonial position upon Massasoit's eldest son:

> Insomuch as Alexander, King of the Wampanoags, did not appear before the duly convened Court of Plymouth on June 1 as he had promised and instead, was seen in the company of the Narragansetts on that date, I hereby call upon you to muster the Marshfield militia and march south to Pokanoket territory where you are to locate the King. Bring him straight away to Duxbury where he shall answer the two charges brought against him before the Plymouth Court, namely, that he is negotiating with the Narragansett nation to engage with him in war against Plymouth Colony and that he is selling land directly to colonists contrary to the agreement between Plymouth Colony and the Wampanoags. If he should resist, you shall force him to come in whatever way serves you best.[255]

Accordingly upon the directions, Wamsutta was forced by gun point at a hunting station to come to discuss his actions and if he refused he was a dead man. Unfortunately, Wamsutta became sick on the way to Plymouth. He got so sick that Winslow let him go before they arrived in Plymouth. Half way before he got home, Wamsutta died.

With the death of Wamsutta, his brother became sachem of the Wampanoag Confederacy. We have become to know him as Phillip, while his Indian name is Metacom. Also known as Pometacom, or King Philip, he seems at first to have been desirous of continuing the friendly relations with the whites, after his brother's death, which his father first began. The friendly relations between white man and Indian were held for forty years within his father's reign after the signing of the treaty with Governor Carver. Within a few months of Philip's succession to the great chieftaincy, he renewed the covenant which Massasoit had made with the colonists; and in the winter of 1663-64 John Eliot sent books for learning to read and to pray unto God. The English were presented an opportunity to continue the friendship that had existed between them and the Wampanoags from the beginning.[256]

However, Plymouth ultimately wanted a contract from Phillip that eliminated any future sale of land without the Plymouth colonies' consent. Phillip recognized, though, that the charter his land lay under pledged subjection to the king of England, not Plymouth. Philip's recognition as subject to the king made him feel as an equal to the colonial authorities. During a visit to Rhode Island by the royal commissioners from England who represented the king, they were received by Philip and intervened in a dispute over land at Mount hope between the Wampanoags and Narragansetts. The royal commissioners sided with Phillip and confirmed his home of Mount Hope or Pokanoket fell in Rhode Island bounds. Thus, Philip's knowledge of his land was in accordance to Rhode Island's royal charter of 1663.

Plymouth challenged the charter and the colonies disputed boundary claims. The boundary claims were a very important issue at the time. The Narragansett country was territory where Connecticut was trying to place its jurisdiction. Massachusetts, Rhode Island and Plymouth conflicted over a region where the three colonies claimed boundaries had overlapped. This area was also the edge of the Nipmuck territory.

In 1667 Plymouth's General Court established the town of Swansea. Located at the western edge of Plymouth's claims and alongside the counterclaims of Rhode Island. Most importantly it trespassed on Phillip's homeland. A year later the general court authorized expansion of Swansea for more inhabitants to purchase lands, which disregarded Phillip's plea to prevent others from seeking his lands. The Wampanoag Indians became angry. The Wampanoag Indians would eventually show an armed force before the Swansea settlers in 1671 and this act then forced Phillip to Taunton.[257]

There were also reports that claimed many Indians were repairing toward Mt. Hope and manufacturing bows and arrows, half pikes, and setting up their guns. These rumors spread rapidly. There was an effort made to remove the chance of a war between Plymouth and the Wampanoags. John Eliot hoped to share the Gospel with the tribe and sent a couple Natick Indians, but Philip was not interested in giving up his life or possessions for peace with the colonies. Philip viewed his relationship to Plymouth as being one of equals, as the two parties had direct ties to the king of England and that relationship was the only avenue to settle disputes within the colony.

The Wampanoag sachem felt Plymouth was as much a subject to the king as himself, but Plymouth did not view the situation as that. Philip was correct in his stance, in all the treaties between the Wampanoags and the Plymouth Colony subjection was acknowledged toward the king, only friendship was declared between the Wampanoags and Plymouth residents, dating all the way back to 1621.

"A very unusual scene was enacted" on April 12, 1671, in the Meeting House on Taunton Green when the English Commissioners from the Bay and Plymouth governments were to meet with King Phillip and his leading counselors. The Indian Chieftain, with his band of warriors armed and painted as if ready for war, first approached within four miles of the town, where he established his camp. He thereupon sent messengers to the English, inviting them to meet with him for a conference.

The Governor preferred Phillip to come into town, and it was finally arranged for him to enter, which resulted because two colonists were left with the Indians as hostages. Phillip then decided it would be safe for him to confront the colonists and with some of his men he approached Crossman's Hill, on the outskirts of Taunton. "Here he again became suspicious, and well he might have felt so, because some of the Plymouth men wanted to attack him then and there, but were restrained from doing so by the cautious representatives of the Bay Colony."[258]

Philip was finally persuaded by the Massachusetts men to attend the conference provided it were staged in the Meeting House and provided also that he and his warriors were stationed on one side of the church while the colonists should occupy the other side. "Philip's complaint was, that the Pilgrims had injured the planting grounds of his people. The Pilgrims said that the charges against them were not sustained; and because it was not, to their satisfaction, the whites wanted that Philip should order all his men to bring in his arms and ammunition; and the court was to dispose of them as pleased."[259]

In this conference it was proved pretty conclusively that the Indian Chieftain was arming, and not against the Narragansetts, but to oppose the colonists. When the English Ambassador asked him why he wanted to make war against them and asked him to make a treaty, he is said to have replied: "Your governor of Massachusetts is but a subject, I shall treat of peace only with the king, my brother; when he comes, I am ready." Plymouth, however, ordered all his people turn in their arms and also fined the sachem.

Thus the claim of "King" began to be added to Phillip's name. Though the sachem of an insignificant tribe, his reputation reached a height never attained by any of the aboriginal race thus far in New England.[260] Finally, on September 29, 1671, Philip and five other Sachems submitted, which recognized Philip as a subject to Plymouth and their laws.

Apparently at some point it became evident to another Indian that Philip was planning a general Indian uprising to drive the English out of the land.[261] In January

1675 a praying Indian named John Sassamon traveled to Governor Winslow's house to explain that Phillip was preparing for war. He informed the Governor of Plymouth Colony that the Wampanoags were organizing a general conspiracy against the English. Sassamon was in dead earnest, and even expressed the fear that his warning to the governor might cost him his life.[262]

How right he was.

John Sassamon was a mysterious man—a Wampanoag by his father, a Massachusett by his mother and a Praying Indian by his parents' decision to convert—not a permanent member of either the English or the Wampanoag society. Orphaned at a young age when his parents died of smallpox in the epidemic of 1633.

Many of the Indians stricken by illness along the coast were converted to Christianity on their deathbeds and as a result their children were fostered by English families. Thus, they were taught English, Christianity, and the European way of life. John Sassamon, who was around thirteen when his parents died, was one of the Indians brought up by English. Sassamon would live in the home of a wealthy Dorchester resident, Richard Callicott, and he would be taught how to read and write through this family. John Eliot, the minister of the neighboring town of Roxbury visited Dorchester often, formed a relationship with Sassamon from the time of his childhood and taught him Christian principles. Sassamon also attended an Indian School in Dorchester, where Eliot regularly taught the pupils.

During the Pequot War, Sassamon served with his master Richard Callicott under Captain John Underhill, and his purpose was not only as an interpreter but also as a soldier. According to Underhill, when Pequots saw Sassamon, who was wearing English clothes and holding a gun, they asked him from a distance, "what are you, an Indian or an English?" "Come hither," Sassamon replied, "and I will tell you." As they came close enough, "hee pulls up his cocke and let fly at one of them, and without question was the death of him." After the war, they returned to Dorchester with Indian captives.

Sassamon continued his relationship with John Eliot after the Pequot War. Eliot understood the Indian language more and more and began to use Indian translators, including Sassamon. Sassamon must have been partly responsible for teaching Eliot their Indian language, while receiving in exchange for his labor the English and the Christian way of life. Eliot could not translate the Bible into the Massachusett language all by himself; he had to rely on Indian translators.

Eliot learned the Massachusett language enough by 1646 to preach sermons in the language. Eliot made Sassamon his principal aide and Sassamon served Eliot until his death. In 1651, while Eliot formed the first praying town in Natick, Sassamon was involved from the start and would become a schoolmaster there.

In 1653, Sassamon studied at Harvard College through his relationship with Eliot. However, he did not stay in long and returned to Natick within a year. He continued there as a schoolmaster, but in 1654 Sassamon left Natick and joined the Wampanoag community. In Wampanoag country he became the translator for the chiefs.

Sassamon labored for the Pokanoket chief sachem, Massasoit, and then his eldest son, Wamsutta, who succeeded him around 1660. By this time Sassamon had a significant role within the tribe, translating in treaty negotiations between the

Wampanoags and Rhode Island. When Philip became the chief sachem after his brother's death, Sassamon's importance grew and he became Philip's interpreter and counsel. Sassamon's knowledge of English was of the most importance to Philip who could not read or write in the foreign language. During the 1660s Sassamon was a witness to Philip's pledges of loyalty to the English and he was also the continual interpreter in treaty negotiations and in land transactions. However, controversy would arise and Sassamon's mishandling of his role led to a falling out with Philip. Being a Wampanoag may have taken second to being a political agent and spy for Massachusetts Bay.

As Sassamon labored for Sachem Philip Eliot became eager to convert Philip. He would use Sassamon as a tool to influence Philip, and in 1664, Eliot requested the commissioners of Plymouth colony to give support to John Sassamon in order to teach Philip and his men to read. Eliot stated that Philip, "did this winter past, upon solicitations and means used, sent to me for books to learn to read, in order to praying unto God which I did send unto him, and presents with all."

Eliot felt that Sassamon was the connection to pull Philip into the missionary work. Neither Sassamon's effort or the books Eliot sent would convert Philip though. The time when Eliot visited Philip and prayed for his redemption, the sachem crossly responded by ripping a button off Eliot's coat and saying "That he cared for his gospel, just as much as he cared for that button."

With the failed attempt, Sassamon did not stay at Mount Hope with Philip much longer. There was one particular incident that broke the bond between Sassamon and Philip. Separation for the two Wampanoags occurred when Philip asked Sassamon to write his will. Sassamon pretended he was writing down everything Philip presented, instead, Sassamon named himself heir to most of Philip's land. Sassamon would be forced to flee when Philip discovered what his translator had done. Furthermore, Sassamon was a Christian Indian and Philip felt those kind of Indians were the most mischievous, as they were subject to no Indian and only the subject to the colony.

In the late 1660s, Sassamon rejoined the Natick Indians. Sassamon would follow John Eliot and may have acted as a spy with ulterior motives for the mission, but obviously his attempt for the Wampanoag Indian conversion failed because Phillip would not convert. However, he may have been the spark that ignited the Indian war.

The downfall of Sassamon began when Plymouth was planning an armed expedition to seize all the Wampanoags guns, until John Eliot mediated. In August Eliot directed the Natick Praying Indians to send Sassamon and two other missionaries to the Wampanoags and invite Philip to Boston. While on this mission, Sassamon viewed Philip joined with leaders of the Sakonnets and many other Indian chiefs, including some Narragansett sachems. It was assumed the meeting was to gain their support and Sassamon described all the chiefs present to the English colonists. Philip would still travel to Boston and humble himself as a subject to Plymouth and the King of England.

A meeting between Sassamon and Philip again occurred at the end of 1674, when Philip and his men were hunting around Sassamon's town, Nemasket, Sassamon would choose to visit his Wampanoag relatives. Through the discussion,

Sassamon claimed he discovered that Philip was planning to attack the English settlers and drive them away forever. Following the brief encounter, Sassamon left right away for Plymouth with a fear for his life. Sassamon would then meet Plymouth Governor Josiah Winslow at his house and disclosed Philip's plan to attack the English.[263]

As he himself predicted, Sassamon never returned to his home after his meeting with Governor Winslow. He was supposedly murdered after the meeting and was stuffed under a pond of ice. This was the official version of Sassamon's death and it was what placed suspicion on Phillip's tribe for his murder. The suspicion of murder was greatly strengthened by the known facts of Sassamon's life. Thus when his death at Assawompsett Pond did occur and word of it spread, the authorities had every reason to be suspicious, and drew the conclusion that Phillip was behind the murder.[264]

John Sassamon became the first Christian martyr of the Indians as it became suspected he suffered death upon the account of his Christian profession and fidelity to the English.[265] Consequently, a praying Indian named Patuckson told authorities he had seen the murder. He named three of Phillip's men as the killers, and that made Phillip responsible. Not many Indians believed this claim because Phillip would have no reason to hide his role in the murder, as it was the right of a sachem to order an assassination upon his own.

Three Wampanoag Indians, Tobias, Mattaschunanamoo, and Wampapaquin, Tobias' son, were arrested on the evidence of an Indian who claimed to have been an eyewitness of the affair. The Indian, however, claimed that Sassamon had been drowned while fishing and that the marks on his body were caused by contact with the ice.[266] It was also declared that Patuckson had a motive for accusing the three Wampanoag Indians, which was to be attributed to a gambling debt. The Indians reported that the informer played away his coat, and these men then sent him that coat, and thereafter demanded payment instead, yet Patuckson chose not to pay and therefore so accused them, knowing it would please the English so to think him a better Christian.[267]

> In connection with the accusation of these men [it must come to] question what authority the English assumed within the jurisdiction of the matter. There is no evidence that Sassamon was subject to them or under their special protection by reason of any treaty or agreement. The three men whom they tried for his murder were Indians, and, if they belonged in the vicinity where the crime was committed, were subjects of the sachem Tuspaquin, and the offence was against the laws of the territory of that chief. It was such acts as this, ignorance for the natives rights to deal with offenders among their own people; men who were not subject to the English and in their own territory. This superiority by the colonists was one of the great provokers to bring the Indians to war. [Alvin Weeks][268]

The Plymouth authorities must have stirred anger in Philip for imprisoning the Wampanoag men for the murder of a Wampanoag, and I am not sure if Philip was aware of how unfair the trial of those men were.

This trial of the three Wampanoag men was different to the records of other trials in the Plymouth Court, "the record of this trial is brief and uninformative". Six Indians were chosen to the jury along with twelve colonists. These were six Praying Indians, Indians who had rejected their Wampanoag heritage and who knew little to nothing of the English legal system, nor they didn't even know enough English to understand the testimony.

The most unfair part of the Wampanoag trial was that there was no defense counsel provided- a long founded rule in the English Court system. Another legal inconsistency was that there was only one eyewitness testimony depended upon, which ignored the rule that, in trials of capital crimes, there are to be two witnesses. Another unfair occurrence in the Indians' trial was the punishment by hanging within a week of the verdict. In the English system, the punishment for capital crimes was carried out at least a month after trial. Plymouth's legal system with this decision ended the fifty years of a legal alliance between Indians and colonists, bringing about a new interpretation on how to prosecute the Indian.

The Wampanoag justice system, on the other hand, would have the two parties involved settle the punishment for the crime on their own and it was a matter to be handled solely within the tribe. No third party existed as in the English system. To Phillip and his tribe, it was inconceivable that Plymouth Colony should be punishing Wampanoags for the murder of a Wampanoag. The trial and death penalty brought upon the three Wampanoag members by a separate party caused an anger in the Wampanoags that led them "to beat their war drums".[269]

The trial and execution of the three Indians incited the Wampanoag warriors to madness and began the second Puritan conquest in Plymouth Colony in 1675. About the time of their trial, Philip was said to be marching his men up and down the country in arms. The tension between the Indians and English colonists was to now spiral out of control. From all sides came reports to the authorities of hostile acts on the part of the Wampanoags. Cattle were shot, corn stolen, houses robbed; in some places, outbuildings were fired. The attitude of the warriors had become defiant, while spies reported that strange Indians were swarming into Philip's villages and the women and children were being sent to the Narragansetts. Alarm and terror spread among the distant settlements.[270]

It must be said, however, that Philip's men limited their damages to the killing of the cattle and hogs of the English and the carrying away of their property, the purpose apparently being to drive the colonists to the first acts of violence against the Indian; it was Wampanoag superstition that the first party to shed blood would be vanquished. Blood soon resulted, an Indian being shot and wounded first, in Swansea, while committing some act of damage began the war, but in this war the committer of the first blow would not become vanquished.[271]

The Wampanoag sachem, many colonists believed, readied his nation for war shortly after Sassamon's accused murderers were executed on June 8th, 1675 fearing that the English intended to destroy him. As tensions increased, some of the whites in the outlying settlements abandoned their farms for the safety of Plymouth; others stayed behind. On June 18th, in Swansea, one of these semi-deserted villages, was invaded by some scavenging Indians, and they took property left by fleeing owners, and were fired upon by settlers who had remained. "Some Indians were seen by an old man and a lad, pilfering from houses whose owners were at church, whereupon the old man bade the young one shoot, and one of the Indians fell but got away."[272] That Indian was to be dead soon. The first blood was thus drawn by the English not by the Indians. The neighboring natives would then visit the local garrison and ask why the colonists had shot their fellow tribesman. The English, in reply, simply wanted to know whether he had died. When the Indians, hoping that the settlers might attempt to make amends for the incident, answered that he had, and a lad of the garrison replied that the death "was no matter".

Rhode Island, alarmed at the state of affairs even before the incident in Swansea, made attempts to compromise the matter and bring Philip to an agreement. Deputy Governor Easton of the colony, and five others, including Samuel Gorton, met Philip and his chiefs at Bristol Neck Point on the 17th of June, a day before the Swansea death, and sought to reduce the chances of a violent reaction to the execution of Philip's Indians for Sassamon's murder, as well as other matters, through negotiations. Philip gave a humble response and nothing was solved.

The war would soon begin after this meeting—but not as the result of a conspiracy on the part of either Indians or English. Philip was hardly masterminding a campaign to drive the English into the sea; Wampanoag actions were reactions to the colonial legal system which was far beyond his control. The rebelling Indians would continue to increase greatly in numbers after the Sassamon trial, some from the neighboring tribes, while others were strangers, and most of the women and children were sent away to the Narragansett country. It was actually the younger warriors who demanded open acts of hostility with the increasing of Phillip's following.

Rather than the presumption of King Philip as the grand conspirator, Philip may have just lost control. Some Wampanoag male youths wanted to take matters into their own hands and on June 17th as some settlers advanced into Phillip's country in search of horses, which had strayed away from their owners and entered into the territory of the Wampanoags, the white men were now side by side with the Wampanoags and one of the young Indians wanted to kill an Englishman. Yet, the men in search of their horses were all released upon orders from Phillip himself. The incident shows that the Wampanoag sachem, unlike his young warriors, was still hesitant to commit violence. [273] [274]

At Swansea the Indians joined together in considerable numbers, yet the settlers were not backing down. On June 24th, one man was so enraged at the shooting of his cattle and the attempt to rifle his house that he shot at an Indian. Upon this the Indians began open and random hostility, and on that day eight or nine of the English at Swansea were killed and others wounded. With this attack the war began in the eyes of the colonists. A speedy gathering was made both at Plymouth and Boston, and on the afternoon of June 26th, five companies were either gathering or already on the march from the two colonies.[275]

Also on June 24th, Massachusetts envoys visited eight Nipmuck villages and thirteen of the Indian sachems there confirmed continual submission to the Massachusetts government and gave their word not to join Philip. Pocumtuck Indians along the Connecticut River also gave their word to a partnership with the

English. Young Indians of these tribes may have fled to Philip, but Sachems and rulers were hesitant to lose an alliance with the English.

Around this time the praying Indians at Marlborough were increased to about forty men, which came to by the additions of several Christian Indians that gathered there: from Hassanamesit, Magunkoag, Manchage, and Chobonokonomum. These praying Indians left their places with the trouble increasing, and came into Marlborough under the English wing which was viewed as safe, and there built a fort, which stood near the center of the English town, not far from the church or meeting-house.

These Indians at Marlborough, some of them having been abroad to scout in the woods to discover the enemy and secure the place; they met with a track of Indians which they judged to be a greater number by the track, and upon discovery whereof they presently repaired to the chief militia officer of the town named Lieutenant Ruddock, and informed him thereof, who presently joined some English with them, and sent forth to pursue the track, which they did, and first seized five Indians and after two more, which were in all seven; these being seized were forthwith sent down to the magistrates at Cambridge, who examined them and found them to be Indians belonging to Narragansett, Long Island, and Pequot, who had all been at work about seven weeks upon Merrimack river; and hearing of the wars they reckoned with their master, and getting their wages, conveyed themselves away, and being afraid marched secretly through the woods, designing to go to their own country, until they were intercepted as before. This act of the Christian Indians of Marlborough was an evident demonstration of their fidelity to the English interest. The seven prisoners, after further examination before the council, told the same thing as before, were for a few days committed to prison, but afterwards released. [Daniel Gookin][276]

Orders were given to Major Daniel Gookin on July 2nd 1675 through the Governor and council to raise a company of the praying Indians to combat the hostile Indian force formed at Mount Hope. The Praying Indians were to be armed and furnished, and sent to the colonial army at Mount Hope. The Major immediately sent for all the praying Indians for one third part of their able men, who all readily and cheerfully appeared, and being enlisted were about 52, as the able men among the praying Indians at this time amounted to about 156. These men being armed and furnished were sent to the army under conduct of Captain Isaac Johnson, the 6th of July, 1675.[277]

Prior to the impressments of the praying Indians, on June 28th the government of Massachusetts carried an official letter to Governor Winthrop of Connecticut, also informing him of the outbreak of trouble with the Wampanoags, including an account of conditions at Swansea. The letter reached New London the following day by John Winthrop Jr., who read it and then sent it to his father in Hartford:

Thomas Danforth, who was then First Commissioner of the United Colonies, wrote the rough draft of Council's letter to the Connecticut Governor:

133

There is reason to conceive if Phillip be not soone [suppressed] he and his confederates may skulke into the woods and greatly anoy the English, and the confederacy of the Indians is larger than yet wee see. (…) Particularly we request you to use your utmost authority to restrain the Mohegans and Pequots.[278]

The position of Uncas' alliance with Connecticut continued through time and the authorities in Hartford joined the Mohegans securely to the English cause in 1675 as the Mohegans offered their assistance on July 9th. The English sent a letter to Uncas that if he will send hostages to the English for the assurance of his faithfulness they shall accept his offer.[279] Uncas sent six of his men to assure friendship and offer his service against Phillip or any other Indian enemies of the English. The result of negotiations with Uncas was that he sent two of his sons to Boston as hostages, and his eldest son and successor, Oneko, with fifty men, to assist the English against Philip. These Indians were sent to Plymouth under the conduct of Quartermaster Swift. They subsequently joined with the Rehoboth men in the pursuit and battle with Philip after he fled Poccasset. The Mohegans received as wages the plunder they seized from Philip and the fleeing hostile Indians. The Mohegan alliance may have determined the Narragansetts' reluctance to join the colonial force against Phillip.[280]

Back in Swansea, the contingent of praying Indians with arms and equipment became the eyes and ears of the colonial forces during the time of their brief impressments by the colony. This request for Indian soldiers and scouts was in accordance with the magistrates' requirements upon the residing Indians' within the colonies' jurisdiction; this was founded on the land submission to the General Court by the Massachusetts Tribe in 1644, "wherein subjection and mutual protection were engaged."[281] They were used positively as scouts, interpreters, and warriors. This compelled many colonial men to live and fight as the Indians fought: stealthily, rapidly, and lightly. However, even after reports of commanders describing the Praying Indians as carrying themselves well, proving themselves as courageous soldiers and faithful to the English interest, by the end of July 1675 half of these soldiers were released from duty and sent home, and the other half soon followed them. Indian soldiers, aside from Connecticut Indians and a handful of others, would not serve on the English side again until April 1676. Indian removal from the colonial force resulted from complaints by English soldiers that the Indians were cowards and skulked behind trees in battles, and that they shot over the enemies' heads.[282]

On July 5th the Massachusetts army began moving toward the Narragansett country and separated from the Plymouth army. It was of most importance to bring the Narragansetts into a relationship with the English by peaceful means even though the English had a strong suspicion of the Narragansetts. Upon arrival, the design was to put upon the tribe a necessity to declare themselves friends or enemies, and to push upon them the performances of former articles of agreement between the English and them.[283] Orders came from Boston for Major Savage's forces to march into Narragansett, to enforce a treaty with that powerful tribe, and prevent their alliance with Philip.

Both parties, however, found the country deserted on July 7th, except the few very aged being left in the villages. Again and again Captain Hutchinson sent for the sachems, yet neither Canonchet nor any of his leading Sachems could be found. The officers, however, spent several days completing a very ceremonious treaty with some of the old men whom they were able to bring together and comply to a treaty of continuing in peace and friendship with the English.[284]

Thus, by the 15th of July a few aged and unimportant Indians were forced to sign a treaty as the Narragansett Indians did finally approve after a great lack of cooperation. Among the articles the Narragansetts were to comply with, they urged that the English should not send any among them to preach the Gospel or call upon them to pray to God. The English refused to compromise to such an article and it was withdrawn and a peace was concluded for that time. In this act they declared that their hearts were to reject Christ and His grace offered to them before. However, in months to follow, it would be viewed by the colonists that the Lord Jesus destroyed the body of the Narragansett nation who would not have him reign over them.[285]

By the terms of the one-sided treaty on the 15th of July the signers on behalf of the Narragansetts agreed:

> That all and every of the said sachems shall from time to time carefully seize, and living or dead deliver unto one or other of the above-said governments, all and every one of Sachem Philip's subjects whatsoever, that shall come, or be found within the precincts of any of their lands, and that with the greatest diligence and faithfulness.

> That they shall with their utmost ability use all acts of hostility against the said Philip and his subjects entering his lands or any other lands of the English, to kill and destroy the said enemy, until a cessation from war with the said enemy be concluded by both the above said colonies.

> The said gentlemen in behalf of the governments to which they do belong, do engage to the said Sachems and their subjects, that if they or any of them shall seize and bring into either the above English governments, or to Mr. Smith, inhabitant of Narragansett, Philip Sachem, alive, he or they so delivering, shall receive for their pains, forty trucking cloth coats; in case they bring his head they shall have twenty like good coats paid them. For every living subject of said Philip's so delivered the deliverer shall receive two coats, and for every head one coat, as a gratuity for their service.

> Pettamquamscot, July 15, 1675[286]

The Narragansetts must have felt there was a disregard of humanity that the Massachusetts colonies held, which was evident through their request for Narragansett hostages in order to show fidelity. By July 17, twenty-one Narragansetts made the journey to Boston. Ultimately, 150 Narragansetts and their refugees were sent away and placed under the colony's protection as an assurance of sincerity. These unfortunate Narragansetts, of all the New England tribes, were most deserving of sympathy. They remained peaceful even after receiving terms of a treaty through the threat of an armed force, which was signed by no sachem.

Canonchet, furthermore, we will see, had no concept of this treaty and suffered at the hands of the English for breaking it. The whole conduct of Massachusetts and Connecticut against the Narragansetts had been often unjust and high-handed.[287]

Meanwhile, as no one knew where the Indians would strike next, other Indians besides the Wampanoags were now trying their hand in the war. On the 14th of July, a war party of Nipmucks from the praying village of Pachackoog led by Matoonas launched a sudden attack against the small frontier town of Mendon in the southern part of Massachusetts, killing five or six of the inhabitants while they labored in the fields. This was the first attack within the Massachusetts Colony.

Following this attack on Mendon, with the Massachusetts army returning from the Narragansett country and rejoining the Plymouth forces, they prepared for a potent attack against the Wampanoags. The combined army moved forward toward the Pocasset swamp country on July 19th where Philip had fled, and they were immediately met with a murderous volley by a band of hostile Indians lying in wait for them in a thicket. Five of the colonial men were instantly killed and many were wounded. Undaunted by this attack, the English forces pushed on toward the great cedar swamp where the Indians withdrew.

The colonial force learned how dangerous it was to fight in such overgrown woods, as their eyes were blinded by leaves and their arms trapped with the thick limbs of the trees and surrounding prickers, and their feet continually bound with the roots spreading every which way. "It was ill fighting with a wild Beast in his own den," and they never were able to get their hands on the Indian warriors.[288]

The English now found themselves deep in the swamp, and obviously at a great disadvantage. Because of the terrain and the tangle of brush, they were seriously handicapped by their equipment. Night was now approaching and a swamp was no place for the large army at night. It was a frustrating day.

It was learned from an old Indian found in one of the wigwams that Philip was nearby. The English attempted to pursue his location, but the night was coming on and in the dusk the soldiers began to fire at every stump and waving bush, and many, made nervous and confused by the darkness, shot in the gloom even at their comrades. Considering that Philip was cornered and as good as captured, the main army disbanded, and Captain Prentice marched towards Mendon where the Nipmucks had began their attacks. Philip, though, was far from being taken, and, while Captain Henchman was building a fort outside the swamp, the sachem evaded the outposts during the night of the 31st of July, and crossing the Taunton River, made his escape.[289] The best they could do was capture the one man who informed them that both Phillip and Weetamoo, a Pocasset noble woman and Wamsutta's former wife, had recently departed.[290]

Many bands throughout were beginning to sway toward Phillip's persuasion, which the Narragansetts had not at the time of the July 15th treaty. Reaction to the first Nipmuc attack on Mendon was felt through the Massachusetts colony, especially concerning to the Governor and Council of Massachusetts. However, prior to the attack, peaceful intercourse was sought with the Nipmucs, as the case was with how the Massachusetts colony handled the Narragansett tribe.

Thirty-five year old scout, trader, and hunter Ephraim Curtis of Worcester was sent into Nipmuck territory previous to the time of the Mendon invasion as he was most familiar with the Nipmucs through encounters at outposts. Curtis was also one of the messengers in June 24-26, 1675, who previously received confirmations of subjection to the Massachusetts government from sachems of the Nipmuck towns of Hassanamesit, Manchage, Chabanakongkomum, Maanexit, Quantisset, Wabquisset, and Pachackoog, all praying towns. Treaties were made with all of these seven principal towns visited.

He was then employed to journey into the Nipmuc country on the 13th of July, a day prior to the Mendon attack, with the purpose of negotiating and spying upon the Nipmucs.[291] Tied into this journey, Curtis was employed by the Massachusetts Government to conduct Uncas and his six men homeward as far as Wabquesesue. Uncas had previously offered Mohegan assistance in Boston and was on his way back to Connecticut. The important prospect for Curtis was to discover the motions of the Nipmucs or "Western Indians".

Governor Leverett and his council of the Bay were in favor of somehow confirming subjection of powerful tribes. It was of most importance to keep other strong Indian forces from joining in the rebellion. The authorities in Boston sent three separate missions to the separate Indian tribes, the Nipmucks, Narragansetts, and Pocumtucks, as part of an overall plan to prevent an Indian war, which at the time proved effective with the Narragansetts. Instead of sending an army to the Nipmucks as the colony had in the case of the Narragansetts, the authorities chose Ephraim Curtis, a young trader who owned a trading post deep in the Nipmuck country, and who knew these Indians firsthand.

Ephraim Curtis and a small party were chosen for the mission. He would spend his time interviewing the rulers of the various villages there, obtaining from them promises of fidelity. Most of these rulers denied any of their men had gone to aid Phillip, and those that did have gone away with the rebellion were promised to be recalled.[292] Yet, Curtis was not aware that an Indian village constable had persuaded many of the Nipmucks that those who did not become praying Indians would be killed.

Upon the arrival of Curtis to separate tribes, he would read to the sachems a message from Governor Leverett, receiving in turn a promise that two of their leading men would visit the governor in the near future, but the promise would never be kept. On reaching Brookfield, Curtis was informed that Matoonas, with Sagamore John, leaders of the party among the Nipmucs friendly to Philip, along with fifty of Phillip's men, had robbed his house at Quansigamug (Worcester). Some Indians, with whom he had traded for many years, told Curtis that it would be dangerous to continue his journey. Curtis reported:

> I conducted Unkeas his men safly while I com in sight of Wabquesesue new planting fielde; first to Natuck, from thenc to Marelborrow, from thenc to Esnemisco, from thenc to Mumchogg, from thenc to Chabanagonkomug, from thenc to Mayenecket, from thenc over the river to Seneksig, while wee cam nere to Wabaquasesu, wher they were very willing that wee should leve them, and returned thanks to Mr. Governer, and to all them that shewed them kindness, and alsoe to us for our company. And in my jorny my chefe indever was to inquire after the motions of the Indians. The first information which I had was at Marelborrow att the Indian fort, which was that my hous

at Quansigamug was robed; the Indians, to confirm it, shewed me som of the goods and alsoe som other goods which was non of mine. They told mee it was very daingerous for mee to goe into the woods, for that Mattounas, which they said was the leader of them that robed my house, was in company of fifty men of Phillips complices rainging between Chabanagonkamug and Quatesook and Mendam and Warwick, and they might hapen to mett mee; and if I mised them, yet it was daingerous to meet or see the other Nipmug Indians which wer gathered together, for they would be reddy to shoot mee as soon as they saw mee. (...)

I speak to many of them in the Governor's name, which I called my master, the great Sachim of the Massathuset Englesh, requiring them to owne ther fidellyty and ingidgement to the Englesh, telling them that I cam not to fight with them or to hurt them, but as a messinger from the Governer to put them in mind of their ingaidgment to the English. I think some of them did beleve mee, but the most of them would not. [History of Hardwick][293]

Despite the grim signs of robbery of his own house and the attack on Mendon, which should have shown Curtis that the Nipmucks were in a most violent state and might even try to kill him, he would still continue his mission among the familiar tribe. The missions of Ephraim Curtis not only had the English authorities reach the ears of the Nipmucks with their message of peace, but other information on the Nipmucks was being produced.

Curtis headed back to Boston on the 16th of July satisfied that he made some progress toward repairing the Indians' anger against the English. He reported on July 24th that the tribe was in better spirits and they "promised that Keehoud and one more of their principle men would come to the Massathusets Bay within four or five days and speek with their Great Sachem."[294]

The Council waited in vain for the Nipmuc embassy. None came, and, thoroughly alarmed, they determined to force matters to an issue. Captains Hutchinson and Thomas Wheeler, with twenty troopers, were accordingly sent from Boston, July 28th, to demand the reasons why the promised Indian embassy had not been sent, and to warn them that unless they delivered up Matoonas, his accomplices and all hostile Indians who came among them, the Council would hold them as aids and abettors. [Ellis and Morris][295]

Boston, 27 July, 1675. The Council, beeing informed that the Narraganset Indians are come downe with about one hundred armed men into the Nipmuck country, — Do order you, Capt. Edward Hutcheson, to take with you Capt. Thomas Wheler and his party of horse, with Ephraim Curtis for a guide, and a sufficient interpreter, and forthwith repaire into those parts, and ther laubour to get a right understanding of the motions of the Narraganset Indians, and of the Indians of Nipmuck; and for that end to demand of the leaders of the Narraganset Indians an account of the grounds of their marching in the country, and require an account of the Nipmuck Indians why they have not sent downe their Sagamore according to their promise unto our messenger Ephraim Curtis. [History of Hardwick][296]

In the period of Phillip's initial revolt, the Nipmucks became divided into a pro-war tribe and an anti-war tribe, until many turned hostile. The colonies instant support of one another, as hysteria increased toward local Indians, showed all the Massachusetts and Rhode Island Indians that an alliance with the English meant nothing; Englishmen from any colony would stick together against any Indian. Upon Curtis' return to Boston, the council thus immediately sent Captain Edward Hutchinson, escorted by Captain Thomas Wheeler and his mounted Company, with Curtis as guide, to find the Indians and bring them to terms.[297]

The authorities were ready to demand that Matoonas and the other Indians who had taken part in the murders at Mendon on July 14th be delivered up to justice, as well as wanting a guarantee of peace with the Nipmuck sachems. Captain Edward Hutchinson, having just returned from the treaty-making mission to the Narragansetts, was given the responsibility of trying to obtain these desired commitments.

On July 28th Captain Wheeler, with about twenty of his troop, reported to the Council, and with Captain Hutchinson, marched from Cambridge to Sudbury, and thence the next three days into the Nipmuck Country. Ephraim Curtis and three friendly Natick Indians, as guides and interpreters, also marched. Traveling toward their destination they passed through a number of Indian villages that were empty, which meant they were at some central location not living scattered as in times of peace. Hutchinson and his party of mounted men rode into the small town of Brookfield, which housed twenty families. Upon their arrival they learned the great body of the Indians were at a place about ten miles northwest of Brookfield.

Thus on August 1st Captain Hutchinson sent Curtis and other men to arrange a parley with the defiant Nipmucs. Ephraim Curtis led the group, two were Brookfield men, and the fourth was probably one of the Indian guides.[298] The convoy was to inform the Indians that they had not come to do harm but to send a message. The group would meet with the Quabaug Indians about eight miles from Brookfield in a swamp. The messengers found the atmosphere at the Indian camp anything but welcoming, the young warriors were threatening at first, however, their sachems agreed to meet Captain Hutchinson and his party next day at eight o'clock. Curtis reported the Quabaugs, whose leader was Mattaump, agreed to come next day to a plain some three miles from Brookfield to meet the English.[299]

The company was now surrounded in a foreign land by the forested domain of the Nipmuc. An ambush was not on their mind when they set out for the place of rendezvous the following day. Captain Hutchinson, accompanied by the troopers, scouts, and three of the chief men of Brookfield, went to the meeting place, but no Indians appeared. At which point the officers suspected betrayal, and were warned by the Indian guides not to go on; but the Brookfield men that came along were so confident of the good faith of the Nipmucks, and urged to trust the local natives, that at last the party marched on.

It was assumed to find the Indians in a swamp several miles away which was in accord with the report as to where the Indians were, the path to which was, at one point, narrow and difficult, having an impassable swamp on one side and steep rocky hill on the other. Here with their skill the Quabaug Indians had placed their ambush.

The English were forced to ride in single file along the conditions of the narrow trail. They entered where a wooded hill rose suddenly from the edge of a swamp, which was covered with thick brush and tall grass. The entire company not knowingly was allowed to pass the first lines of the ambush, which then closed up to cut off a retreat; and when the foremost of the troopers had ridden forward some sixty or seventy rods, the Indians, from their hiding places on either side along the whole line, poured in upon them a sudden and terrible volley. Eight men were killed on the spot.[300] Unable to retreat by the way they had come or to enter the swamp, a few of the colonial party, dismounting, held the savages from rushing and overpowering them in a hand-to-hand conflict until the rest rallied.[301]

When the company reached the ambush they were unable to move forward because of the ground, the men turned and fled the way they came in, yet the Indians closed in behind them. With great confusion and eight men dead or wounded, miraculously, the three Indian scouts knew the way to Brookfield without following the main trail. Their safe journey to Brookfield was the result of the Nipmucks lacking horses. After a difficult ride of ten miles, the troopers rode into Brookfield, where they fortified one of the largest houses. The alarm immediately spread through the town, and the inhabitants left their own houses and fled to the house held by the troopers.[302] The return of the defeated and wounded troopers made clear the deadly force which was now approaching the little settlement. The frightened residents of Brookfield prepared to defend themselves against a Nipmuc attack, setting the stage for the great battle of Brookfield.

Barely had the preparations for the garrison's safety been completed when the Quabaugs poured into the village, plundering and burning the deserted houses and surrounding the garrison on all sides. Reinforcements would be crucial for Brookfield's survival. Ephraim Curtis and Henry Young mounted their horses and attempted to travel east to Marlborough to notify the garrison there. Yet they spotted Indians after barely reaching the further end of the street and returned to the garrison, which the Indians began to attack.

The Indians were well supplied with ammunition, and they shot through the walls of the garrison. As the attack went on, the strength of the enemy seemed to grow. Ephraim Curtis made another attempt to get help, but again was forced back. On August 3rd, he tried a third time, crawling through the darkness on his hands and knees. Finally he would make it through the lines of the Quabaugs and safely arrived at Marlborough thirty miles away exhausted. However, news of the Nipmuck attack on Brookfield reached Marlborough earlier by travelers who were travelling towards Connecticut, they saw the burning houses and the killing of some cattle, and turned back and spread the alarm at Marlborough. Immediately, Major Williard was sent after and greeted by messengers on his march from Lancaster to Groton that day.[303] Help finally was approaching. It was a long ride to Brookfield, but the troopers covered the distance quickly. [304]

In Brookfield, the Nipmuck warriors continued the attack and shot flaming arrows into the roof of the garrison house as the Brookfield men fired back at the Indians, but the people inside cut holes in the roof, and put out the flames before they could spread. Though the Indian bullets occasionally pierced the walls of the garrison house, they inflicted few casualties among the fifty women and children and the thirty-two men within.[305]

By now it was the 4th of August, and the siege had been under way for almost forty-eight hours, as the Nipmuc would continually receive large reinforcements. The invading Indians proceeded to fortify the meeting-house nearby, and also the barn belonging to an overtaken house, which served as protection from the English muskets. In short time, they invented a machine of war, of a style unheard of before or since in warfare. It was a sort of rolling wheelbarrow fourteen rods long, a pole thrust through the heads of a barrel for a front wheel, and for a body, long poles spliced together at the ends and laid upon short cross-poles, and truckle wheels placed under at intervals. They constructed two of these centipede-like carriages and loaded the fronts with quantities of combustibles, such as flax and candle wood. These were almost completed, however, when a heavy shower fell and wet all their combustibles, eliminating any threat to burning the garrison.[306]

In the meantime, Major Williard and his force arrived, and so intent were the Indians about the machines, that his company, coming about an hour after dark, positioned the force outside the garrisoned house before the enemy received them. There was a large body of Indians posted about two miles away, on the road by which the Major's company had come, and another party of over one hundred nearer the garrison. The Indian watch post had let the company pass unharmed, most likely depending upon the larger group to strike the blow; and these Indians of closer proximity depended upon the others from a distance for an alarm, which was not heard. Thus both groups missed the opportunity to attack Williard's company. As soon as they saw their mistake the Indians attacked Major Williard's party with fury, but without much avail, and all were soon safely within the garrison house. The Indians seeing their devices defeated and the garrison reinforced, set fire to the barn and meeting-house they occupied, and in the early morning of August 5th withdrew.[307] The Indians decided to disappear into the forest. Thus following the Brookfield battle it was decided by the settlers to completely abandon the town.

Growing confidence by the recent successes led the Indians to lurk more about those western towns and Philip, for some time, was among them:

> He had met the Quabaugs retiring from their invasion of Brookfield in a nearby swamp, on the 5th of August, and, giving them wampum as a pledge, praised their success. He told their chiefs how narrow his escape from capture or death in the fight at Nipsachick had been. Two hundred and fifty men had been with him, besides women and children, but they had left him; some were killed and he was reduced to forty warriors and some women and children. After this encounter, aside from rumors, there is little heard of Philip for some months. [Ellis and Morris][308]

Hysteria now spread into neighboring towns with news of the Brookfield attack. The English chose to seize the guns from the Pocumtuck tribe, who neighbored the Brookfield affair. The Pocumtucks chose to flee instead of losing their defensive means. Thus some rebelling Pocumtucks took part in devastating attacks. There were few Wampanoags participating in August attacks, it was the Nipmuc and Pocumtuks that increased the strength of Philip's force within

141

Massachusetts. Maybe the tribes within Massachusetts reacted violently based on the Massachusetts authorities persistent precautionary preventions.

The war was now spreading throughout the region as well. Enemy Indians were reported south of the Merrimack River, and the frontier villages in that vicinity pleaded for help. On the 22nd of August, violence broke out at Lancaster when a group of unidentified Indians killed seven inhabitants of that town. At first, suspicion fell upon the local peaceful Indians then residing at Marlborough, but the truth seems to be that surrounding Nipmucks, encouraged by the presence of Philip in their country, were extending the field of war.[309]

Things growing to this height among the English, the governor and council, against their own reason and inclination, were put upon a kind of necessity, for gratifying the people, to disband all the praying Indians, and to make and publish an order to confine them to five of their own villages, and for them not to stir above one mile from the center of such place, upon peril of their lives. The copy of which order here follows:

At a council held in Boston, August 30th, 1675.

The council judging it of absolute necessity for security of the English and Indians in amity with us, that they be restrained their usual commerce with the English and hunting in the woods, during the time of hostility with those that are our enemies; do order, that all those Indians, that are desirous to approve themselves faithful to the English, be confined to the several places underwritten, until the council shall take further order, and that they so order the setting of their wigwams that they may stand compact in one place of their plantations respectively, where it may be best for their own provision and defense, and that none of them do presume to travel above one mile from the center of such of their dwellings unless in company of some English, or in their service, excepting for gathering in their corn with one Englishman in company, on peril of being taken as our enemies, or their abettors. And in case any of them be taken without the limits aforesaid except as above said, and do lose their lives, or be otherwise damnified by English or Indians; the Council do hereby declare that they shall account themselves wholly innocent, and their blood, or other damage by them sustained, will be upon their own heads. Also it shall not be lawful for any Indians, that are now in amity with us, to entertain any strange Indians, or to receive any of our enemies' plunder, but shall from time to time make discovery thereof to some English that shall be appointed for that end to sojourn with them, on penalty of being accounted our enemies, and to be proceeded against, as such.

Also, whereas it is the manner of the heathen that are now in hostility with us, contrary to the practice of civil nations, to execute their bloody insolences by stealth, and skulking in small parties, declining all open decision of the controversy, either by treaty or by the sword; the council do therefore order, that after the publication of the provision aforesaid, it shall be lawful for any person, whether English or Indian, that shall find any Indian travelling in any of our towns or woods, contrary to the limits above named, to command them under their guard and examination, or to kill and destroy them as they best may or can. The council hereby declaring, that it will be most acceptable to them, that none be killed or wounded, that are willing to surrender themselves into custody.

The places of the Indians residence are, Natick, Punquapog, Nashobah, Wamesit, and Hassanamesit. And if there be any that belong to other places, they are to repair to some one of these.

By the Council

Edward Rawson, Secretary[310]

By this order the Christian Indians would undergo even more great changes: being hindered from their hunting, securing their corn from the cattle and swine, and even laboring among the English to get food and clothes. The converts, also, would be subject to being slain or imprisoned daily, if found outside their sanctioned bounds. I've heard some English took away their guns and kept them, which left the Christian Indian helpless.

The result of what the committee presented to the Court for consideration that those Indians of Natick be removed to Noddle's Island; Nashobah Indians to Concord; Hassanamesit, Magunkog, and Marlborough Indians to Mendon; Punkapog Indians to Dorchester neck of land, resulted in nothing, for the English inhabitants refused to admit them to live so near them. The Court declined the consent to the committee's proposals.

Therefore the Court took another means. Some people were angered at the committee on how they dealt with the Indians, and it was said "some men were more a friend to the Indians than the English, but it was no strange thing for men's reason to be darkened, if not almost lost, when material and temptation do prevail."[311] It was thus ordered and intended by the Council, that two or three Englishmen should be kept at each of the Indian plantations, to judge their conduct, but there were only a few men who were willing to live amongst the praying Indians.

Some of the English that inspected the Indians at Punkapog, and in particular Quarter-Master Thomas Swift, testified concerning the Praying Indians living there, and it became obvious to him that the jealousies and suspicions of many of the Englishmen about the Christian Indians was unsupported. Another man appointed to live among the Christian Indians was named John Watson, who, before he lived with these Christian Indians, judged all Indians with prejudice and displeasure. Yet after he had lived with them, he received such joy, and became convinced of the ill of his prior judgment, he was ashamed of himself for his former accusations of them because of common rumors. The good John Watson testified this before the governor, general court, and many others that wondered how the Indians conducted themselves.

Despite the Council's attempts in consolidating the praying Indians into five villages, or the testimony of these English witnesses on behalf of the Christian Indians, the hatred among the majority of people grew daily. The anger was not only against those Indians, but also towards the English who chose to be charitable to them. Many harsh speeches were made against Major Daniel Gookin and Mr. John Elliot. It was unfortunate even as Gookin had the highest of representation backing his efforts. He had been appointed by the authority of the General Court of Massachusetts and the Honorable Governor and Corporation for Gospelizing those Indians to rule and govern those Indians for about twenty years. Eliot had been their teacher and minister about thirty years. Anger should have only been justified if these men did support and protect those hostile toward the English.[312]

On the other side of the war, many hostile Indians were gathered in great numbers on the west side of the Connecticut River, and were probably under the direction of Philip, although it is unlikely he took part in any of the assaults. Small parties were constantly lurking near the frontier towns, Hatfield, Northampton, and as far as far south as Springfield, where, on September 26th, they burned the farmhouse and barns of Major Pynchon on the west side of the river.

Up to this time the Springfield Indians had been friendly and remained quiet in their large fort on the east side of the river towards Longmeadow. Just below Springfield, near the river bank, there had been for many years a village of the Agawams. It had existed when the first settlers of Springfield selected the site for their town, and its inhabitants had lived on friendly terms with the settlers for forty years.[313]

Some change, though, had been noticed in those Agawams, and Major Pynchon had turned to the commissioners about disarming them. The Connecticut Council advised against the measure, and suggested rather to take hostages from them. The hostages would be sent to Hartford, for security. This plan was taken up and the hostages were sent; but the Agawams, excited by the successes of the revolt in Western Massachusetts, as well as possibly being encouraged by agents of Philip, decided to join the war against the English. They somehow facilitated the escape of their hostages, and waited for an opportunity to strike a significant blow.

On Monday, October 4th, a large body of the enemy had been reported some five or six miles from Hadley, and immediately all the soldiers were withdrawn from Springfield. Springfield was thus defenseless and invaded the following day by the local Indians, and our town was near destroyed.[314]

We sure felt the wrath of the angry Indians in Springfield. It is true the Agawams and Springfield residents enjoyed excellent relations for a long time, mostly a result of the fair John Pynchon. For as long as I could remember, the local natives were living in a sort of fort about a mile below the town, where they could be closely supervised by local officials. Most men in Springfield refused to believe that the sachem, Wequogan, and his people could wrong the people of Springfield.[315]

There would be Indian terror in Springfield by these same Indians, however. I was in my house, bordered on a wood line, when I heard the sounds of screaming and I immediately, as a coward, ran into the woods. I hid in the woods during the Indian invasion of Springfield and watched the entire ordeal as I thought the rumors of an Indian invasion were heresy and did not think to fortify in the garrisoned house. This is my rendition of what I remember and have been told:

The burning of Springfield by the Indians October 5, 1675, nearly forty years after its settlement, has been the most horrific event witnessed here. With open hostilities now spreading to the Connecticut valley. Hadley, Deerfield, and Northfield had already been invaded and Major John Pynchon had gone to Hadley with a small force on the 4th of October because of reports of a large body of Indians. Springfield was left unprotected. Many of the people in Springfield had not been happy to see the troops march out of town on the 4th of October, and the very next evening these same people, as they rummaged through the ruins of the town, were shouting, "We told you so!"316

On Long Hill in the south part of the town, overlooking the valley, a fort had been constructed for the protection of the friendly Indians, who were dwelling in peace in the neighborhood. Into this a large number of hostile Indians, including some who had previously been on terms of intimate friendship with the whites, had secreted themselves. Toto, a friendly Indian, who was living with Henry Wolcott, Jr., a Windsor farmer, revealed a violent Indian plot by the Agawams to Wolcott, and that night the farmer named Wolcott risked his life and rode swiftly into Springfield bringing the warning, which roused the inhabitants and cautioned them of the threatened danger. Everyone was notified who had not gone to Hadley with Major Pynchon, and immediately took refuge in the three fortified houses. Among the numbers were some of the older men of the community including:

Deacon Samuel Chapin
Rev. Pelatiah Glover
Jonathan Burt
Lieut. Thomas Cooper
Thomas Miller
and others.

A messenger was dispatched to Hadley to notify Major Pynchon of the great danger that was reported by Toto, but the morning of the 5th opened without any indications of an attack upon the town, and Toto's statements began to be discredited. Lieutenant Thomas Cooper, long engaged in this region, set out on horseback for the Indian fort. Thomas Miller accompanied him. They had approached Mill River, within less than a half a mile of the Indian fort, when the Indians fired upon them. Miller was instantly killed and Cooper severely wounded. Cooper's horse galloped back to town and stopped in front of Major Pynchon's house and at this point Lieut. Cooper fell dead to the ground. The Indians then followed up this attack, and soon the dwellings which had been temporarily deserted by the residents of Springfield, for places of greater safety, were set on fire and destroyed.

Pentecost Mathews, wife of John Mathews, was shot and killed in the south part of the town, and her house set on fire and consumed. With the work of destruction unfolding, the Indians in this most tragic attack were familiar spirits. They proved to be some of the friendly Indians—one of them an old Sachem who had been on the most intimate terms of friendship, almost from the time of the first settlement. The house of correction, some of Pynchon's mills and many other dwellings and barns, were burned to the ground. Major Pynchon, hurried back from Hadley as soon as informed of the contemplated plot, but did not arrive until the town was in ashes and stated that about thirty houses were burned.

During the attack Edmund Prygrydays and Nathaniel Brown were severely wounded and both died soon afterwards. Major Treat of Connecticut who had been stationed at Westfield with an armed force, and Major Pynchon and Captain Appleton with their two hundred soldiers all arrived and prevented further destruction.[317]

After October 5th the morale of the people in the upper Connecticut Valley, especially Springfield, reached a new low. The inhabitants and soldiers were now living crowded together in the houses. The people of Southern New England were especially shocked at the Springfield area Indians, who had long been considered among the most peaceable and dependable. Now their dissent caused the English to be increasingly suspicious of neutral or praying Indians everywhere, and made the lives of such Indians even more difficult than before.[318]

This was Springfield's first introduction to fire and blood in this Indian war, and although we were greatly disheartened, we immediately set about repairing our broken fortunes. This great destruction of life in a single year reflects the danger that existed within the western settlements. With the destruction of Springfield and the other Hampshire County towns great concern was now directed towards the intentions of all Indians:

At Brookfield August 2- 13 killed

Above Hatfield, August 25- 9 killed

At Deerfield, September 1 and after- 2 killed

At Northfield, September 2- 8 killed

Near Northfield, September 4- 16 killed

At Deerfield September 18- 71 killed

Of Captain Mosley's Company September 18- 3 killed

At Northampton, September 28- 2 killed

At Springfield, October 5- 4 killed

At Hatfield, October 19- 10 killed

At Westfield, October 27- 3 killed

At Northampton, October 29- 4 killed [Henry M. Burt][319]

The Indian rebel attacks against Springfield in October worsened matters for all Indians, with the exception of the Mohegans. The attack not only led to the internment of Christian Indians, but it also triggered a chain reaction that eventually resulted in the United Colonies' invasion of the great swamp fort in the Narragansett territory. Because the Indians who had assaulted Springfield had for so long showed their loyalty to the English, their actions left the English confused and suspicious of Indians who held a neutral position. Some in Springfield actually blamed the Praying Indians for this attack. The Springfield invasion simply turned the English distrustful of all Indians, friendly or hostile.[320]

An incident then occurred to increase the colonial panic. Around the end of October, the General Court received a complaint from the officials of Dedham claiming that some of the praying Indians of Natick were responsible for setting fire to a house and barn in that town. It was, however, suspected by the Superintendent of Indian Affairs Daniel Gookin that the rundown structures, which he said were deserted and of no use to the owner, had been burned on purpose by some of the residents who wanted the local Indians banished. They assumed it would be easy to accuse the Natick Indians of such a crime in order to force the General Court to have them removed. After hearing the evidence, court officials voted toward an immediate removal of Natick Indians to Deer Island in Boston Harbor.[321] Deer Island would be used as a place of detention as early as October 1675, the island would intern about five hundred Praying Indians after months of war.

The situation for these praying Indians was very difficult, the non-converts thought of them as untrustworthy and the colonists to whom they submitted and whose religion they had adopted were also distrustful of them. Furthermore, those Indians who were hostile to the English intruders upon their lands made attempts to create trouble between the praying Indians and the colonists and many false accusations were made. The praying Indians knew of this hatred and placed their hopes and reliance upon the English. The English settlers, however, were in a struggle for their very existence and chose not to trust any Indian. The praying Indians had the support of neither side in this war.

Though many of the Christian Indians remained faithful, there were others who joined the hostiles. Philip's first real allies did come from a praying village led by Matoonas. This revolt of the Nipmuck converts is a show of the dislike by some of the Indians within Massachusetts toward conversion.[322] The English, on the other hand, came to regard the Praying Indians with such suspicion that the General Court passed severe regulations that none should be allowed to enter any town unless under the guard of two musketeers, and anyone found without such a guard might be arrested.

The question arose if the English should have trusted the praying Indians more and made greater use of their fighting prowess and knowledge of Indian methods of warfare. The aborigines often said that in action they had the advantage of their white enemies in several ways; they themselves in their marches and battles always spread out, whereas the English usually kept "in a heap together," so that it "was as easy to hit them as to hit a house."

On the contrary to the attack by Matoonas and the Nipmucs, the Natick Indians behaved particularly well on the side of the colony in one of the first encounters with Philip. Incredibly, the Natick Indians fought against their own tribesmen on behalf of the colony, and yet, some of the colonists accused their allies of skulking and of shooting over the heads of the enemy, and although some of them brought four Indian scalps as proof of their loyalty, they were still distrusted and they would be punished for false accusations made by the townspeople. There is no doubt that in several cases the fires were set and damage was done by inhabitants living near the Praying villages, who hated these Indians and desired their removal; or often by hostile Indians who were skulking about in the neighborhood, and knew they had more to fear from the scouts of these Christian Indians than from all the troops of the English.[323]

Upon the 26th of October, the reports were raised and stirred up against the Christian Indians of Natick, upon pretence that some of them had fired a house or old barn at Dedham, not worth ten shillings. This house, all probability, was set on fire on purpose by some that were back friends to those poor Indians; thereby to take an occasion to procure the removal of all those Indians from Natick; the engineers of which well knew that the magistrates generally were very slow to distrust those poor Christians, this trick was therefore used to provoke them. Hopefully one day the consciences of those persons that have been active to defame and trouble those poor innocent Christians, without cause, will transform into a mind clear of prejudice and hatred. The body of them, the Naticks, were always true and faithful to the English; and I never saw or heard any substantial evidence to the contrary. Besides this burning of the house, there was other false information presented at the same time to the General Court, to stir them up to a sharp procedure against those Indians.

This scheme against the Natick Indians achieved what it was designed for, the passing of an order in the General Court to remove them from their place unto Deer Island; having first obtained the consent of Mr. Samuel Shrimpton, of Boston and owner of Deer Island. In pursuance of this order, Captain Thomas Prentice was commanded to bring them down speedily to a place called the Pines, where boats were appointed to be in readiness to take them on board, and take them to the aforesaid Island.

Good Mr. Elliot, that faithful instructor and teacher of the praying Indians, met them at the Pines, where they were to be embarked, who comforted and encouraged and instructed and prayed with them, and for them; pushing them to patience in their sufferings, and confirming the hearts of those disciples of Christ; and encouraging them to continue in the faith, for through many tribulations we must enter into the kingdom of heaven. There were some other Englishmen at the place called the Pines with Mr. Elliot, who were much affected in seeing and observing how submissive and Christianly and affectionately those poor souls carried it, seeking encouragement, and encouraging one another with prayers and tears at the time of the departure, being, as they told some, in fear that they should never return more to their habitations, but be transported out of the country; of this I was informed by eye and ear witnesses of the English nation that were upon the place at the time. In the night, about midnight, the tide serving, being the 30th of October, 1675, those poor creatures were shipped in three vessels and carried away to Deer Island, which was distant from that place about four leagues. [Daniel Gookin][324]

When those Indians at the Natick settlement became aware of what was contemplated, they first sent a petition requesting the court to show them respect. They asked the court not to listen to any false charges against them. They also suggested that either more Englishmen should be sent to live with them as witnesses of their proper behavior, or else that they should hand over some of their leading men as hostages. They would beg not to be taken from their wigwams just as winter was approaching, because it would be impossible conditions for the aged and ill. They would declare innocence and loyalty to the colonists. These proposals seemed fair, but the colonists became still more angered. The General Court passed a vote in October that all the Natick Indians be sent for, and disposed of to Deer Island, as their present residence. It was first necessary to get the permission of the owner of the island, Samuel Shrimpton, of Boston, who would grant permission provided no wood should be cut or any of his sheep killed.

An Englishman named Captain Prentice, of Roxbury, who was a friend to the Indian people, carried out the removal of the Naticks. With the aid of several others he brought along, the Naticks were to be marched down to the Bay. Upon reaching Natick he told the Indians of the decision for their removal, and in one or two hours they packed up a few possessions and left in a quiet sadness. The group of two hundred men, women and children started forth with six carts carrying their possessions and the ill, first to a place then called "The Pines," on the banks of the Charles River. Hereafter, all the Indians were loaded on boats to the island and were brought over to their new home on October 30, 1675.

The great uproar raised against the Naticks for burning an empty barn was the false tool that devastated them, but enabled the colony to succeed. The justification of the authorities and the friends of these Indians was that it would be the best to get them down to Deer Island away from the enraged townspeople.

If only the people of Massachusetts understood the value and faithfulness of these praying Indians, there would have been far fewer deaths sustained by the colonial forces upon the Massachusetts frontier. These Praying Towns were so located that they might have formed a line of defense for the greater part of the Massachusetts towns upon the frontier; and it was proposed and urged by those who knew most about these Christian Indians that the forts, which in most cases they had built for themselves under the direction of the English, should now be garrisoned by them, with English officers and about one third of the garrison English soldiers; and that these would be a great asset in scouting and guarding the frontiers. There is little doubt that this course would have saved most of the destruction and bloodshed which took place in Massachusetts during the war; but there was a furious popular prejudice against all Indians, and the majority of the population had no confidence in any attempt to employ Indians in military movements. [Bodge][325]

The magistrates were in a troubling state throughout the war. They had to negotiate between English settlers certain that the neighboring Christian Indians were enemies, and, the supporters of the Christian Indians—John Eliot and Superintendent of Indian Affairs Daniel Gookin. The magistrates attempted but could not please both sides. They spoke of remorse, while at the same time they paid no attention to the pledge of 1644 for mutual protection.[326] It became the popular feeling of the body of people within the towns to banish all Indians.

With many examples of grave destruction at the hands of friendly neighboring Indians upon different towns, the fate of the Christian Indians and the neutral Narragansett Tribe would be a matter of most importance.

Canonchet, standing distant from participation in the war and the supposed previous July 15th treaty, would be summoned to Boston in September 1675 to reconfirm the July treaty. He appeared before the Council and received the same threats from the Council as the previous treaty. He was to sign a treaty guaranteeing his tribe to fight against the hostile Indians, and to seize and turn over all those Indians who had taken part in the war and were in his territories for shelter. This demand was impossible for him to perform, yet he finally accepted on October 18th. The English gave Canonchet the deadline of October 28th to deliver all hostile Indians. The Narragansett Sachem must have left Boston knowing well that his refusal to perform their demands would result in war.[327]

He signed the treaty on October 18th agreeing to surrender Weetamoe within ten days and was rewarded a silver-trimmed coat. Also in accordance with the July 15th treaty, which was pressed upon the old Narragansett men by Captains Moseley and Savage at the sword's point. The surrender of all Philip's subjects, even women and children who should take refuge with the Narragansetts; was agreed to by Canonchet through the treaty in October. The July treaty was disobeyed by Canonchet for a long time, yet on the demand of the commissioners of the United Colonies, Canonchet confirmed to deliver all the men, women, and children to the Governor or Council at Boston before October 28th. However, if the friendly praying Indians were distrusted, a neutral tribe, such as the Narragansetts, was not to be considered favorable; waiting for a justification for war seemed to be the general colonial approach of the Narragansett. Peace with the colonies, pursued by Canonicus and Pessacus, was broken. Attempts at submission and subservience had not improved the white man's opinion of the Narragansett, nor made the English less industrious in furthering their own interests and those of Uncas.[328]

On the 2nd of November, it was decided that the Narragansetts failed to obey the agreement as refugees were not delivered within the specified time. Thus the United Colonies agreed the Narragansett sachems had violated their solemn engagements with the English, and accordingly Plymouth Colony officials sold 144 of the Narragansetts and refugees who had come in as security of the July treaty, although it was known that they had nothing to do with the hostilities. They were sent to Cadiz, Spain, and averaged a price of two shillings and two-pence each.[329]

The distrust of the Narragansetts and the temper of the young warriors had not gone away, and the commissioners of the United Colonies called an emergency meeting to discuss the situation. It was decided rather than to be patient, the best course of action would be to destroy the Narragansett people immediately, before the tribe could join Philip.[330] "On November 12, 1675, the commissioners of the United Colonies unanimously agreed to discipline the Narragansetts for their defiance of the treaty formed on October 18 which ordered the tribe to provide Wampanoag refugees to the English. Canonchet had no intent on keeping his promise in this treaty, probably because his experience with the English in former treaties led him to have no trust in the English word.[331]

With the Narragansetts being people not so acquainted with such ways as handing over refugees, the United Colonies raised [over] a one thousand man army under the command of Josiah Winslow to march into Narragansett country and demand that they hand over all Indians who had sought their shelter."[332]

"The [colonist also believed the] Narragansett Indians favored Philip and seemed on the point of joining his alliance. The Narragansett's had gathered their winter's provisions and fortified themselves in the center of an almost inaccessible swamp[333]." There came information that the hostile Indians with Philip were retreating towards the south and to winter quarters amongst the Narragansetts, and that information compelled the United Colonies to carry out war against this powerful tribe.

The veteran troops were recalled and reorganized; small towns in various parts of the colonies were garrisoned, and an army of one thousand men was equipped for a winter campaign. General Josiah Winslow, Governor of Plymouth Colony, was appointed commander-in-chief of the Army; Major Samuel Appleton was to command the Massachusetts regiment, Major William Bradford that of Plymouth, and Major Roger Treat that of Connecticut.

General Winslow, upon his appointment to the command of the army in this expedition, rode to Boston for consultation with Governor Leverett and the Council. Thence on Thursday December the 9th, he rode to Dedham, having Benjamin Church as aid.

On December 18th, this, the largest army ever assembled in the colonies, after a day of fasting and prayer on the 2nd when the people were told by the government of the Bay Colony that they were suffering judgment for their sins of frivolity, [they] started at daylight for the Narragansett swamp where some 1,200 warriors were fortified with their women and children. And it was Sunday.

In this December, most of the Narragansetts did not follow the old winter tradition of separating into "smaller bands and hunting-camps". The number of refugees with them, as well as the lack of food, made this impossible. Instead, the Narragansetts gathered themselves with huge stores of corn at a hidden village in the Great Swamp near Kingston, Rhode Island. Narragansett families assumed safety within the fort as it was out of the way. Their concealing was a sign that they had no intention of warfare.[334]

Hartford no less than Boston can count this as one of the gravest moments in its history. As they marched, three feet of snow would cover the ground before the night was through. Upon arrival at the edge of the swamp, the English encountered a party of Indians who quickly returned the fire of the Massachusetts army's advance troops, and then withdrew into the swampland. The leading companies followed into the swamp after the retreating enemy. Fortunately for this colonial force, the cold of the past few weeks had completely frozen the muck and water of the swamp, so that the English were able to advance across land which under warmer conditions would be impassable.[335]

The onrushing troops suddenly saw before them within the swampland a small piece of upland and upon it a great walled Indian village. The wall itself was constructed of tall impenetrable hedge of almost a rod in thickness set upright in the ground, and around its perimeter was piled a thick mass of tree limbs and brush several yards thick. The fort had been raised upon an island of four or five acres of rising land in the midst of a swamp. Its place of entrance was over a long tree stretching over a pool of water. The bridge was made up of a long log laying four or five feet from the ground over which men could enter. There was a block-house opposite to it. The English thus filed into this as the only means of cover and entrance. From the block house, as well as within the entrance, they were shot down nearly as fast as they arrived.[336] It is true the English were shot down at first, but they continued to pour in.

151

As fate would have it, the first English troops to arrive came upon the one vulnerable spot in the entire structure, at the one corner of the palisade that was not complete, there was a gap which had been temporarily blocked by the trunk of a tree placed in a horizontal position.[337]

Within the palisade, the Indians began to fall back as the company continued to enter and the colonial force was now somewhat protected by the sharpshooters in the nearby blockhouse, but many men still continued to fall, and the Narragansetts, rallying again, began to pressure them violently, and the Connecticut force suffered from the enemy's fire. A short time later, the Plymouth men made their entrance. Little by little the attack of the English finally had driven the Narragnsetts out of the village, yet they still hung on the outskirts of the swamp, firing continuously at the English from the shielding woods.

Either through chance or deliberately fired by some English hand, the Indian wigwams caught fire, and the wind swept the fire in a mighty wave of flame through the crowded fort. The victory had been won, but the price paid had been heavy.[338] The many weary troops were thus forced to march back through the snow, carrying their wounded, to the head quarters, where they had marched in the morning. The suffering was incredible.[339] The numbers of Indians that had escaped, and were still in the woods close at hand, were unknown, but supposed to be several thousand, with report of a thousand in reserve about a mile distant.[340]

How many Indians had perished was not determined, but it must be assumed that the Narragansett force had been greatly reduced. At least twenty of the New Englanders were killed in this war that the Narragansetts were forced into because they would not subject themselves for any of the United Colonies demands.

Consequently, the number of Indians killed has been greatly exaggerated. One thousand perished I have been told by some.[341] "The Naragansetts had lost at least 97 warriors and between 300 and 1,000 women and children is told by another account."[342] However, most of the Narragansett warriors escaped, enraged, and now chose to join the Nipmucks.[343] The English did not realize that their mishandling of thousands of peaceful neutral Indians eliminated the greatest weapon of all and turned the Narragansetts toward an alliance with Philip. Unfortunately paranoia prevailed and many men died that should not have; as violence spawns more violence.

Meanwhile, Phillip was not even in New England. He had left for New York sometime around December 1675 with a band of warriors to recruit Mahicans, north of Albany. Philip, with the remnant of his Wampanoags and Pocassets, had spent the late fall and early winter at Quabaug, but late in December, joined by his own followers and a following from the valley tribes, went west and established winter quarters, some twenty miles northeast of Albany.[344] It is probable that he was there negotiating with the Mohawks for their cooperation in a spring campaign, as well as, to speak with a mediator outside of New England with royal authority, and it is believed that he had assurance from the French of ammunition and arms, together with a body of Canadian Indians to re-enforce him.[345] The removal from the scene of war let Philip gain apparent advantages: communication with the French and Mohawks; and also access to the Dutch traders, who ignored bans on sales to hostile Indians, for obtaining supplies of powder. However, many of the traders refused to sell direct, but the Mohawks took the furs from Philip's warriors and traded them off as their own, for powder, lead, and guns.

On January 5, 1676, New York Governor Edmund Andros received word of Phillip's whereabouts and was urged to send Mohawks to attack Phillip. Philip had the ability to cause hostility in New York and the Mohawks accepted Governor Andros' encouragement to attack, and fell upon their old enemies in a brutal surprise attack that broke and scattered the great force that Philip had collected to ravage New England in spring. The Mohawks fell upon Philip's men and killed fifty of them; driving Philip and the remaining force back to New England.

Meanwhile in New England, success for the English began to show in several expeditions, especially in that of the Narragansett Swamp. The Indians, on the other hand, were distressed for want of food, while their ammunition began to disappear. The sudden reverses of fortune on both sides abundantly shows how quickly the advantage in war can change. Accordingly, with Philip and his diminished force fleeing back to the east, the spring of 1676 in New England would open with terror.

Though Philip and his force were weakened when they returned to the upper Connecticut River Valley, the hostile Indians, altogether, had increased. A new and momentous desire was now within the Indian spirit. The scouts and advanced parties of the Narragansetts began to come among the Nipmuc tribe following their retreat from the swamp, bringing to the western Massachusetts tribes news of their defeat and the destruction of their swamp fortress. At first they were not believed and were not received by the Nipmucks and their allies, because the Narragansetts had looked upon the English to remain neutral; and, as the great leader Canonchet and his tribe chose for Narragansett indifference in all the great war councils of the supporters of Philip, so now these bands fleeing for their safety were not believed, and when they came to the camp at Menamest, they were rejected and their messenger shot at, being accused of treachery and of being friends of the English, although they brought English scalps and heads in proof of their story. But when larger bands came, bringing more proofs of the same kind, and provided confirmation from other sources, there was great rejoicing by the Indians that they had acquired the assistance of the strongest tribe in Southern New England and their chief. And as they had been last to choose violence against the settlers, so their reasons for hatred and revenge were deeper.[346]

The praying Indians interned on Deer Island had no intention to join the hostile Indians even though they were living in dire circumstances. Many other praying tribes would join the Naticks on Deer Island in the winter due to the same colonial reasoning that interned the Naticks. Near the end of December, orders were issued to have the Indians of Punkapoag interned on the Boston harbor islands, sent there for as little a cause as the Naticks were.

Near the end of February, 1676, the Indians of the peaceful tribe from Nashobah were removed to Deer Island. The citizens of Concord found the Nashoba Indians unbearable and feared an Indian attack, and the town quietly sent for Samuel Mosley. When Samuel Moseley arrived he entered the congregation in Concord with a company of volunteers while the town was at worship. He entered the church and waited until the Minister finished his sermon, and Moseley then addressed the Concord people and offered to remove the town's Indians. He received praise and as soon as the services were finished Moseley and his men marched to a local resident's house where the Indians lived. Moseley and his company were followed by most of the congregation—"a hundred or two of the people, men, women, and children." There would be an armed mob outside the home where the Indians lived that night. The townspeople entertained themselves with foul speeches to the Indians.

The next morning, Moseley stated that he was to take the Nashobahs to Boston. Mr. Hoar, who housed the Nashobah Indians at his residence, insisted that Moseley show an order from the Council for their removal from his land. Moseley felt that his commission to kill and destroy the enemy was justification enough for the Indians removal. Hoar, in turn, protested that the Nashobahs were not foes but friends and sanctioned under his care. However, Moseley ordered his men to break down the door and remove all the Indians.[347] The Indians were taken and Moseley's soldiers would steal all the Indian belongings. The Nashobah's were then marched down to Boston, where the court would send them to Deer Island in February of 1676.[348]

Their sufferings on the Island during the winter were very severe, for their rude shelters were inadequate, their clothing scanty and their food, consisting chiefly of shell-fish and clams, was unhealthy and also insufficient, in spite of almost continuous fishing and digging. There was little wood because they were prohibited by the owner of the place from cutting any of the standing timber. Many of course died, but they uttered few complaints and two of these Indians left the Island to serve as spies for the colony. John Eliot often visited Deer Island to comfort the prisoners and to look after their wants. This interest caused the white people to condemn Eliot severely.[349]

Other praying tribes had faced far different conditions. About the first of November 1675, an enemy force of nearly three hundred armed Indians came down to Hassanamesit and pressured the Christian Indians to go away with them. The Indians living within the Hassanamesit Praying village had already been disarmed by the English and threatened by their English neighbors that some had already left to join the enemy willingly.[350]

These Christian Indians at Hassanamesit were gathering their crop of Indian corn in Indian barns when they were told that the visiting Indian group would steal what corn they had and leave them to starve if they didn't satisfy the requests. The enemy Indians explained to the Christian Indians that if they followed the English, they would suffer as those Praying Indians of Natick. The good Christians were unable to combat the enemy Indians and, also probably, in fear of future sufferings by the English; that upon these considerations, many of them at last chose to join the enemy into their quarters, under their promise of good treatment and protection; and perhaps if Englishmen, and good Christians too, had been in their case and under like temptations, possibly they might have done as they did.[351] Thus the Christian converts submitted to the enemy Indians and joined their camp.[352] The broken Indians of Hassanamesit joined the enemy's quarters about Wenimesset (Tewksbury), where portions of the Nipmuck, Quabage, and Wesakam Indians now would keep their rendezvous.

In the early months of internment on Deer Island, King Philip was successful in his warfare and many dissenters befell the English settlements and after the fight which was between the English and the Indians at Narragansett, December, 1675, the Council of Massachusetts were very desirous to use means to gain intelligence of the state of the enemy; and, in pursuance thereof, passed an order empowering Major Gookin to use his best endeavor to procure two persons of the Praying Indians, from Deer Island, to undertake that service, and to promise them a reward for their duty. Accordingly, upon the 28th of December, Gookin went down to Deer Island, and advising with two or three of the principal men, they approved the design [for spying on the enemy] and of the persons he had pitched upon for that employment of intelligence, if they could be procured, Job Kattenanit and James Quannapohit. These, being spoken to by the Major about this matter, answered, that they were very sensible of the great hazard and danger in this undertaking; yet their love to the English, and that they might give more demonstrations of their fidelity, they being also encouraged by their chief men, they said, by God's assistance, they would willingly adventure their lives in this service. The same day, the Major brought them up with him, and conveyed them privately, in the night, to his house at Cambridge, and there kept them in secret until all things were fitted for their journey, and instruction and orders given them.

Upon the 30th of December, before day, they were sent away, being conducted by an Englishman unto the falls of Charles River, and so they passed on their journey undiscovered. These spies, Job Kattenanit and James Quannapohit, [carried] themselves in this service prudently, and faithfully brought the intelligence which might have conduced much to the advantage of the English had their advice been wisely believed. They first fell among the enemy's quarters about Wenimesset, where the Nipmuck, Quabage, and Wesakam Indians kept their rendezvous, among whom were most of the praying Indians that were captivated from Hassanamesit, as was previous mentioned. These spies were instructed to tell a fair, yet true story to the enemy during their labor; that they were some of the poor Natick Indians, confined to Deer Island, where they had lived all this winter under great sufferings; and now these being gotten off, they were willing to come among their countrymen and find out their friends that had lived at Hassanamesit, and to understand the numbers, strength, unity, and estate of their countrymen, that were in hostility with the English, that so they might be the better able to advise their friends at Deer Island and elsewhere, what course to steer, for the future; and that one of them had all his children among them. Upon the 24th day of January, James Quannapohit returned, and was led to Major Gookin's house, from the falls of Charles River, by an Englishman that lived near that place.

The main matters of the enemy described to Gookin was that the enemy quartered in several places this winter and Philip and his soldiers were not far from Fort Albany. They intended a general rendezvous in the spring of the year, and then they would prosecute the war vigorously against the English, burn and destroy the towns. They heard of the fight between the English and the Narragansetts, and rejoiced much at that breach, hoping now to be strong enough to deal with the English, when the Narragansetts and they were joined. That there were messengers sent from the Narragansetts to the Nipmucks, that quartered about them, declaring their desire to join with them and Philip. That the enemy gloried much in their number and strength, and that all this war their loss of men was inconsiderable. They seemed to be very high and resolute, and expect to carry all before them. He said, they lived this winter upon venison chiefly, and upon some corn they had got together before winter from several deserted plantations. The enemy boasted of their expectation to be supplied with arms and ammunition and men from the French, by the hunting Indians. He declared the enemy purposed, within three weeks, to fall upon Lancaster. [Daniel Gookin][353]

The two spies remained near a month amongst the enemies. After an absence of three weeks and walking eighty miles through deep snow James Quanapohit returned to the Falls of the Charles. He reported to the Council that he had met the enemy beyond Lancaster, and under the pretense of getting information for their friends on Deer Island, he learned considerable news, including the intended attack upon Lancaster, which proved true. The spies also discovered the Sachems and old men were inclined for peace whereas the young men were too proud and vain to pursue peace.

James escaped from the enemy with the aid of Job, but Job remained, as he could not carry his children away yet, who had fallen into the hands of the enemy. James escaped as so: Job and he pretended to go out hunting, killed three deer quickly, and, went over a pond and lay in a swamp till before day; and, after they had prayed together, James ran away.[354] Job would later return and his children would eventually join him in Deer Island.

It was understood that these two spies were to return to their prison camp in spite of the valuable service they had rendered. In fact, they were accused of bringing in false information. Although they had risked their lives, and done such important service, it was still said that all they informed were lies, and that they held correspondence with the enemy and that is why they came back to the island safe.[355]

The war still continued and the colonists found it necessary to make still further use of the interned Indians on Deer Island. The General Court voted in February 1676 to raise an army of six hundred men and Major Savage was chosen Commander-in-Chief. Before the General Court adjourned, which was not until the 28th of February, Major Thomas Savage, as Commander-in-chief, wouldn't accept the duty until Christian Indians within Deer Island were sent with him for guides.

In the months of February, March, and April, the enemy Indians were very violent in their attempts and assaults upon all the frontier English plantations, burning several villages or part of them, and murdering many people in the highways; Warwick, Lancaster, Medfield, Weymouth, Groton, Marlborough, Rehoboth, Providence, and many other places were among those destroyed or damaged. Almost daily, messengers with sad news were brought into the Council. It was feared and judged that seed-time and harvest would be hindered, and may result in a famine to follow the war. These thoughts upon those at the head of government, along with the need to end the success of the enemy, brought the Council, to arm and send in a company of the Christian Indians that were at Deer Island. The Indians throughout had appeared very desirous and willing to engage against the enemy.

> Captain Daniel Henchman was appointed by the Council to look to the Indians at Deer Island and to put them upon employment. This gentleman made motions to the Council of his readiness to conduct these Indians against the enemy; declaring that he had great confidence in God, that if they were employed they might, with God's blessing, be instrumental to give check to the enemy and turn the alarm; testifying that he found them very willing and desirous to serve the country, and leave their parents, wives, and children under the English power, which would be rational security to the English for their fidelity. But those motions were not accepted at first. The people generally distrusted those praying Indians, and were not willing to have any of them employed to serve the country; which was the principal reason why the Council complied not with those and former motions of this nature, for many of the Council were otherwise opposed to it. Though afterwards the motion to arm and employ the Christian Indians was embraced and put in practice. [Daniel Gookin][356]

Captain Henchman, who had been chosen to look after the interned Indians, urged the magistrates to permit him to lead a small company against the enemy, explaining that the children and relatives left on the island would be ample security for their loyalty. His recommendation at first wasn't accepted, but later, towards the end of April, the Council voted to arm and send out a Company of seventy men under Captain Samuel Hunting and Lieutenant James Richardson, who knew the Indians well. Arms could be procured for only forty. As soon as the men were selected and gathered they headed out on April 21 first reaching Charlestown on their way to Chelmsford.

Upon the 21st of April, Captain Hunting had drawn up and furnished his company of forty Indians, at Charlestown, they were ordered by the council at first to march up to Merrimack river near Chelmsford, and there to form a fort near the great fishing-places, where it was assumed the enemy would come at this time to get fish. This fort was to keep their scouts about daily and to seize upon the enemy. If they should be overpowered by greater numbers, their fort was also for their retreat, until assistance might be sent them. However, for just as those Indians soldiers were ready to march, upon the 21st of April, about mid-day came many messengers, they expressed that a great body of the enemy, around fifteen hundred, had assaulted a town called Sudbury, that morning, and set fire on houses and barns. Thus they would change their plans and be called upon the scene of a great disaster.

With the townspeople deserting from Groton, Billerica, Lancaster, and Marlboro, it was Sudbury that had become the important frontier town of the Bay settlements. Situated on the east bank of the Sudbury River it was a point of considerable importance, the roads were opened to the settlements, east, south, and

157

west. Small parties of soldiers with supplies were continually passing through it on the way to and from the valley.

The tale of the attack on Sudbury is as follows:

Captain Samuel Wadsworth was dispatched by the Council with a company of foot to relieve the garrison at Marlboro. Unfortunately, the full force assigned to him could not be collected, because many of those impressed into the war failed to appear and he began his march with only seventy troops, many of them boys. The advance parties of the Indian warriors were already in the woods about Sudbury when Wadsworth, in the evening of the 20th of April, passed through the town unmindful of the large number of Indians near by, for during the day, some of the Sudbury settlers had been fired upon and a house or two upon the distant outskirts had been burned. It was believed, however, that this was the work of only a small party, and Wadsworth was ignorant that over five hundred warriors, Philip among them, was waiting in ambush.

These soldiers that had been sent from Boston, under Captain Samuel Wadsworth of Milton, who, on their way toward their destination to Marlborough, took the trail of Philip, and followed it through the woods to Sudbury and within a mile of the town they discovered a body of a hundred Indians. These Indians fled as if through fear, leading the English into a place convenient to be surrounded by five hundred savages, who sprang forth and destroyed them. Most of this English force of about seventy men were slain; but a few of them were left alive to be tortured.[357]

Following the massacre, Captain Hunting with his Indian company, being on foot, got to Sudbury around nightfall and the enemy had retreated unto the west side of the river of Sudbury at the time of the praying Indian companies arrival, which several English were joined. Upon the 22nd of April, early in the morning, forty praying Indians, having stripped themselves, painted their faces like to the enemy. They traveled over the bridge to the west side of the river without any Englishmen, the Indian soldiers soon felt a great grief as they witnessed so many English dead.[358]

It was the hostile Indians usual manner to remove themselves "when they had done any mischief, lest they should be found out; and so they did at this time. The [Sudbury invaders] went about three or four miles; and there they built a great wigwam, big enough to hold a hundred Indians; which they did in preparation to a great day of dancing." (Mary Rowlandson)

From this time forward, the Christian Indian soldiers were constantly employed in all expeditions against the enemy, while the war lasted; and after the arrival of the ships from England, which was in May, arms were bought to furnish the rest of the able men; and then Captain Hunting's company was made up to the number of eighty men; those did many services in the summer, 1676. During this summer, the company destroyed or captured a very large number of the enemy and performed most effective work in the closing operations of the war. [Ellis and Morris][359]

Still, the sufferings of the four hundred or so older men, and of the women and children who were left on the islands continued, although spring with its warmer weather had already arrived. In this condition of want and sickness they were, after their men were sent for to fight in the wars. It was

158

until mid-May when the Lord must have been pleased to satisfy the hearts and minds of men towards them, little by little; partly because of the true reports brought to the General Court, of their distressed estate, and the great unlikelihood they were to plant or reap any corn at the Islands; and partly from the success God was pleased to give their brethren, abroad in the country's service. The hearts of many were in a degree changed to those Christian Indians; and the General Court then sitting passed an order, giving liberty to remove them from the Islands, cautioning their order, that it should be done without charge to the country. This liberty being given, Major Gookin, their old friend and ruler, by the authority and encouragement of the right Honorable "The Corporation for Gospelizing the Indians", residing in London, and by authority of the General Court of Massachusetts in New England, immediately hired boats to bring them from the Islands to Cambridge, not far from the house of Mr. Thomas Oliver, a virtuous man, and of a very loving, compassionate spirit to those poor Indians; who, when others were shy, he freely offered a place for their present settlement upon his land, which was very commodious for the situation, being near Charles River, convenient for fishing, and where was plenty of fuel; and Mr. Oliver had a good fortification at his house, near the place where the wigwams stood, where they might retreat for their security. This deliverance from the Island was a jubilee to those poor creatures. [Daniel Gookin][360]

Fortunately the excellent record of the fighting men from Deer Island caused the English to deny internment and in May, as aforementioned, the General Court passed an order for their removal to Cambridge by hired boats. In Cambridge the Indians were much relieved, especially as some were ill at the time. Eliot and others provided the sick ones with food and medicine and all recovered.

The war was now nearing its end and the help of the Indian allies and Christian Indians contributed much towards bringing it to a conclusion. The colonists had suffered the loss of about six hundred of their best men, thirteen towns had been destroyed, and six hundred dwellings laid low, but destruction would have been much worse had it not been for their Indian converts, who, through their knowledge of the country and the method in war, were able to sacrifice such precious services. The war was a sad blow to the cause of Christianity among the natives, many of them seemed to disappear or desert, chiefly from the more recent Praying Towns; some became heathen again, some were killed in conflict, some died on the islands during captivity and were buried there, some proved untrustworthy and were executed as rebels, and some died of starvation.

It has been estimated that four hundred of the English Indian Allies were either captured or killed, and it has been said that they actually killed over three hundred of their very own countrymen. Their fidelity to the English is rather to be marveled at, particularly when one considers they were drawn against their own kind. There are some interesting testimonials that were made by some of the English officers serving over them. The Christian Indians conducted themselves well, and proved themselves courageous soldiers, and faithful to the English interest. The Praying Indians must be judged to have provided a great influence in the positive outcome of this war for the United Colonies.[361]

The outcome of war for the bands of hostile Narragansetts, Wampanoags, and Nipmucs was not favorable. Canochet, the son of Miantonomo, and the chief sachem of the Narragansetts, had escaped the destruction of his principal fort, and had many brave fighting men with him in the early spring of 1676. Some time in March he had ventured down from the north to Seekonk, near the seat of Philip, to get seed-corn with which to plant the towns upon the Connecticut River that had been deserted by the English. [362] Necessity brought Canonchet and a band of Indians to find corn, for it was a hungry winter.

This spring of 1676 Connecticut was conducting independent military operations of her own, mostly in the Narragansett country. From time to time during this period parties of Narragansetts made their way down into the Connecticut territory in search of food, and it was these Indians who became the objects of Connecticut's military efforts east of the Pawcatuck. These expeditions were well manned with English volunteers together with Mohegan, Pequot and Niantic Indians.[363]

In a raid around Seekonk and Pawtucket in the spring of 1676, Canonchet was crossing the Blackstone River, when his foot slipped, throwing him into the water and wetting his gun so that it became useless. This misfortune so weakened him that he was overtaken by a swift-footed Pequot who was with a pursuing party of whites and Indians. After his capture, the first Englishman to approach him was very young. When this young man attempted to interrogate him, Canonchet replied, "You much child. No understand matters of war. Let your brother or your chief come. Him I will answer." His capture occurred on March 27th and he was taken to Connecticut.[364] Canonchet, son of Miantonomo, would soon share a similar fate as his father.

To the offer of his life if he would secure peace, Canonchet replied that he wished to die before his heart was made soft and before he had spoken unworthy of himself. On April 8, the council at Hartford formally acknowledged the receipt of his head from the Mohegans and Pequots to whom he had been turned over for execution."[365] Thus as Canonchet's father was killed by Uncas, the son of Uncas superintended the execution of the son of Miantonomo.[366] The death of Canonchet was really the death-blow of the war for the Indian and turning point for the colonies, for he was the real leader of all active operations in early 1676. Canonchet led many devastating attacks on English towns from February through early March. Philip was still chief instigator, however, following Canonchet's death, more than before, he became, for the time, the controlling mind of a larger number than ever before.[367]

The success gained through such a major blow to the enemy, which the Connecticut troops had obtained because of their use of the Mohegans and Pequots, may make it appear that the conduct used by the Massachusetts colonists during the majority of war was foolish. For the numerous disasters Massachusetts withstood, how many could the Christian Indians have prevented if they had been trusted and employed sooner.[368] The Mohegans had been accused of being untrustworthy,

160

however, Connecticut continued to use their services and never once demanded seizure of their arms. The Mohegans were faithful throughout the war.

The remaining operations of the war in these parts mostly became, simply, the hunting down of almost defenseless enemies. The colonial authorities eventually issued a proclamation calling all those Indians who had been engaged in the war to come in and surrender, submitting themselves to the judgment of the English courts. Many parties sought to take advantage of this, but were captured upon their approach by scouting parties, and were treated as captives.

Following this proclamation which had been made for the peaceful surrender of all Philip's supporters, the squaw sachem of Saconet, an ally of Philip, had first sent three messengers to the governor of Plymouth, asking for life, promising, under that proclamation, submission; and accordingly surrendered herself and tribe to Major Bradford. But, sad to tell! They were slain, the entire one hundred and ten, that very day.[369]

It may be said in truth, that God made use of these poor, despised, and hated Christians, to do great service for the churches of Christ in New England, in this day of their trial; after the Indians went out, the balance turned in favor of the English side; for after the attack of Sudbury and the addition of the Christian Indian soldiers, the enemy went down the wind; and, about July, one hundred and fifty surrendered themselves to mercy to the Massachusetts government, besides several that surrendered at Plymouth and Connecticut. [Daniel Gookin][370]

Philip and his warriors at this point had become desperately weakened by a combination of disease, starvation, and attacks; while the settlers began to have much optimism. By June, most Indians had no intention of war and most alliances scattered. It was finally a volunteer force of English and Indians under Benjamin Church that found and killed King Philip to end the war in Southern New England.[371] Church had discovered the perfect kind of military unit for dealing with the scattered remnants of the enemy- a small, volunteer company including Indians and English. Even captured enemy Indians were sometimes given the opportunity to join Church's band, and these traitors made excellent scouts and preying soldiers.

The force which finally got a hold of Philip was this volunteer force, as the men pressed into the war during the later stages were solely impressed for defense of local garrisons. The source for offensive power for New England's military came from the special companies like Benjamin Church's Plymouth-based volunteer company. Church had come to value the Indians' skulking way of war and adapted it to English custom. The companies of colonial volunteers, as Connecticut had, were convinced to join because of promises of wages, pillage, and bounties.

It was in July when Captain Church's mixed band of Indians and English captured Philip's wife and nine-year-old son. When he got the news, Philip, it is said, was ready to die. Philip's family being captured at last and his force surrendering, he fled, broken-hearted, to his old home.[372] King Phillip, who had been a deadly inciter, that had once three hundred men barbarously inclined, was reduced to ten, and now was to be killed.

161

Philip hid in a swamp on Mount Hope Neck, with his little party, yet unfortunately for the Wampanoag Sachem, one of his Indians being discontented with him made an escape from him, and was joined by Church and informed Captain Church of Philip's whereabouts. The Wampanoag deserter spoke of Philip's condition, as Philip had killed the Wampanoag exile's brother for advising surrender. This Indian offered to pilot the English to Philip's hiding-place.[373]

The men were with the required weapons and supplies to combat the great chief as they had the understanding of where King Philip was. Captain Church and his company searched for him with the Indian guide, and fell upon the swamp, where they heard he was. It was very mucky, and the ground so loose, that the men sunk and the passage was too difficult. However, in the dark the party of men crawled into position and came within sight of the enemy's camp. An order was made to lie hidden until daybreak, and then open the day with a surprise attack. However, with being undetected and instead of taking patience at the Wampanoag camp, one of the company fired a shot at an Indian who appeared as if he glanced at Church's party.

While they were at first overwhelmed with difficulties in this attempt, the providence of God wonderfully appeared, for by chance the Indian guide and the Plymouth man being together, the guide spied an Indian running for his very life and bids the Plymouth-man shoot, whose gun went not off, only flashed in the pan. With that, on August 12, 1676, the Indian looked about, and was going to shoot, and shot the enemy through the body, dead, with a brace of bullets; and approaching the place where he lay, upon search, it appeared to be King Philip, to their no small amazement and great joy.

A Plymouth Man and the guide named Alderman had been stationed by Captain Church at a point where Philip was thought likely to appear, and according to Church it was the guide whose shots took effect, causing Philip to fall upon his face in the mud and water, with his gun under him.

This seasonable prey was soon divided. They cut off his head and hands, and conveyed them to Rhode Island, and quartered his Body, and hung it upon four trees. One Indian more of King Philip's company they then killed, and some of the rest they wounded, but the Swamp being so thick and miry, they made their escape. [Charles Lincoln][374]

Sadly in the end, over a thousand Indians were sent into slavery in the West Indies with the closing of the New England hostilities. It was such an unfortunate situation for Indians, the Wampanoags for instance, who surrendered to Plymouth were all sold out of the country as slaves. This action forced many peaceful Indians not to surrender and turn to other hostile Indians for security. Philip, however, would not surrender.

The moment of fatality for Philip also signified the closing of the rapid decrease in hostile Indians still in the open frontier. In June 1676, Massachusetts and Plymouth granted mercy to Indians who surrendered. Indians immediately surrendered carrying such a weak condition. Philip's Indian brethren thus deserted his cause and submitted themselves to the English by the hundreds. On July 17, Sagamore John of Pachackoog and one other Nipmuck sachem, with four braves.

162

came in seeking peace. John and his followers were ordered by the court to be put under supervision of the Cambridge village. The Nipmucks may have not wanted to dishonor themselves by surrendering to the English, yet the possibility of death at the hands of the English made self-preservation the only option.[375]

Sagamore John, of the Indians on Pakachoag Hill, who had been induced by the wily King Philip to join with his men in the war against the white settlers, alarmed at the dangerous condition of affairs, (…) prudently sought safety by timely submission to the colonial authorities. July 13, Sagamore John ventured to visit Boston to deliver himself up and make terms for his men. The Governor and Council had issued proclamations offering pardon to the Indians who voluntarily came and surrendered.

Sagamore John expressed sincere sorrow for taking part against the English, promised to be true to them in the future, received assurances of security and protection, and was permitted to depart. On the 27th of July he returned, bringing with him 180 of his followers. To propitiate favor and purchase peace by an acceptable offering, he had treacherously seized Mattoonus and his son Nehemiah and brought them down bound with cords to be given up to justice. Mattoonus, having been examined, was condemned to immediate death. Sagamore John, with the new-born zeal of a traitor and turncoat, in order to signalize his devotion to the cause he adopted by extraordinary rancor against the cause he deserted, entreated for himself and his men the office of executioners. Mattoonus was led out, and being tied to a tree on Boston Common, was shot by his own countrymen, his head cut off and placed upon a pole opposite to that of his son. [The Nipmuck Indians, Caleb A. Waei., Esq., 1898][376]

In my final thoughts, I must ask, could peace have existed if compromise and respect to the Indian culture had existed on the mainland as it did in Martha's Vineyard, where there was not one Indian revolt during King Philip's War? Or was the vast wilderness of western Massachusetts an impossible land to tame?

Preserving their people and land, as Massasoit and Uncas had tried, became of no option for proceeding Indian generations. Indians that chose the most peaceable relationship with the white men were still sent to an isolated Island. Would there be a change in history if the Indian conduct had been different throughout the two Puritan conquests?

The past Indian war has eliminated any chance at furthering the gospel amongst the Indians. The great irony in all this is that the loss of Indian authority in New England didn't strengthen the Puritans in Massachusetts, instead, the Puritans, as a group, are now looked upon as servants for the Crown of England. Thus, the Indians were all considered servants and now so are the Puritans. It's unfortunate that a universal understanding of true Christian conduct could not be the most important interest of all nations, in which no one had to dominate over others. With that being said, I hope the reader does not overlook the many men in London who held the highest divinity and shared their purses in order to sponsor an effort to share Christianity with the Native.

The idea of faith does not serve any purpose if man does not evolve his spirit toward the divine principles which faith defines. The solution for greed and delinquency will be found in religion, if used in accordance with the true intentions of the gospel. Unfortunately, a parasite has arisen that craves excess. Expansion of property, expansion of wealth, expansion of power, have become the influence during the building of the Unified Colonies. The enhancement of one's own material wealth has become precedent, with the natural well being of the whole becoming denied.

As the use of military increased with land acquisition, representation, and ownership, a sense of invincible expansion has become the direction of our government. Even the Indians who have joined this cause have been enslaved, killed, and even segregated to a reservation, but most importantly, they lost their homeland, never to be returned. My wonder is how far this will spread and how long it will last. Is material wealth more important than natural wealth? For humanity to progress we must evolve morally not simply adapt to a corrupt people.

Chief Massasoit questioned what the entitlement of property truly was: "It cannot be the earth for the earth is our mother, nourishing all her children, bears, birds, fish and all men. The woods, streams, everything on it belongs to everybody and is for the use of all. How can one man say it only belongs to him."[377]

I will conclude by asking the reader one simple question.

Would you prey or pray?

Bibliography

A Brief History of the Pequot War, John Mason

A Brief History of the Unites States, Joel Dorman Steele and Esther Baker Steele, American Book Company

A History of the Indian Wars with the First Settlers of the United States, to the Commencement of the Late War, Daniel Clarke Sanders, 1828

After King Phillip's War: Presence and Persistence in Indian New England, Colin G.Calloway, University Press of New England, 1997

Cotton Mather: The Puritan Priest, Barrett Wendell, Harbinger Books, 1963

Epochs of American History: The Colonies 1492–1750, Reuben G. Thwaites, Longmans, Green, and Co., 1894

Eulogy on King Philip, William Apess

Flintlock and Tomahawk, Douglas Edward Leach, Parnassus Imprints 1958,

Historic & Archaeological Resources of the Connecticut River Valley, The Massachusetts Historic Commission, 1984

Historical Account of the Doings and Sufferings of the Christian Indians in New England in the Years 1675–1677, Daniel Gookin

History of Hartford County, Charles W. Burpee, S. J. Clarke Publishing, 1928

History of the Indian Wars of New England, with Eliot the Apostle Fifty Years in the Midst of Them, Robert Boodey Caverly

Indian History, Biography and Genealogy: Pertaining to the Good Sachem Massasoit, Ebenezer Weaver Peirce & Mrs. Zerviah Gould Mitchell

Indian Wars of New England: Topography of Indian Tribes, Herbert Milton Sylvester

King Phillip's War: Civil War in New England, 1675–1676, 1999 James D. Drake

King Philip's War, George W. Ellis & John E. Morris, Grafton Press, 1906

Leift Lion Gardener His Relation of the Pequot Warres, Lion Gardener

Massacre at Hurtleberry Hill: Christian Indians and English Authority in Metacom's War, Jenny Hale Pulsipher, The William and Mary Quarterly, 1996

Massasoit of the Wampanoags, Alvin Weeks, 1920

Missionary register, Volumes 2-3, By Church Missionary Society

Mystic Fiasco: How the Indians Won the Pequot war, 2010, David Wagner and Jack Dempsey, 7–8

Narratives of The Indian Wars 1675–1699, Charles H. Lincoln, Charles Scribners's Sons, 1913

New England Frontier: Puritans and Indians 1620-1675, Alden T. Vaughn, 1965

New England on Fire! Margaret Barton, Poppet Publications, 2008

News From America; or A New and Experimentall Discoverie of New England; Containing, A True Relation of Their War-Like Proceedings These Two Yeares Last Past, With a Figure of The Indian Fort, or Palizado, Captain John Underhill, 1638

Of Civil Government Second Treatise, John Locke, A Gateway Edition, 1955

Other Indian Events of New England, Allan Forbes, State Street Trust Company of Boston, 1941

Roots of American Racism: Essays on the Colonial Experience, Alden T. Vaughan, Oxford University Press, 1995,

Rhode Island's Founders: From Settlement to Statehood, Patrick T. Conley, History Press, 2010 18–20

Roger Williams: Prophet and Pioneer, Emily Easton, Houghton Mifflin Company, 1930

Soldiers in King Philip's War, George M. Bodge, 1891

Springfield, Massachusetts: Volume I, Henry M. Burt. Printed and Published by Henry M. Burt, 1898

Stories of Wethersfield, Nora Howard, White Publishing 1997

The Beginnings of New England, John Fiskes, Houghton Mifflin Company, 1902

The Beginnings of New England, John Fiskes, 1889,

The Colonial Mind, Main Currents in American Thought Vol. 1 1620–1800, Vernon Louis Parrington

The Enslavement of the American Indian, Barbara Olexer, Library Research Associates, 1982

The Gentle Radical: A Biography of Roger Williams, Cyclone Covey, The Macmillan Company, 1966

The History of Ancient Wethersfield: Volume 1, Sherman W. Adams & Henry R. Stiles, New Hampshire Publishing Company, 1904

The History of Connecticut, From the First Settlement of the Colony to the Adoption of the Present Constitution Volume 1, G. H. Hollister, 1857

The Indian and The White Man, Chandler Whipple, The Berkshire Traveller Press, 1974

The Indian Land Titles of Essex County, Massachusetts, Sidney Perley

The Indians of the Nipmuck Country in Southern New England, 1630–1750, Dennis A. Connole, MacFarland & Company, 2001

The Invasion of America, Francis Jennings, Norton and Company, 1975

The Indian Wars, Robert M. Utley & Wilcomb E. Washburn, American Heritage Publishing/Bonanza Books, 1977

The Memorial History of Hartford County, Connecticut, 1633–1884. Volume 1, edited by James Hammond Trumbull

The New England Company

The New–England Indians: a bibliographical survey, 1630–1700 By Justin Winsor,

The Nipmuck Indians, Caleb A. Waei., Esq., 1898

The Pequot War, Alfred A. Cave, University of Massachusetts Press, 1996

The Puritans, A Sourcebook of Their Writings, Edited by Perry Miller and Thomas H. Johnson,

The Puritan Dilemma: The Story of John Winthrop, Edmund S. Morgan, Longman Inc., 1999

The Reformed Doctrine of Predestination, Loraine Boettner

The Story of Connecticut Vol. 1, Charles Burpee

The United States to 1865, Michael Kraus

Thomas Hooker: Preacher, Founder, Democrat, 1891, George Leon Walker, Dodd, Mead, and Co.

Thomas Mayhew: Patriarch to the Indians, Lloyd C. M. Hare, AMS Press, 1969

Uncas: First of the Mohegans, Michael Leroy Oberg, Cornell University Press 2003

[1] Historical Collections of the Indians in New England, Daniel Gookin, 1

[2] Historical Collections of the Indians in New England, Daniel Gookin, 178

[3] A Historical Account of the Indians of New England, Daniel Gookin, 170

[4] The Colonial Mind, Main Currents in American Thought Vol. 1 1620–1800, Vernon Louis Parrington, 84

[5] Cogely, 238

[6] A Praying People, Dane Morrison, 1995, Peter Lang Publishing

[7] The Story of Connecticut Vol.1, Charles Burpee, 107–109

[8] The United States to 1865, Michael Kraus, 48

[9] Eulogy on King Philip, William Apess, 7

[10] The Reformed Doctrine of Predestination, Loraine Boettner, 382

[11] The Reformed Doctrine of Predestination, Loraine Boettner, 17

[12] Missionary register, Volumes 2-3, By Church Missionary Society, 189

[13] Boettner, 119

[14] The Beginnings of New England, John Fiskes, 1889, 258–59

[15] Indian History, Biography and Genealogy: Pertaining to the Good Sachem Massasoit, Ebenezer Weaver Peirce & Mrs. Zerviah Gould Mitchell, 7

[16] Massacre at Hurtleberry Hill: Christian Indians and English Authority in Metacom's War, Jenny Hale Pulsipher, The William and Mary Quarterly, 1996, 472–473

[17] Soldiers in King Philip's War, George M. Bodge, 1891

[18] Historical Account of the Doings and Sufferings of the Christian Indians in New England in the Years 1675–1677, Daniel Gookin

[19] King Philip's War, George W. Ellis & John E. Morris, Grafton Press, 1906, 27

[20] Historical Account of the Doings and Sufferings of the Christian Indians in New England in the Years 1675–1677, Daniel Gookin

[21] The Nipmuck Indians

[22] The Nipmuck Indians

[23] Historical Account of the Doings and Sufferings of the Christian Indians in New England in the Years 1675–1677, Daniel Gookin

[24] King Philip's War, George W. Ellis & John E. Morris, Grafton Press, 1906, 18

[25] Historical Account of the Doings and Sufferings of the Christian Indians in New England in the Years 1675–1677, Daniel Gookin 433–437

[26] Gookin, 454

[27] A Brief History of the Pequot War, John Mason, 44

[28] The Indian and The White Man, Chandler Whipple, 242

[29] Bodge

[30] The Memorial History of Hartford County, Connecticut, 1633–1884. Volume 1, edited by James Hammond Trumbull, 11–15

[31] Mason, 5

[32] A Brief History of the Pequot War, John Mason, vii–viii

[33] Boettner, 61

[34] Boettner, 365

[35] Boettner, 367

[36] The Puritans, A Sourcebook of Their Writings, Edited by Perry Miller and Thomas H. Johnson, 88

[37] The Story of Connecticut Vol. 1, Charles Burpee, 11–12

[38] The Beginnings of New England, John Fiskes, 76–77

[39] Daniel Clarke Sanders, 15

[40] Sanders, 15, 1828

[41] The Puritans, A Sourcebook of Their Writings, Edited by Perry Miller and Thomas H. Johnson, 103

[42] Ibid, 101

[43] A Brief History of the Unites States, Joel Dorman Steele and Esther Baker Steele, American Book Company, 55,

[44] Thomas Mayhew: Patriarch to the Indians, Lloyd C. M. Hare, 8–9, 1932

[45] Thomas Mayhew: Patriarch to the Indians, Lloyd C. M. Hare, 8–9, 1932

[46] Ibid, 11–15

[47] The Indian Wars, Utley & Washburn, 45

[48] The Story of Connecticut Vol. 1, Charles Burpee, 16

[49] The History of Ancient Wethersfield: Volume 1, Sherman W. Adams & Henry R. Stiles, New Hampshire Publishing Company, 1904, 56–60

[50] The Story of Connecticut Vol. 1, Charles Burpee, 28–78

[51] Thomas Hooker: Preacher, Founder, Democrat, 1891, George Leon Walker, Dodd, Mead, and Co. 40–51

[52] The Story of Connecticut Vol. 1, Charles Burpee, 87

[53] The Gentle Radical: A Biography of Roger Williams, Cyclone Covey, The Macmillan Company, 1966, 150

[54] G. H. Hollister, 27

[55] Historic & Archaeological Resources of the Connecticut River Valley, The Massachusetts Historic Commission, 1984

[56] Historic & Archaeological Resources of the Connecticut River Valley, The Massachusetts Historic Commission, 1984

[57] Sanders, 27, 1828

[58] The Indian and The White Man in New England, Chandler Whipple, 98

[59] Historic & Archaeological Resources of the Connecticut River Valley, The Massachusetts Historic Commission, 1984

[60] Cave, 50

[61] The Story of Connecticut Vol. 1, Charles Burpee, 25

[62] The Memorial History of Hartford County, Connecticut, 1633–1884. Volume 1, edited by James Hammond Trumbull, 11–15

[63] Stories of Wethersfield, Nora Howard, White Publishing 1997 12–13

[64] Covey, 159

[65] Hollister, 113–114

[66] Adams & Stiles, 60

[67] Roots of American Racism: Essays on the Colonial Experience, Alden T. Vaughan, Oxford University Press, 1995, 201–203

[68] The Indian and The White Man in New England, Chandler Whipple, 155

[69] Adams & Stiles, 62–65

[70] Ibid, 201–203

[71] Hollister, 54

[72] Adams & Stiles, 23

[73] Cave, 136–137

[74] Hollister, 127

[75] History of the Indian Wars of New England, with Eliot the Apostle Fifty Years in the Midst of Them, Robert Boodey Caverly, 78

[76] Covey, 95

[77] Mason, 16–17

[78] Drake, 101

[79] Cave, 57–68

[80] The Indian Wars of New England, With Eliot the Apostle Fifty Years in the Midst of Them, Robert Boodey Caverly, 83

[81] The Indian Wars of New England, With Eliot the Apostle Fifty Years in the Midst of Them, Robert Boodey Caverly, 83

[82] Hollister, 44

[83] Ibid, 70–71

[84] The Indian and The White Man in New England, Chandler Whipple, 213

[85] Francis Jennings, 196

[86] Hollister, 20

[87] Vaughan, 117

[88] Underhill, 63–64

[89] History of Hartford County, Charles W. Burpee, S. J. Clarke Publishing, 1928, 44

[90] The Story of Connecticut Vol. 1, Charles Burpee, 48

[91] Cave, 96–97

[92] Cave, 100–101

[93] Cave, 95–100

[94] The Indian and the White Man, Chandler Whipple, 218

[95] The Indian and the White Man, Chandler Whipple, 218

[96] The Indian and The White Man in New England, Chandler Whipple, 220

[97] Underhill, 56–57

[98] Covey, 159–160

[99] Underhill, 61–62

[100] Ibid, 161

[101] Covey, 162

[102] Covey, 162

[103] History of the Indian Wars of New England, With Eliot the Apostle Fifty Years in the Midst of Them, Robert Boodey Cavalry, 73

[104] Covey, 163–164

[105] History of the Indian Wars of New England, With Eliot the Apostle Fifty Years in the Midst of Them, Robert Boodey Cavalry, 73

[106] History of the Indian Wars of New England, With Eliot the Apostle Fifty Years in the Midst of Them, Robert Boodey Cavalry, 73 & 93

[107] Wagner and Dempsey, 15

[108] The Story of Connecticut Vol. 1, Charles Burpee, 51
[109] Adams & Stiles, 71
[110] The Story of Connecticut Vol.1, Charles Burpee, 51
[111] The Story of Connecticut Vol.1, Charles Burpee, 52
[112] The Story of Connecticut Vol. 1, Charles Burpee, 52
[113] The Story of Connecticut Vol. 1, Charles Burpee, 52
[114] The Story of Connecticut Vol. 1, Charles Burpee, 52
[115] Hollister, 54–55
[116] Gardener, 135–137
[117] Mason, 21
[118] Wagner and Dempsey, 42
[119] Ibid, 198
[120] Ibid, 25–31
[121] Ibid, 38–49
[122] Underhill, 51
[123] Hollister, 55–56
[124] The Indian and the White Man, Chandler Whipple, 227
[125] Hollister, 57–58
[126] The Indian and the White Man, Chandler Whipple, 228
[127] Hollister, 57–58
[128] Ibid, 60
[129] Hollister, 59
[130] Cave, 98–141
[131] Mason, 26
[132] Mason, 27
[133] Ibid, 139
[134] Mystic Fiasco, Dempsey & Wagner, 90
[135] Hollister 61–62
[136] Mystic Fiasco, Wagner & Dempsey, 117
[137] Ibid, 107–109
[138] Underhill, 82–83
[139] Ibid, 113
[140] Ibid, 133
[141] Hollister, 64
[142] Underhill, 84–85
[143] Mason, xix
[144] Ibid, 129
[145] Sanders, 32–33
[146] Hollister, 147
[147] Cave 158–160
[148] Wagner and Dempsey, 139
[149] Mason, (John Fiske, Beginnings of New England) xviii
[150] The Story of Connecticut Vol. 1, Charles Burpee, 53
[151] Mason, 37–40
[152] Ibid, 163

[153] Vaughan, 340–341
[154] Weeks
[155] The Indian and the White Man, Chandler Whipple, 238
[156] Alvin Weeks
[157] The Indian and The White Man, Chandler Whipple, 238
[158] Adams & Stiles, 69
[159] Vaughn, 205
[160] Forbes, 8
[161] King Philip's War, Ellis & Morris, 29
[162] Jennings, 257–261
[163] Steele, 57
[164] Rhode Island's Founders: From Settlement to Statehood, Patrick T. Conley, The History Press, 45–46 2010
[165] The Story of Connecticut Vol. 1, Charles Burpee, 111
[166] The Indian and The White Man, Chandler Whipple, 239–240
[167] King Philip's War, Ellis & Morris, 30–32
[168] Odberg, 102
[169] The Indian and The White Man, Chandler Whipple, 164
[170] Weeks
[171] King Philip's War, Ellis & Morris, 32
[172] Hollister, 124
[173] Alvin Weeks
[174] Hollister, 123–124
[175] King Philip's War, Ellis & Morris, 33
[176] Jennings, 260–263
[177] Forbes, 8,12
[178] Jennings. 255
[179] Indian Wars of New England: Topography of Indian Tribes, Herbert Milton Sylvester, 457
[180] Indian Wars of New England: Topography of Indian Tribes, Herbert Milton Sylvester, 472-473
[181] The Indian Land Titles of Essex County, Massachuestts, Sidney Perley, 36–37
[182] The Story of Connecticut Vol.1, Charles Burpee, 165
[183] Historical Collections of the Indians of New England, Daniel Gookin, 202
[184] Hare, 27–28
[185] Hare, 62–63
[186] Ibid, 64
[187] Ibid, 41
[188] Ibid, 116–117
[189] Hare
[190] Ibid, 58–59
[191] Hare
[192] Hare, 98
[193] Mathew Mayhew, Hare 101
[194] Hare, 108

[195] Historical Collections of the Indians in New England, Daniel Gookin, 206
[196] Hare, 111
[197] Hare, 112
[198] Leach, 18
[199] King Philip's War, Ellis & Morris, 9
[200] Historic & Archaeological Resources of the Connecticut River Valley, The Massachusetts Historic Commission, 1984

[201] Odberg, 167
[202] Historic & Archaeological Resources of the Connecticut River Valley, The Massachusetts Historic Commission, 1984

[203] Drake, 39–41
[204] Cogely, 28–30
[205] The New–England Indians: a bibliographical survey, 1630–1700 By Justin Winsor, 12
[206] The New England Company of 1649 and John Eliot, Publications of the Prince Society, 1920
[207] The New England Company
[208] Cogely, 178
[209] Leach, 6
[210] Jennings, 249
[211] A Brief Narrative of the Progress of the Gospel amongst the *Indians* in *New England*, in the Year 1670, given in by the Reverend Mr. JOHN ELIOT, Minister of the Gospel there, in a LETTER by him directed to the Right Worshipfull the COMMISSIONERS under his Majesties Great-Seal for Propagation of the Gospel amongst the poor blind Natives in those United Colonies. *LONDON*, Printed for *John Allen*, formerly living in *Little-Britain* at the Rising-Sun, and now in *Wentworth street* near *Bell-Lane*, 1671.
[212] Connole, 88–89
[213] Historical Collections of the Indians in New England, Daniel Gookin, 168-169
[214] Historical Collections of the Indians in New England, Daniel Gookin, 169
[215] Historical Collections of the Indians in New England, Daniel Gookin, 169
[216] A Brief Narrative of the Progress of the Gospel amongst the *Indians* in *New England*, in the Year 1670, given in by the Reverend Mr. JOHN ELIOT, Minister of the Gospel there, in a LETTER by him directed to the Right Worshipfull the COMMISSIONERS under his Majesties Great-Seal for Propagation of the Gospel amongst the poor blind Natives in those United Colonies. *LONDON*, Printed for *John Allen*, formerly living in *Little-Britain* at the Rising-Sun, and now in *Wentworth street* near *Bell-Lane*, 1671.
[217] Historical Collections of the Indians in New England, Daniel Gookin, 180-181
[218] Cogely, 105–107
[219] Cogely, 140
[220] Bodge
[221] Connole, 141–144

[222] The Indians of the Nipmuck Country in Southern New England, 1630–1750, Dennis A. Connole, 109–110
[223] Historical Collections of the Indians of New England, Daniel Gookin, 172
[224] The Nipmuck Indians
[225] Drake, 94–95
[226] Historical Collections of the Indians of New England, Daniel Gookin, 189
[227] The Indians of the Nipmuck Country in Southern New England, 1630–1750, Dennis A. Connole,109–111
[228] The Indians of the Nipmuck Country in Southern New England, 1630–1750, Dennis A. Connole,112
[229] Historical Collections of the Indians of New England, Daniel Gookin, 192
[230] Historical Collections of the Indians of New England, Daniel Gookin, 191
[231] The Nipmuck Indians
[232] The Indians of the Nipmuck Country in Southern New England, 1630–1750, Dennis A. Connole, 113
[233] Historical Collections of the Indians of New England, Daniel Gookin, 177
[234] Drake, 50
[235] Historical Collections of the Indians of New England, Daniel Gookin, 177
[236] Ibid, 118–119
[237] The Indians of the Nipmuck Country in Southern New England, 1630–1750, Dennis A. Connole, 118
[238] Ibid, 120
[239] Connole, 84–121
[240] The Indian and The White Man, Chandler Whipple, 157
[241] Historical Collections of the Indians of New England, Daniel Gookin, 195
[242] Gookin, 439
[243] Bodge
[244] Gookin, 462
[245] Bodge
[246] Connole, 113
[247] Connole, 164–165
[248] Leach, 1
[249] The Story of Connecticut Vol.1, Charles Burpee, 214
[250] Bodge
[251] The Indian and The White Man, Chandler Whipple 170–171
[252] Barton, 48
[253] Weeks
[254] Indian History, Biography and Genealogy: Pertaining to the Good Sachem Massasoit, Ebenezer weaver Peirce
[255] Ibid, 5
[256] Weeks
[257] Jennings, 289–293
[258] Forbes, 45–48
[259] Eulogy of Philip, William Apess, 29–30
[260] Forbes, 45–48

[261] Epochs of American History: The Colonies 1492–1750, Reuben G. Thwaites, Longmans, Green, and Co., 1894, 170–171
[262] Leach, 31
[263] Vaughan, 76–85
[264] Leach, 31–32
[265] Gookin, 440
[266] King Phlip's War, Ellis & Morris, 48
[267] Jennings, 294–295
[268] Weeks
[269] Barton, 48–49
[270] King Phlip's War, Ellis & Morris, 49
[271] Weeks
[272] King Phlip's War, Ellis & Morris, 57
[273] Drake, 70
[274] Leach, 35
[275] Bodge
[276] Gookin, 441–444
[277] Gookin, 441–444
[278] Bodge
[279] Bodge
[280] Leach, 44–45
[281] Pulsipher, 466
[282] Pulsipher, 466
[283] Gookin, 439
[284] King Phlip's War, Ellis & Morris, 70–71
[285] Gookin, 439
[286] King Phlip's War, Ellis & Morris, 72
[287] King Phlip's War, Ellis & Morris, 73
[288] King Phlip's War, Ellis & Morris, 77–78
[289] King Phlip's War, Ellis & Morris, 77–78
[290] Leach, 50–69
[291] King Phlip's War, Ellis & Morris, 84
[292] Leach, 40–41
[293] History of Hardwick, Massachusetts with a Genealogical Register, Lucius R. Paige, 1883
[294] History of Hardwick, Massachusetts with a Genealogical Register, Lucius R. Paige, 1883
[295] King Phlip's War, Ellis & Morris, 84–89
[296] History of Hardwick, Massachusetts with a Genealogical Register, Lucius R. Paige, 1883
[297] Bodge, xiii
[298] Bodge
[299] Bodge, xiii
[300] Bodge
[301] King Phlip's War, Ellis & Morris, 90

[302] Bodge

[303] Bodge

[304] Leach, 77–84

[305] King Phlip's War, Ellis & Morris, 92

[306] Bodge

[307] Bodge

[308] King Phlip's War, Ellis & Morris, 96

[309] Leach, 84

[310] Gookin, 450–451

[311] Daniel Gookin, 470

[312] Gookin, 451–453

[313] King Phlip's War, Ellis & Morris, 117

[314] Bodge

[315] Leach, 89

[316] Leach, 95

[317] Springfield, Massachusetts: Volume I, Henry M. Burt. Printed and Published by Henry M. Burt, 1898, 130–135

[318] Leach, 96

[319] Springfield, Massachusetts: Volume I, Henry M. Burt. Printed and Published by Henry M. Burt, 1898, 130–135

[320] Pulsipher, 465–466

[321] Connole, 174

[322] Jennings, 308–309

[323] Bodge

[324] Gookin, 469–474

[325] Bodge

[326] Pulsipher, 467

[327] Bodge

[328] King Phlip's War, Ellis & Morris, 136

[329] Olexer, 57–58

[330] Connole, 178

[331] Bodge

[332] Burpee, 118

[333] Steele, 58–59

[334] Mystic Fiasco, David Wagner & Jack Dempsey, 95

[335] Bodge

[336] History of the Indian Wars of New England, with Eliot the Apostle Fifty Years in the Midst of Them, Robert Boodey Caverly, 186–87

[337] Leach, 129

[338] King Phlip's War, Ellis & Morris, 151–152

[339] Bodge

[340] Bodge

[341] Ibid., 58–59

[342] Drake, 119

[343] Jennings, 312

[344] King Phlip's War, Ellis & Morris, 165
[345] Bodge
[346] Bodge
[347] Pulsipher, 472
[348] Ibid, 175
[349] Gookin, 486–488
[350] Bodge
[351] Gookin, 475–476
[352] Connole, 175
[353] Gookin, 486–488
[354] Gookin, 489
[355] Gookin, 491
[356] Gookin, 500–507
[357] History of the Indian Wars of New England, with Eliot the Apostle Fifty Years in the Midst of Them, Robert Boodey Caverly, 205
[358] King Phlip's War, Ellis & Morris, 207–208
[359] King Phlip's War, Ellis & Morris, 212
[360] Gookin, 516–517
[361] Forbes, 57–64
[362] Hollister, 282
[363] Leach, 171
[364] Weeks
[365] Burpee, 131
[366] Hollister, 284
[367] Soldiers in King Philip's War, Bodge
[368] Bodge
[369] History of the Indian Wars of New England, Col. Robert Boodey Caverly, 73
[370] Gookin, 513–519
[371] Zelner, 215–216
[372] Ibid., 59
[373] Bodge
[374] Lincoln, 104–105
[375] Connole, 208–212
[376] The Nipmuc Indians
[377] Barton, xxiii

Made in the USA
Charleston, SC
09 June 2012